THE
MICROBREWERS
Contributing Editor
Tim Hampson
HANDBOOK

8TH EDITION

First published in Great Britain in 2007 by Navigator Guides
Eighth edition published in 2021 by Paragraph Publishing Ltd,
6 Woolgate Court, St Benedicts Street, Norwich, Norfolk, NR2 4AP
Previous editions: 2011, 2013, 2015, 2017, 2019

www.paragraph.co.uk

Copyright © Paragraph Publishing 2021
ISBN 978-1-9998-4084-6-0

The publishers have made every effort to ensure the accuracy of information
in the book at the time of going to press. However, they cannot accept
responsibility for any loss, injury or inconvenience resulting from the use of
information contained in this guide.

Acknowledgements
The publishers would like to thank all those microbreweries and suppliers who
provided information for their case studies, Ted Bruning for his original work, and
Tim Hampson for updating this eighth edition.

Editorial: Bethany Whymark
Design: Tim A'Court
Photography: Mandy Chettleburgh
Production manager: Anita Johnson
Audience director: Richard Drake
Commercial manager: Joanne Robertson
Head of content: Christopher Coates
Managing director: Damian Riley-Smith
Printed in Great Britain by Page Bros, Norwich

Cover images, front: © Adrian Tierney-Jones
back: © elevatebeer.com | © adam wilson | © helena lopes

THE
MICROBREWERS'
HANDBOOK

Contents

CASE STUDIES

Foreword

O ver the last decade, the craft beer revolution has done much to raise the profile of beer and brewing, bringing innovation and premiumisation to the sector. The high reliance of these artisanal producers on pubs and bars has, however, made them particularly susceptible to the impacts of Brexit and Covid-19.

In its 2021 report "Why will beer prove resilient in the aftermath of Covid-19?", drinks research company IWSR asserted, "Many of them may not survive in the coming months. However, the consumer's appetite to explore and experiment is unlikely to diminish post Covid-19, and when the green shoots of recovery do emerge, we can expect a new generation of craft players to appear as well, replacing those that did not make it through."

IWSR is confident that beer will show resilience, believing the category will rebound better than wine and spirits post pandemic. "Globally, beer grew 0.3 per cent in volume and +2.2 per cent in value in 2019, led particularly by increases in non-alcoholic beer (+15.2 per cent in volume, vs 2018). Though the beer category has taken a hit in 2020, in total, beer is expected to reach 2019 volumes by 2024, rebounding better than wine and spirits."

The company cites a number of factors which will drive growth, including growing demand for low-alcohol beers: "Until relatively recently, no-alcohol beer was often seen as a distress purchase, but improving taste, innovation, substantial marketing support and widening availability helped sales to jump by 15 per cent globally last year. The segment is a good fit with the contemporary consumer, and is predicted to expand by nearly 50 per cent over the next five years."

The firm's researchers also believe e-commerce will grow, as Covid-19 lockdowns led online shopping to become the norm for large swathes of consumers. IWSR's head of beer Richard Corbett said: "As an antidote to the pandemic, players in the industry are revamping their online capabilities, upgrading their online shops and partnering with digital sales platforms. This will help to offset any sluggish recovery of the on-trade channel and allow the sector to reach out to increasingly more drinkers."

As brewers look to refine their online presence, it is important to remember that strategies will differ based on the channel of distribution. IWSR said: "One size does not fit all, and brewers need to deploy brands in their portfolio in different ways."

A notable bias towards men continues to exist among beer drinkers. However, in recent times, helped in part by the craft movement, the sector has become a broad church of tastes, styles and flavours. IWSR claims that, as a result, beer's appeal has increased to a wider, and often more female, audience: "Added to this, the lower ABV level of beer could resonate with women looking to migrate from stronger alternatives like wine and spirits. Marketing and glassware should help to facilitate this as well."

One of the main revenue generators for growth in craft beer has been taprooms. They enable the brewer to have a closer relationship with their consumers. The beers are sold with an added margin enabling brewers to invest in their business and look to new markets such as exports.

According to the small brewers' trade association SIBA, good planning is key to surviving and prospering in the post-Brexit world. A spokesman for SIBA said: "Brewers will need to make sure they get an EORI number, consider appointing a customs intermediary or make sure you have all the skills and requirements to do customs declarations yourself."

There are also changes to labelling and new glassware requirements. Brewers that employ EU nationals or intend to do so should also be aware of the new immigration changes. The government has produced a series of videos and guides, and you can also create a personalised tracker to help you prepare. There are also several grants available for training.

The UK government's international trade secretary Liz Truss says in the last 12 months she has seen a number of brewers which have made a significant investment in new products and equipment. In particular, brewers are investing in canning lines – much needed as consumers look to cans as a greener form of packaging and worldwide the demand to drink beers at home continues to grow. She said: "British brewing is renowned for its quality across the globe, and our industry serves some of the biggest international brands in the business."

Tim Hampson 2021

Preface

The boom and interest in locally made beers continues to be unsatiated. But there is more to running a brewery than understanding how to brew beer using the basic ingredients of malted barley, hops, water and yeast. Today, brewers have to understand sustainability, the environment, taxation, consumer law and marketing. A brewery is more than just a place where beer is brewed. To do so effectively means having access to a wide range of expertise.

We are experiencing a growing consumer interest in craft and local beers. Many of these beers will be drunk in a brewery tap or a pub. However, more people will drink at home. Today's drinkers demand quality, choice, innovation, provenance and a range of styles and formats. This environment together with a favourable regime of tax relief via Small Brewers Relief introduced in 2002 has led to a growing number of people realising there is a business opportunity for them to set up a brewery.

Sadly, too many still embark on this endeavour with their eyes wide shut. It is a tough world and one in which the larger brewers are squeezing prices and routes to market to maintain market share. Add to this the effect on some established businesses of the months of lockdown due to the pandemic.

History tells us that the strongest willed and most flexible will survive. Today's aspirant microbrewers need a clear business plan, a willingness to be flexible and set the highest standards if they are to prosper. Consumers are becoming more demanding in what they buy, and tend to want something different every time.

All the evidence points to a shift in drinking habits towards quality, and away from the volume drinking of years gone by. This should be welcome news for independent brewers who produce interesting craft beers. There is also a need to create an experience around beer. Today this has to include the whole lifecycle: where and how were the ingredients grown? Does the brewery support diversity and inclusion? What is the brewer's policy on recycling and sustainability?

On one level making beer is easy, and many people have joined in the craft beer revolution. They gave up their day job, bought some brewing equipment and are brewing batches of foaming beer which their friends are more than happy to drink pints of, for free. But such largesse is not a business model.

Too often after launching their breweries, many find the initial wave of optimism and enthusiasm wanes, sales start to slip and there is no money to fund new products or much-needed equipment. Others have leapt head-long into their own brewery business without realising how hard it is. Many don't realise how tight margins are. Growing competition also means the bar is constantly being raised on quality. The brewing of boring, bland beer is no passport to success. Some have made the mistake of growing too fast and end up owing HMRC money. That said, those who succeed love the industry for its comradeship and the fact they can make some money from making a product they love. Compared with some businesses, brewing isn't that regulated. You can just register with HMRC and away you go; you are a commercial brewer.

Today's craft brewers draw inspiration from across the world. Unfiltered, cloudy beers are being widely produced, and it is not just flavoursome hops which are being added to beers – brewers are experimenting with ingredients such as coriander, lemongrass and grape must. The only limit is the extent of brewers' imaginations.

The best advice for any aspirant brewer is to go on a brewing course. If you are really keen, volunteer and work in at least one local microbrewery for six months. Brew at home and keep at it until your recipes are refined and perfected. Amid all of this, plan how you will finance your business venture.

Running any business is risky. Studies show 60 per cent of business start-ups do not make it past the first year and 80 per cent go under in five years. However, with hard work, high standards and a rigid adherence to best practice, running your own brewery can be emotionally and financially rewarding.

New entrants into brewing will have to balance the opportunities offered by consumer demand for new, innovative beers with supply challenges, and will quickly have to focus on quality and excellence. The mediocre will not survive.

Tim Hampson 2021

Introduction

How it All Started

n 1965 Peter Maxwell Stuart, the 20th Laird of Traquair, unwittingly started a revolution. He had rediscovered the 18th-century brewhouse that once kept masters and servants alike at his ancestral pile at Innerleithen, Peeblesshire, supplied with ale, and decided to restore it. A period of hard work followed, and before long the beer started flowing again at Traquair House.

Neither Peter Maxwell Stuart nor anyone else thought at the time that the establishment of the first commercial brewery in Britain in half a century was any more than a mere curiosity, a one-off. Then seven years later another former brewery, this time at Selby in North Yorkshire, also recommissioned its vessels. Founded in 1894, Selby had stopped brewing in 1954 to become a licensed trade wholesaler. But, said owner Martin Sykes, "I foresaw a revival of interest in real ale and got in early." In November 1972 the first brew was released; this time, it was no one-off curiosity.

Less than a year later the third of the new wave of "microbreweries" – and the first truly new brewery in more than 50 years – was founded by former rocket scientist Paul Leyton at the Miners' Arms at Priddy in Somerset. It sounded like a pub but was actually a restaurant, where you could only drink Paul's home brew with a meal; and all the beer was bottled rather than draught. The year after that a fourth micro – and nobody now remembers who coined the term – was set up at the Masons Arms at South Leigh in Oxfordshire, and the microbrewing revolution was well and truly on.

True, it got off to a faltering start. Nearly all of the country's 55,000-odd pubs were either owned by existing breweries or were loan-tied, having accepted the exclusive supply agreement that came with low-interest brewery loans. Half of the 300 small breweries started in the 1970s and '80s failed, most often for want of free-of-tie pubs to sell their beers to.

Campaign for Real Ale (CAMRA)

But the 1970s was also the founding decade of the Campaign for Real Ale (CAMRA), fomentor of the great consumer revolt against the weak, gassy, keg beers the brewing industry was foisting on the public. CAMRA and the microbrewers were symbiotic from the start – in fact, Martin Sykes, the refounder of Selby Brewery, was a member of CAMRA's first National Executive Committee. CAMRA's *Good Beer Guide* pointed drinkers to pubs that stocked traditional beer, including real ale from new brewers; and the beer festivals staged by its rapidly expanding web of local branches allowed the public the opportunity to try the new brewers' ales for themselves. So, with growing support from enthusiastic beer-lovers and from the handful of publicans who could and would stock their beers, the luckiest and pluckiest of the pioneers clung on. Slowly their numbers grew, and within a decade local independent brewers had become an established, if often penurious, fixture of the nation's beer and pub scene.

Who were they, though, these pioneers? Not the counter-cultural hippy good-lifers you might suppose. Most of them, in fact, were already brewers.

Throughout the 1950s and '60s big breweries had been buying up smaller ones and closing them down. This concentration in the industry was the delayed effect of the economic conditions of the preceding four decades: war followed by depression followed by war followed by rationing had left scores of small family breweries hopelessly uncompetitive. Their pubs and breweries hadn't had a bean spent on them in generations and were in many cases near-derelict; and the owners were desperate to sell, sometimes for ludicrously small sums. Bass once recouped the entire purchase price of a brewery it had bought simply by auctioning the contents of the new acquisition's wines and spirits warehouse. In other cases, buyers found that their acquisitions hadn't had their pub estates revalued since before the First World War, and covered their outlay just by sending round a team of surveyors.

That is, perhaps, another story. The upshot, for our purposes, was that hundreds of experienced staff – executives as well as brewers – were thrown out of work as old-established breweries were rationalised out of existence. Most of them simply disappeared into the general labour force; but a few decided to carry on making a living at their chosen trade and, following the lead of Traquair, Selby and the rest, set up breweries of their own.

The Pioneers

Some of the early trailblazers were pretty senior figures. Bill Urquart founded the Litchborough Brewery in a barn at his Northamptonshire home in 1974 having been laid off by Watney after 40 years in the business. His last assignment had been to run down the old Phipps Brewery in Northampton, which was earmarked for demolition to become the site of Carlsberg's brand-new lager plant. Part of his job was to decide who would be made redundant and who would get a job at the new plant. At 58, he had a feeling that his own name was on the list for the chop, so he seized the opportunity to acquire the skills he would need to set up on his own. At Litchborough he not only brewed a bitter so popular that his own golf club sold it, but he also helped many other new brewers set themselves up.

Another senior brewer who set up for himself but spent as much time helping newcomers as running his own brewery was Peter Austin, founder of Ringwood in Hampshire in 1978. Peter had just retired as head brewer of the Hull Brewery, but his new life took him all around the world, installing small brewing plants as far afield as China.

Other highly experienced pioneers included Simon Whitmore, managing director of Courage's western region, who founded Butcombe Brewery in Somerset in 1978 after being made redundant. Peter Mauldon, who in 1982 refounded his family brewery in Sudbury, Suffolk (established by his great-grandfather in 1795, bought and closed by Greene King in 1960), had been a senior brewer at Watney in Mortlake, Surrey. David Bruce, who opened the first of the Firkin chain of brewpubs in 1979, had worked in management and brewing at both Courage and Theakston's. Martin Ayres, Ted Willems, John Bjornsson, Chas Wright, Pat Glenny, James Johnstone, Gerry Watts, Roger Catte, Geoff Mumford, Bruce Wilkinson, Tony Allen, Peter Yates, Peter Amor, Bryan Wilson and John Gilbert were other industry veterans who set up on their own in the 1980s and whose ventures are still going strong today, often under second- or even third-generation ownership.

Despite the newcomers' résumés, the established brewers – both the surviving older-established family firms and the new Big Six national brewers – were at first rather scornful of their potential. It was hard to believe they could produce anything decent on brewing plants thrown together from scraps of old dairy equipment and the like, and the older firms were armour-plated, or so they believed. Their tied estates, and the number of free houses they controlled through low-interest loans, surely meant that the upstarts would never gain more than a toehold in the retail trade and could never become a threat. A semi-cordial relationship based on amused condescension soon developed. Pitfield Brewery used to get its fresh yeast from Charles Wells of Bedford, turning up at the back gate with a galvanised bucket which a worker would obligingly fill with barm scooped straight from the fermenter. No one saw Pitfield as anything but a harmless eccentric – until 1987, that is, when its Dark Star strong old ale became the first microbrewer's beer to win the Campaign for Real Ale's Champion Beer of Britain competition.

For these chaps could brew, whatever the mainstream thought. Brewing is, after all, not that complicated a process (although brewing consistently good-quality beer is extremely painstaking and demanding). A chef-turned-microbrewer I know tells me it is far easier than cooking in a restaurant. Nor does the equipment itself have to be expensive and gleaming, so long as it's well maintained and only has the holes in it that you actually want. Anyway, most of the new wave had actually been brewing all their working lives, so to find them consistently turning out beers of seriously commercial quality should have come as no surprise.

Actually, in terms of quality they had some key advantages over their much bigger competitors. With no accountants counting the farthings, they didn't have to skimp on the raw materials they used. With no tied estates to guarantee a base level of sales, they could only survive by brewing consistently better beer. With no marketing departments telling them what the public supposedly wanted, they were free to brew whatever they fancied. Some rifled the recipe books of the past and reinvented vanished beers such as porters and old ales (like Dark Star); others experimented and came up with entirely new styles. The cumulative effect was to arouse in the beer-drinking public an appetite for novelty and variety (and, paradoxically, so far had mass-produced beer fallen by then that a thirst for the traditional and a thirst for novelty were virtually identical) that older, more staid breweries couldn't or wouldn't satisfy – or in many cases even acknowledge.

Throughout the 1970s and '80s the trickle of newcomers accelerated thanks to a house-price boom that gave most middle-aged people the equity to invest in a new life of their choice, and an economic recession that left many middle-aged people with no choice but to invest in a new life. Fewer and fewer of the second wave came from within the brewing industry itself; but many of them were experienced businesspeople of considerable acumen, so although the retail trade remained largely closed to them, the rate of business failures slowed even as the rate of start-ups increased. By the end of the 1980s the number of new breweries had reached three figures.

Society of Independent Brewers (SIBA)

The Society of Independent Brewers was established in 1980 to represent the interests of the growing number of independent breweries in Britain.

It currently represents around 830 independent craft breweries and its vision is "to deliver the future of British beer" as the "voice of British independent brewing".

It operates the "Assured Independent British Craft Brewer" initiative. Beers which carry the Independent Craft Brewer logo are relatively small, independent and brewing quality beer.

The logo is used on pump clips, beer bottles, can labels, and at many beer festivals across the UK, and wherever it appears the beer will have been made by a truly independent craft brewery.

More information on the initiative can be found via **www.indiecraftbrewers.co.uk**

Marketing: The days when sexist imagery could be used to market beers have gone. SIBA is moving forward with plans to create a marketing "Code of Practice" for its members. It has stated there is "no place in the beer industry for sexist or offensive marketing".

The code provides an opportunity for SIBA and SIBA members to lead the brewing industry in moving away from any past discriminatory materials in branding and labelling.

Product safety: Generally speaking, our modern consumer culture and retailers, especially multiple retailing groups, demand food safety and quality assurance from professional brewing businesses. SIBA has introduced a food safety and quality management programme for its members with a target to help at least 500 brewers gain the accreditation within two years.

Monopolies and Mergers Commission (MMC)

In 1988, as a result of pressure from SIBA, CAMRA and licensees' associations, and with the help of a handful of supportive MPs, the Office of Fair Trading ordered a Monopolies and Mergers Commission (MMC) enquiry into the supply of beer. The mainstream brewers had been here before and had always escaped with no more than cosmetic changes. But this time their complacency proved ill-founded, for much to their surprise the MMC found there was a "complex monopoly operating against the public interest" and recommended measures to smash it. To the brewers' even greater surprise and indeed fury, the then Trade Secretary Lord Young proposed to implement measures in full. He quickly disappeared in a reshuffle, and although his successor, Nicholas Ridley, watered down the MMC's proposals considerably, the 1990 Beer Orders still had the desired effect.

The Beer Orders

The Beer Orders contained two key clauses. The first was that the Big Six (Bass, Allied, Grand Met, Whitbread, Courage, and Scottish & Newcastle) must either sell or lease free of tie half of their pubs above a 2,000 ceiling; the second was that their tenants should be allowed to stock one guest real ale of their choice. The first measure led, eventually, to the demise of the Big Six and the emergence of giant non-brewing pub companies such as Punch Taverns and Enterprise Inns. The second led to a huge increase in the number of microbreweries, thanks to the opportunities it opened up in the retail trade.

The early 1990s were halcyon days for the micros as they saw their beers go on sale in pubs owned by the Big Six (and served, to add insult to injury, through handpumps and beer engines also owned by the Big Six, much to the Big Six's disgruntlement). One of the country's most successful local brewers, Wickwar of Gloucestershire, was founded in 1990 by Courage tenant Ray Penny expressly to supply himself and fellow tenants with guest ale. It wasn't long before Ray got rid of his Courage tenancy to concentrate on running his brewery, which has since moved to bigger premises and supplies around 350 free houses in the region. He is also developing a small tied estate of his own.

End Product Duty

Small brewers were boosted still further three years later when the archaic system of levying duty on the unfermented wort was scrapped. This system, which dated back to Gladstone's introduction of malt duty in 1880, put the smaller brewers at a serious disadvantage. All brewers – however large – were allowed six per cent duty-free wastage allowance, which meant that the more efficient big brewers were in effect selling four or five per cent of their beer tax-free, whereas smaller brewers were sometimes charged duty on beer they couldn't actually sell. In 1993 this system was replaced by end product duty calculated according to the beer's percentage alcohol by volume. It meant there was no longer any need for a wastage allowance: brewers were charged only for what they had actually sold, and could even claw back the duty on beer spoiled or returned as unfit for consumption.

So end product duty meant a more level playing-field as far as prices were concerned. The party didn't last, though. By the late 1990s the Big Six had disappeared, and the guest ale market had disappeared with them. But the microbrewers had made plenty of hay during the brief period of sunshine. Consumers had got used to the idea that Courage pubs didn't only stock Courage beer and Whitbread pubs didn't only stock Whitbread beer. Choice had been put in front of them, and they liked it. The new non-brewing pub companies saw this and started stocking cherished traditional ales from big-name family brewers such as Adnams, Fuller's and Young's alongside national brands such as Bass and Tetley. Once the idea of choice had caught on, it gradually became easier for microbreweries to find outlets, and by the time the Beer Orders were finally scrapped in 2002 as no longer relevant, they had trebled in number.

Progressive Beer Duty (PBD)

The scrapping of the Beer Orders was mourned by CAMRA but not by anyone else. For as luck would have it, the very same year saw the next great legislative boost for microbrewing in Britain when after years of hard lobbying by SIBA (aided by CAMRA) the chancellor introduced the same system of progressive beer duty (PBD) that was already common in Europe. PBD or "sliding scale" allowed a 50 per cent duty rebate to producers of less than 5,000 hectolitres or 3,000 barrels of beer annually (a brewer's barrel is 288 pints or 1.63 hectolitres). Brewers of more than 3,000 but less than 18,000 barrels a year got progressively smaller rebates. It was a step that enraged established brewers; and even those few micros that had grown to near the 18,000-barrel ceiling were less than pleased, describing it as a disincentive to growth. But the proof of the pudding is in the eating: PBD made possible an enormous increase in the number of micros in Britain, of which there are, at time of writing, approaching 2,200 – a figure that would have seemed incredible even five years ago. HM Treasury is currently reviewing Small Brewers Relief to determine if reform is needed, and if it is needed, what this reform might look like.

Direct Delivery Scheme (Beerflex)

Following the hat-trick of the 1990 Beer Orders, end product duty, and PBD, SIBA scored again with its Direct Delivery Scheme, now called Beerflex.

The withering away of the guest ale market as the Big Six were one by one snuffed out threatened to close the pub trade to small brewers again thanks to the appearance of non-brewing pub companies or "pubcos", as they are inelegantly abbreviated. Most of them were founded with estates of discards bought wholesale from the Big Six. Often they were set up by ex-Big Six personnel, financed by Big Six loans, and stocked only Big Six beers. But one by one they were bought out by aggressive predators funded by venture capitalist houses, in many cases foreign-owned, and very soon the links between the pubcos and the old national brewers were severed.

Next, the Big Six themselves were targeted; as we have seen, all of them have now gone, bought out by Carlsberg from Denmark, Molson Coors from the USA, Heineken from the Netherlands and the multinational Anheuser-Busch InBev.

At the same time, many old-established regional breweries were succumbing to a fad for separating their brewing operations from their pub estates. The near-universal business model in the industry had always been "vertical integration" – that is, the ownership of both manufacture and retail. One of the effects of the Beer Orders, though, had been the driving down of wholesale beer prices as the pubcos shopped around for their beer. In the light of this, the City of London decreed that brewing was no longer profitable, and that the regionals should become pure retailers. Those that gave in to the siren song and got shot of their breweries – Usher's, Gibbs Mew, Morland, Greenall Whitley, Morrells, Brakspear, Eldridge Pope, Burtonwood and others – have by and large been taken over, either by other pubcos, or by those rival regionals that still believe in vertical integration. For its opposite, as things turned out, has proved to be total disintegration.

Today's big pubcos source their beers more widely than either the national or regional breweries to whose estates they succeeded ever had. But they have always found it difficult to deal with local microbrewers. They own no drays or depots of their own; their pubs are supplied either directly by the brewers themselves or, more commonly, by third-party wholesalers. Micros were at first generally too small to deal direct with such giants nationally – Punch Taverns at its peak owned 9,000 pubs, 1,200 more than Bass ever did, and Enterprise Inns in its heyday had almost as many; and few of the new wave of brewers could supply even a fraction of such vast estates. And even when microbrewers' beers were listed by a pubco for regional distribution, it was always galling to have to deliver to a depot 100 miles away or more to get into a pubco-owned pub just down the road – and even more galling to have to return to the depot for the empties!

SIBA's Beerflex has created software that allows local brewers to deal directly with pubco-owned pubs that want to stock their ales. The scheme may appear cumbrous in that it's still the pubco that actually buys the beer from the brewer and sells it to the pub; but the transaction is entirely electronic, and in practical terms it's the brewer who makes the sale, delivers the beer, and collects the empties. (No small matter when the 72-pint firkins most commonly used cost £80 apiece, and the longer they stay out in trade, the more you need to own.)

Beerflex has grown into a business which in 2019 achieved a turnover of more than £12 million. It currently buys more than 4,500 draught and bottled beer from around 450 participating SIBA brewers and sells them to 12 national pub companies and off-trade retailers – companies with which, until the establishment of Beerflex, brewers of local beers found it extremely difficult to trade.

The Future of Microbrewing

In a nutshell, then – rather a large nutshell, granted, but the story of 40 years can't be told in 40 words – that's how we got where we are. The question is: where do you fit in? Indeed, given the amazing growth spurt of the last few years, will there be room for you to fit in at all?

The answer, counterintuitively, seems to be yes. After its turbulent first decade the microbrewing sector developed a remarkable stability, and in the 30 years since then many small independent breweries have changed ownership as the first generation has retired or, as in cases such as Ringwood, Wychwood, Sharp's, Caledonian, and Harviestoun, bigger brewers eager for credible new brands have bought them out. But despite fairly regular predictions of a shake-out due to market saturation, there have been remarkably few outright business failures – and this despite the slow-unfolding crisis in the on-trade which has seen maybe a quarter of Britain's pubs close in the last five years.

Microbrewing seems to have developed a momentum of its own, separate from other trends. Microbrewers have always had to innovate to suit and indeed lead changes in consumer tastes; to find and exploit niches in a heavily restricted licensed trade; in short, to make their own markets. In this respect, small has always been not only beautiful but nimble. The decision-makers in big breweries and pubcos sit far from the scene of the action – trade intelligence is relayed upwards through a chain of business development managers and regional offices, and their responses (if any) flow back through the same slow and often hidebound channels. Similarly, brand decisions are taken centrally after months of R&D followed by prolonged and weighty deliberations; so much is invested in them in terms both of resources and of prestige that they are hard to reverse. The microbrewer, by contrast, is (theoretically, at least) flexible enough to exploit whatever local opportunity arises more or less instantly and to create new beers ad hoc without losing too much if they don't catch on.

The latest manifestation of the agility of small brewers is the current craze for craft beers. The descriptor was turned down as implying kitchen-sink amateurism when SIBA was choosing a name for itself. It resurfaced more recently when a growing number of new brewers started following the example of German-trained brewmaster Alastair Hook, first of Freedom Brewery of Fulham and now of Meantime Brewing Company of Greenwich, in rejecting the old shibboleth that only cask-conditioned (or bottle-conditioned) beer was "real" and that keg dispense (of which much more later) necessarily meant an inferior product. So toxic had the word "keg" become, however, that some bright spark had the idea of calling it "craft" (a term imported from the USA) instead. The term has no intrinsic meaning, but it quickly caught on – especially in London, which was (rather belatedly) developing a dynamic and innovative small brewing scene of its own. Other micros started calling themselves craft brewers; then imported American beers were marketed as craft beers; now the term is near-universal – even regional and national brewers use it – and it is still pretty well meaningless. Nonetheless, it's the perfect example of smaller, more flexible, and more imaginative brewers leading the mainstream industry by the nose.

The craft craze will undoubtedly plateau and perhaps even dwindle in due course, just as previous micro-led trends – the porter revival, the golden ales explosion – have done. But another trend will emerge to take its place... and you may very well be the one to lead it.

Chapter One
How to Brew

Brewing beer, as I mentioned in the Introduction, is not actually all that complicated. Not in theory, at any rate. You simply steep malt in hot water until its starch content turns into sugar and dissolves; you strain off the resulting thin syrup and boil it up with hops; you add yeast and when it all stops bubbling and foaming, you drink it. (Or, in your case, sell it for someone else to drink.) How hard can it be? But as with any craft, success depends on absolute mastery of materials and processes; and within the simple framework outlined above the possible variations are almost infinite. So before you can present the public with a product of consistently good quality (and achieving consistency will be one of your key skills), you're going to need a lot of training, both theoretical and practical.

You can learn the brewing skills you will need on courses run by formal training providers such as Brewlab (**www.brewlab.co.uk**). You can learn the basic engineering skills needed to keep your plant running (if you don't already possess them) from the fabricator who installs it. But before you take either of those risky and expensive steps, you can teach yourself most of what you will need to know about beer by reading, tasting widely and intelligently, visiting working breweries and by brewing at home. And you can start the reading part of your home-learning course right here.

In 40 years of pub-going, I have never got over my surprise at how little the public actually knows about its beer. Many regular drinkers don't even know what it's made of; and public ideas about alcoholic strength are hopelessly confused. So let's start with a potted description of what beer is and how it's made.

The Basics of Brewing

Most alcoholic beverages have three components. The first is a liquid medium. The second is the sugar that the yeast will digest, alcohol and carbon dioxide (CO_2) being its waste products. Finally, there are the aromatic or flavour components. If you're making wine, all three come in one handy little package – the grape (or the strawberry or blackberry or whatever soft fruit you're using). All you have to do is crush your fruit, strain off the juice, add yeast – or let naturally occurring wild yeasts do the job for you – and let it ferment. Hard fruits such as apples and pears are harder to crush – you have to pulp them in a mill before you can press the juice out of them – but the principle is the same. Everything you need is in the fruit. With beer, things aren't so simple. In fact, cereal grains are so hard to ferment it's a wonder that beer was ever invented. For in their natural state, grains contain almost none of the required components: no liquid, no sugar and not much in the way of flavour. All three have to be painstakingly brought together before you can even think about introducing yeast.

Malt

Malt is usually made from barley, but brewers also use other grains, both malted and unmalted. You will probably be familiar with wheat as a brewing grain already, but oats, rye and even rice are also added for particular purposes. In essence, malt is cereal grain that has been tricked into germinating by being steeped in warm water to mimic spring weather. During germination, enzymes in the grain start to convert its insoluble starch into sugar, which the plant needs in order to fuel its growth. This sugar, maltose, is soluble, and is what you want as your fermentable material. So, soon after the grain has started to germinate, it's dried in a kiln to halt the process before it goes too far. Different kilning times and temperatures produce pale, amber, chocolate, crystal, roast and other types of malt, each with its own properties. You will almost certainly be using blends of malts, so you will need to be familiar with all their characteristics. You may also want to use brewing sugars in some brews: these have flavour characteristics of their own and are perfectly respectable adjuncts in many brewing traditions.

Liquor

Once the little sprouts have been shaken off, the malt is ground into a coarse flour (grist) ready to be "mashed' in hot water (referred to as liquor – water, in a brewery, is for washing and cooling). Mashing both completes the conversion of starch into sugar (saccharification) and dissolves the sugar to produce a thin malt syrup or wort. The mineral content of the water is critical: gypsum-rich water from the artesian wells beneath Burton-upon-Trent produced the classic pale ales that succeeded the darker stouts and porters brewed with London water in popular favour in the 19th Century. British ales require hard water, while continental lagers require soft water, for reasons explained later on. Some breweries have their own wells or boreholes; you will probably have to settle for mains water, but analyse it and alter its mineral content first.

Hops

Next, the boil and the addition of hops. Hops contain acids that kill bacteria and protect the beer from infection, and were introduced to British brewing in the 14th or 15th century chiefly as a preservative. But they are vital for flavour, too: their acid may give beer its bitterness, but they also contain oils and resins that produce much of its taste and aroma. Some hops are more acidic than others; some are more aromatic. The aroma characteristics vary hugely from strain to strain: Goldings, for example, produce a citric tang, while Bramling Cross are said to give an aroma of blackcurrants. Again, you will need a thorough knowledge of hop varieties if you are to become a master of your craft.

Yeast

A microscopic fungus, yeast digests the maltose in the wort and excretes alcohol and the CO_2 that puts the fizz into the beer. Every brewery has its own strain, and every strain is different both in its handling characteristics and in the flavours it produces. Yeast is tricky stuff to handle and is very prone to infection. At the University of East Anglia in Norwich is the National Yeast Bank, where brewers send samples of their yeast from which to propagate fresh supplies if problems occur at the brewery. Brewers are very proud of their yeast strains, saying they give their beers their house character, so the strain you choose at the outset will define your brews for years to come.

Other Ingredients

More and more these days, you will come across other ingredients, especially fruit. Fruit has been used for centuries by brewers, especially in Belgium, where some beers are fermented by naturally occurring wild yeasts rather than cultured brewing strains. Wild yeasts and the other microfauna and flora that accompany them often produce sour flavours that are not to everyone's taste: adding pulped cherries or blackcurrants to the mash of sour brown ales and lambic beers is a traditional method of tempering their sourness. In the last 20 years or so these Belgian fruit beers have become more widely available in Britain, and many British brewers have been inspired to experiment with fruit as well. Grapefruit beer from the St Peter's Brewery of Suffolk is one unlikely but surprisingly palatable example.

Almost as important as the raw materials to the character of the beer are the processes by which it is made. The grist must be mashed at a specific temperature for the starch to be fully converted and the sugars to be fully dissolved. The boil can be long or short – a long boil caramelises some of the sugars in the wort and produces a richer, darker beer – and hops are added in different quantities and at different points in the process. The hopped wort has to be cooled before the yeast is pitched, and there are various methods of fermentation which each produce different results. All of this you must learn thoroughly.

Vessels

The vessels can be critical too, especially the shape and size of your fermenters and conditioning tanks. We'll come to the number and type of vessels you'll need in a later chapter. But as an example, take fermentation. It's a biochemical process which, like all biochemical processes, generates a certain amount of heat. This can dictate the speed of fermentation and help or hinder the creation of by-products such as phenols and esters, all of which will affect the finished product; and the thermodynamics of different-shaped fermenters will give different results. Modern cylindro-conical lager fermenters produce more heat and work more quickly than old-fashioned horizontal ones, so a lager conditioned in a cylindro-conical will be detectably sweeter and less clean than one aged in a horizontal. There are plenty of other similar examples, so even before you build your brewery, you will have to have made critical decisions about what sort of beers you want to brew. And it's important to make these decisions from a position of knowledge, which you can get right now – assuming, that is, that your local is open. Because the best way to learn about beer is to drink it, but to drink it intelligently. That means sampling as many different examples of as many different styles as you can get hold of. And sampling is not the same as swigging!

Tasting Beer

The first time I was invited to an organised beer tasting, on a press trip to Bruges nearly 30 years ago, I thought someone was taking the mickey. Arriving at a bar called 't Brugs Beertje, the party was shown into the function room in which was a huge table garnished with an astonishing array of glasses (you shouldn't use the same one too often), and bottles of mineral water and dishes of dry crackers to cleanse our palates between samples. Once seated, we first held up each sample to the light to check its colour, clarity and head. There followed a thorough swirling and nosing à la Jilly Goolden, with tasters detecting aromas of leather, tobacco, new-mown hay et al. A meagre mouthful was then ritualistically swilled; air was sucked; and mouthfeel (i.e. residual sugars, if any, coating the tongue) and flavours were pronounced upon. Finally, we swallowed (you don't spit out beer as you do wine, since the bitterness receptors are at the very back of the tongue). A long hush ensued, with expressions of intense concentration while the length and bitterness of the finish (or aftertaste) were thoroughly cogitated. Finally, there followed a brief but intense discussion of each sample – Was it true to style? Were there any off-flavours? How complex was it? – and each beer was marked.

Well, it seemed daft to me at the time. But after many years of attending such tastings, I have discovered the value of really concentrating on what you're drinking; and at tastings you have to strain your tastebuds in exactly the same way you have to strain your ears to hear a distant melody. Conveying your experiences is difficult, because you have to describe the flavours you detect in terms of others that are commonly recognisable; hence the descent into vocabulary such as "green fruit", "treacle toffee", "marmalade" and other comparables. It all sounds incredibly pretentious, yet the language of tastings is expressly not intended to exclude the uninitiated. In fact the very opposite is true: it's meant to allow a group of individuals (normally brewery staff) to describe their personal experiences of a range of sensations in a format that can be shared. But the difficulty of translating tastes and smells into words even affects skilled and experienced brewers. You might expect, perhaps, that professionals who live and breathe diacetyls, esters, phenols and sulphites would describe their beers in those terms. They do, but only to a limited extent. The flavour wheel used by brewers all around the world since the 1970s to delineate the aromas and tastes of their products includes those terms, but also uses expressions such as liquorice, chocolate, butterscotch, toffee, pineapple, catty, papery, leathery, grassy – even Horlicks!

It struck me quite early on in my beer-tasting career that there's a metaphysical dimension to it, especially in the attempt to explain your findings. You're trying to do two things, both of which are impossible: to objectify the subjective, and to describe one set of sensory experiences in terms of another. You might as well try to paint Beethoven's Fifth, or describe red. Nevertheless, you have to do it. You have to explore all the different possibilities of beer with your intellect as much as with your tastebuds, and for two good reasons. First, having chosen what you want to brew you have to be able to recreate your choice exactly, every time you brew it. And second, you need to upgrade from mere organolept – that is, a dilettante who just likes beer – into a ruthlessly efficient sensory analyst whose finely honed papillae (Latin for "tastebuds") can instantly and accurately detect and identify imperfections and variations from brew to brew.

From a practical point of view, though, wide-ranging tastings of a good selection of beers aren't that easy to arrange. To be meaningful, tastings need to be comparative: you need to be able taste and decide between a range of at least half-a-dozen bitters or best bitters or old ales or stouts or whatever. Very few pubs stock more than one example of any one beer style other than British-brewed lager, of which they might have two or three. Even the handful of real ale Meccas that carry 10 or 12 cask beers at a time will try to stock as wide a spread as possible. The same is true, if to a lesser extent, of supermarkets. They may carry a bewildering variety of pilsner-style beers, from cheap "slab-packs" of canned French or Belgian lager brewed mainly from corn syrup to top-notch Czech beers such as Budweiser Budvar, but of bottled ales they will have only one or two examples of each style. But by shopping around you can assemble wide enough selections of styles to hold meaningful tastings of your own, possibly inviting friends round to make an event of it. And don't exclude women! It's long been known in the industry, and recently confirmed by medical research, that by and large they have more accurate sense-memories than men. So a serious beer-tasting is not merely an excuse for a night in with the lads.

You should also join the Campaign for Real Ale (CAMRA) (**www.camra.org.uk**). Each CAMRA branch is supposed to field an official tasting panel to help select entries for the *Good Beer Guide* and to judge the branch's annual beer competition. Members of these panels receive free expert training, which will be invaluable to you later on. But for some reason, branches are often short of volunteers to serve on their tasting panels, so if you put yourself forward you will undoubtedly be a very welcome member of the team.

Further Reading

There is a host of good and informative books about beer styles and traditions by authoritative writers on the market; you may not find them in bookshops, but there's a specialist bookseller called Beer Inn-Print (**www.beerinnprint.co.uk**) which, despite its title, also has a good selection of out-of-print titles.

Visiting Breweries

You should also visit as many breweries as you can. Twenty years ago it used to be almost impossible to tour a working brewery unless you were in the licensed trade. Visitors were generally considered a nuisance who only got in the way, and most old-established breweries were such a jumble of pipework, narrow spaces, uneven floors and steps and stairs, mostly awash with water, that tour parties were a health and safety nightmare. Today, it's all different: most of the older regional breweries run conducted group tours, and some even have visitors' centres with shops, bars and museums or, at least, displays of antique brewing equipment and brewery ephemera. This change of attitude has been driven mainly by marketing considerations. Smaller breweries with little to spend on advertising have come to see the benefit of drawing the public in. As a result, most brewery visitor centres are aimed more at the tourist than the would-be brewer; even so, they will acquaint you with the sights, sounds and, indeed, the smells that will surround you every day once you have opened a brewery of your own.

For more informal tours, often conducted by the brewer themselves, which gives you a chance to ask questions and get full and informed answers, your CAMRA membership will come in handy yet again. All local branches organise regular trips to breweries large and small in their areas and sometimes further afield. You may even get the chance to do a bit of real hands-on brewing: most branches have a special beer made by a local brewer for their annual beer festivals, and sometimes branch members are allowed to do the actual mashing. This could be you! And if you get friendly enough with a local brewer, they may even allow you to help out occasionally (don't expect to be paid, though!).

CASE STUDY

Abbeydale Brewery
Investing in a brewery is rarely a one-off activity – it's for life

Over time, most brewers come to realise that to expand and improve the quality of their beers requires continued investment in equipment and design.

Sheffield was once famed as a steel city; now it is widely regarded as one of the UK's brewing capitals, such has been the success of its new wave of brewers. It is home to the Abbeydale Brewery, which has just launched a rebrand for its renowned core range of cask ales.

With the previous artwork having been in use since the brewery's formation in 1996, the new look is intended to refresh the range whilst paying homage to Abbeydale's rich history and ensuring that the familiarity with its most popular beers is not lost.

The new artwork has been created by local artist, well-known print maker James Green, in conjunction with Field Design, a small design agency based at the Workstation in Sheffield.

Abbeydale Brewery director Dan Baxter said of the rebrand: "Whilst we are thrilled that the original artwork had such longevity, we know the time has come to reinvest in our artwork for our treasured core beers.

"We hope this will enable us to best provide the right support and backbone for our business and those of our customers, as well as ensuring the people who drink and enjoy our beer will recognise that the branding reinforces the quality of our beloved brews."

The rebrand comes as part of Abbeydale Brewery's plan for continued expansion, in conjunction with the ambition to cement its reputation as Sheffield's foremost craft beer brewery. In recent years, alongside the traditional cask ales Abbeydale is well known for, it has also released numerous innovative beers in both cask and keg.

Inspiration from American brewing styles is a common theme, with Abbeydale having worked on collaborations with celebrated American breweries including Founders, Dan Rogers of Griffin Claw, NoDa and Kuhnhenn Brewing Co.

This is coupled with a commitment to the local community – many of its beers contain locally sourced ingredients (neighbours Birdhouse Tea Co have worked with the brewery on multiple occasions, and Sheffield coffee purveyor Pollard's supplied the key ingredient for a collaboration with award-winning local bottle shop Hop Hideout).

The new-look core range will shortly be joined by a second series showcasing beers using new ingredients and further expanding Abbeydale's outlook on exciting beer styles, including a new barrel souring programme.

In order to expand to the next level and develop beyond a microbrewery, the company needed more space and more investment. For that reason, it made sense to work with NatWest, which could provide a mortgage, while Finance Yorkshire could provide the £100,000 cash boost needed to buy the equipment and employ a new member of staff.

Abbeydale Brewery director Susan Morton said: "The extra space and new equipment will allow us to increase our capacity and make us more efficient and as a direct result of the investment we have been able to take on a new employee. We now have 13 members of staff and we are pleased to bring job opportunities to the community."

www.abbeydalebrewery.co.uk

Brewing at Home

Would-be brewers are luckier in one enormous respect than people considering new careers in other industries. For brewing is one of the few trades, along with baking and one or two others, in which you can coach yourself almost up to professional level in your own home, without giving up your job and without investing too much of your savings.

Many of today's local brewers started off as home-brewing enthusiasts who finally tipped over and turned their hobby into their living. But even if you're not a frequent and regular home brewer yet, you should become one: it's the single most important step in your preparations for your new career. If you are already a home brewer, you'll understand the advantages: for instance, that it's possible to start slowly, with a kit that requires little more than the addition of hot water to make a passable beer. From the all-in-one kit you can graduate step by step through the various phases of difficulty until you're quite at home with all-malt, whole-hop brews. Home-brewing kits can also be upgraded piece by piece from a bucket in the airing cupboard to a miniature tower brewery complete with mash tun, copper, hop back, wort cooler, fermenter and conditioning tank, all of gleaming steel and copper, perfect in every detail. One is always reading of enthusiasts whose garden sheds or garages are home to lovingly constructed brewing plants that need only an excise licence to start operating commercially – indeed, there are one or two cases where this has actually happened.

Brewing at home will familiarise you with brewing materials and techniques, with faults and their cures and with different beer styles. It will also give you the chance to experiment with recipes; and I have heard of local brewers who perfected their entire ranges during their amateur days and were able to turn professional with enviable smoothness. But there's more to it than that. Home brewing will help you in practical terms, yes, but also in psychological terms. Have you really got what it takes to be a brewer? Are you a true enthusiast, or merely a dabbler? If you find your interest in brewing as a hobby palls after a few months, you can be sure it's not going to be a wise move to try and make a living at it. By the same token, if you find the bug is really biting, you can be more certain than many others in your position that the step you're about to take is the right one.

Boots stopped stocking home-brewing and wine-making equipment and materials some years ago, but the Wilko chain now carries a limited supply of essentials. There are also specialist home-brew supply shops in many towns; a site such as **yell.com** will tell you where your nearest is, or you could simply look it up on Google. Internet shopping means that almost anything you require is now but a few clicks away; Googling "home brewing and winemaking" will turn up a galaxy of suppliers selling a huge range of stock and equipment from the most basic to the professional level. The drawback with the internet, though, is that shopping on the net deprives you of the opportunity to talk in person to an expert, which is invaluable. The Craft Brewing Association (CBA), founded in 1995, can fill this gap. Its website, **www.craftbrewing.org.uk**, lists local home-brew supplies shops and, for those who don't have one in their area, mail-order suppliers too. It's a mine of information in other regards as well: anyone with even a passing interest in beer could browse its technical pages for hours. In addition to that, the CBA offers training for beer tasters, runs competitions, helps with recipe designs, has beer style guidelines of its own and has a quarterly newsletter, *Brewer's Contact*. It's divided into local groups covering most of the country; if there isn't one near you, use the link on the site to the National Association of Wine and Beer Makers (**www.nawb.org.uk**), which is more wine-oriented but still lists many home brewers among its membership.

Other groups, especially the UK Craft Beer Network, also flourish on social media. The Network is actually a Facebook page, which gives it the advantage of immediacy but the drawback that you can't easily access previous conversations. What you can do, though, is pose questions and get answers in real time, and as there are at time of writing nearly 7,000 members – many of whom have turned professional – you can be pretty much guaranteed a lively and informative online chat.

Formal Training

So you've drunk intelligently; you've read up on the subject; you've toured breweries; you've brewed your own beer. Now you're ready for your formal training. But where are you going to get it?

Fundamentals of Minibrewing

The obvious answer is that you'll get all the information you need from an experienced brewer, but choosing the right person to teach you the best brewing practice can be as difficult as finding the right brewing equipment. What you need is a person with a good practical brewing pedigree and knowledge, with decades of experience in designing and installing breweries. One of the UK's leading brewers and microbrewery designers is David Smith of Brewing Services Ltd (**www.brewingservices.co.uk**). David spent more than 20 years working for Samuel Smith's in Tadcaster, first as a production brewer and then in a quality assurance role, before leaving to set up his brewing consultancy in 1988. This was just as the microbrewing industry was starting to gain traction and people with a good brewing knowledge were in high demand. Since then, he has designed and installed many breweries but never lost sight of the fact that the equipment isn't much use without the know-how. Having initially set up his consultancy to provide technical assistance and quality assurance services to brewers, it soon became apparent there was a significant skills shortage and that training brewers was therefore of paramount importance..

With this in mind, David set up his own training course: The Fundamentals of Mini-Brewing. Billed as "the course designed by brewers for brewers", The Fundamentals of Mini-Brewing started out in 1989 as the first training course dedicated to those working, or wanting to work, in microbreweries.

David, together with his son Rob who joined the company in 2015 after many years working with Dartmoor, Freedom and Meantime breweries, runs this highly successful four-day course twice yearly. It is firmly rooted in the experience that David, Rob and their guest lecturers have gained in their working lives. The aim of the course is to pass on that practical knowledge and provide the essential first step for anyone planning a microbrewery. It combines lectures and workshops by brewers and industry specialists with visits to a local maltings, other microbreweries and packagers. For those wanting to increase their practical experience there is also the opportunity to help with a complete brew at a working brewery before the course begins. Topics discussed encompass the whole brewing process, from the importance of the correct brewing equipment and good brewery design to selecting the right raw materials and recipe formulation, from mashing in through to packaging and quality control. The purpose of the course is to instill a greater insight into the art and science of brewing while emphasising the need for consistently high quality and good brewing practice.

Following on from The Fundamentals of Mini-Brewing and once your brewery is up and running, Brewing Services Ltd offers tailored on-site training for brewery staff of all levels, as well as mentoring for other exams. The demand for experienced brewers is high and training novice brewers is a great way to ensure that each brewery's training needs are met. More information, current prices and an application form are available at **www.brewingservices.co.uk/ training**. Alternatively, contact Rob on +44 (0) 7966 693 097 or David on +44 (0) 7970 629 552, or email enquiries@brewingservices.co.uk.

Heriot-Watt University

At the other end of the scale is the Bachelor of Sciences course Brewing and Distilling at Heriot-Watt University (**www.hw.ac.uk**) in Edinburgh, one of the world's leading brewing schools since 1903. The BSc course has an annual intake of 10–14 undergraduates who in their four years (this is a Scottish university, not an English one) at Heriot-Watt will learn not only how to make beer but how to turn it into whisky as well. It is a complete course training graduates for employment in both the craft and larger brewing companies. Heriot-Watt is also world-renowned for its Master's degree in brewing and distilling – so world-renowned, in fact, that usually less than a quarter of the annual on-campus intake of 35–45 are British.

If you fancy the letters MSc after your name, you need a first degree in chemistry, chemical engineering, biochemistry, microbiology or something similar, and if you are applying from outside Scotland, a substantial sum for the fees. Again, it is a complete course training graduates for employment in both the craft and larger brewing companies.

Heriot-Watt's Postgraduate Diploma distance learning programme, though, is a different matter altogether. Consisting of eight courses at £1,100 to £2,400 depending on country of origin, it's tailored for busy working people and you can take up to four years to complete it. You can choose only the courses that seem most useful to you, getting a separate certificate for each course you complete, or a Postgraduate Certificate on completion of four courses. On completion of the PG Diploma it is possible to continue to complete the MSc. Seven courses are taught entirely electronically via an online portal, and email and telephone contact is encouraged with course directors. The cohort of approximately 100 attracts brewers from all over the world and all students attend a two week practical workshop to gain hands-on experience in brewing, distilling, malting and microbiology during their studies. For more details, go to **www.postgraduate.hw.ac.uk/prog/119**.

LOOKING TO
FREE UP CAPITAL?

CASE STUDY

Premier Systems

Premier Systems and Serious Brewing: The benefits of brewery management software

In June 2021 BrewMan Version 7, the new web-based version of brewery management software used by 250 breweries in the UK, was launched publicly.

Over the past two years, Premier Systems has completely rebuilt BrewMan to combine the features and functions that have been developed alongside its brewery customers for 20 years with new modern interfaces and intuitive controls that can be accessed through a web browser on any device. This allows users to calculate duty, track production, place orders, manage stock and track casks, all from their smartphones as well as at the office.

As part of this rebuilding process, several breweries signed up to a test version of the system to provide feedback on any improvements that should be made to help their daily processes, as well as spotting and reporting any bugs in the developing system.

The Serious Brewing Company was one of these companies who have managed their business with BrewMan V7 for the last few months, giving Premier Systems invaluable feedback to help steer the development of the system.

Serious Brewing Company is a six-barrel independent microbrewery, based in Rochdale. The brewery was founded in 2015 by husband and wife team Ken and Jenny Lynch. They brew a range of cask and bottled beers, including traditional British ales, pale ales, an award-winning stout and several Belgian-style beers. Consistency and quality are at the heart of everything that Serious Brewing Company is about from the brewing equipment to the careful selection of ingredients.

We spoke to Ken Lynch, co-founder at Serious Brewing, about their experience with the new platform.

What were some of the issues you faced before installing BrewMan?

We were using another system before we switched to BrewMan; it was a Windows application that lived on one laptop at home, which meant that I had to keep notes at the brewery and remember to bring them home to enter in when my wife wasn't using the laptop

15

for sales or accounts. It wasn't a bad system, but we'd outgrown it and it didn't provide the features we felt we needed. The main attraction to BrewMan was that it was cloud based, meaning my wife and I could both have access from any device, wherever we were. After seeing the demonstration, I was impressed at how clean and modern the interface is and that it even works well on a small mobile screen.

How has it helped the business since going live?
As there are only two of us running the brewery, our time is very important, and BrewMan has helped free up time spent on administration to allow us to focus more on production and sales.

Which functions have you found most useful that you didn't realise were available?
The distribution app has totally changed the way we do deliveries. It's much more streamlined than the way we used to do it; the app guides you through the delivery from scanning items off the van, collecting empties and taking a signature. It even integrates with your phone's navigation, which is a pretty cool feature.

How did you find the set-up process and working with the Premier Systems team?
The set-up was very straightforward and having the demo brewery data to play around with helped in figuring out anything that I didn't understand at first. The support from the BrewMan team has been first class.

Would you recommend BrewMan to others?
Definitely! I've already recommended it to a number of breweries.

www.premiersystems.com

Brewlab

Brewlab (**www.brewlab.co.uk**) is a centre for brewing studies and analytical, microbiological and consultancy services, based within the Sunderland City boundary. It teaches courses such as StartUp Brewing and British Brewing Technology, while also supplying specialist training in taste evaluation, microbiology and small-scale bottling services. Courses range from one-day introductory workshops in bottling, tasting and practical brewing to three-week and three-month programmes in brewing theory and practice. It also runs a range of "after sales services" to assist brewers with quality control requirements, tax and excise compliance, yeast storage and propagation. Due diligence packages can be tailored to individual brewery needs, helping to maintain quality and compliance with the industry codes of practice.

Brewlab was founded at the City of London Polytechnic in 1986 to provide laboratory analysis for brewers large and small; the training side of the operation was only developed later to enable staff in the microbrewery sector to understand and interpret analysis results. In 1992 Brewlab moved to the University of Sunderland to take advantage of its extensive biotechnology laboratory facilities. In 2008 Brewlab moved out of the university into temporary brewing and educational facilities, and then in 2011 it settled into a purpose-built modern headquarters incorporating facilities for teaching, analysis, brewing and consultancy services. Its laboratories provide up-to-date facilities for practical work alongside dedicated equipment for detailed studies. There is a fully operational 100 litre (22 gallon) pilot training plant and 25–40 litre kits for recipe development and training. Small-scale bottling facilities allow practical experience and are an opportunity for students to brew beers for sale in local outlets. Students also have access to other research facilities.

Brewlab operates a fully commercial three-barrel showpiece brewery which can provide an industrial setting for student placements and allow them to experience full-scale production. There are also strong links to local microbreweries, allowing for the opportunity for student placements in a variety of plant types, sizes and settings.

Managing the teaching programme and laboratory activities are Dr Keith Thomas, Arthur Bryant, Mike Hitchen and Alison Hedley, with many years' industry experience. In addition to the scheduled Brewlab courses, they occasionally lecture on local university courses and practical sessions such as microbiology, biotechnology and food science. Dr Thomas's specialist research areas are yeast physiology, beer analysis and bioremediation. He is often a judge at major beer festivals and competitions, both within the UK and internationally, and a regular contributor to the SIBA journal. All of the above team are members of the Institute of Brewing and Distilling (IBD). Additional staff provide specialist support for both teaching and analytical services, while students also benefit from the expertise of visiting lecturers, who work in the brewing industry or allied trades.

The Practical Brewing and British Brewing Technology courses are accredited by the Open College Network (OCN). This follows official assessment of Brewlab's course structures and teaching quality. Brewlab students may also study for external qualifications through the Institute of Brewing and Distilling, notably the General Certificate and Diploma exams. Students can also focus on developing practical skills using the varied brewing capabilities available on site.

Brewlab Training Courses

- Brewing Skills Development for production personnel
- Start Up Brewing
- Certificate in Practical Brewing
- Diploma in British Brewing Technology
- Microbiology Workshop
- Advanced Craft Brewing Workshop

For further information contact **info@brewlab.co.uk** or go to **www.brewlab.co.uk**

The course options include one day workshops for craft brewers who want to develop their skills and knowledge, three or four day start-ups, residential three week and three month courses for those who wish to make a career in brewing, either to manage their own brewery, to seek employment in the industry or to further their career prospects.

For many of the courses, groups are limited to 12 students to enable staff to spend more time with individuals. Although some knowledge of maths, chemistry and biology would be beneficial on the more detailed courses, Brewlab provides full student support and additional tuition.

There is a range of professional and development courses for those who already work in the brewing industry wanting to improve their technical and brewing skills.

Students successfully completing course assessments and examinations will receive a Certificate in Practical Brewing or a Diploma in British Brewing Technology accredited by the Open College Network equivalent to NVQ Level 3.

For the following courses, all dates and fees are published on the Brewlab website.

Brewing Skills Development for Production Personnel

Brewlab has created this course following requests from clients for training to enhance the knowledge of existing staff. The course is aimed specifically at those involved in the brewing and production processes and those wanting to improve their understanding of:

- The key factors on which quality ale production depends
- The brewing process – from raw materials to final product
- Production problems, enabling them to be addressed on site, leading to more consistent quality products

The course starts with targeted sessions on the four main raw materials – liquor, malt/adjuncts, hops and yeast. Each session discusses the raw material, its specifications and commonly encountered problems with its usage. The fundamental brewing processes are covered in brewer's terms, along with current industry best practice.

The processes covered include malting, mashing, sparging, boiling, cooling, fermentation, maturation, finings, racking, casking, cleaning, hygiene, quality control and tasting.

Course Programme

- Day One – Recipe formulation, brewing liquor, malt, mashing and sparging
- Day Two – Hops, boiling, cooling, yeast, fermentation, maturation, cask racking and fining
- Day Three – Quality control, food safety and beer flavour profiling
- Day four – Food safety and practical brewing

It is not necessary to attend the full four days and participants can choose which days they wish to study.

Start Up Brewing

Start Up Brewing is a comprehensive three-day course with an optional fourth day of hands-on brewing in a working microbrewery. The course provides a realistic introduction to the brewing process and the requirements of commercial brewing. It is suitable for potential or recently engaged brewers and those looking at brewing as a possible career change or business opportunity.

No background knowledge of brewing is required for the course and the aim is to provide you with a sound overview of the industry and an understanding of the requirements of operating a commercial brewing venture. Opportunities are offered to view the stages of a commercial brew, to study the basic steps of brewing and to discuss business start-up issues with working brewers and specialists.

Certificate in Practical Brewing

A detailed three-week examination course in the theory and practice of brewing. The Certificate in Practical Brewing has an emphasis on traditional procedures and provides up-to-date knowledge, with a strong practical element through laboratory work and placement brewing opportunities. Course work is extended with a series of site visits and external placements. Additional subsidiary components cover:
- Basic microbiology
- Taste training, cellar craft
- Food safety
- Marketing, sales and business start-up

Students completing the course will be awarded a Certificate of achievement comparable to an NVQ Level 3. Accommodation is provided at the University of Sunderland halls of residence as part of the course fees.

Diploma in British Brewing Technology

The three-month examination course offers extensive practical experience with regard to recipe formulation and practical brewing, allowing in-depth use of theory gained on the course. External placements are timetabled throughout the course and additional time is dedicated to self study and research for assessments where relevant. Students are also extended the opportunity to study marketing, business planning and sales techniques and experience group presentations.

Assessments include brew to specification technique, quality assurance plan construction and brewing log records. The module supporting the course, Brewing Technology, has no formal prerequisites for study, but students are advised to anticipate some basic biology, chemistry and maths; also some experience of home brewing or commercial plant would be beneficial. Students completing the course will be awarded a diploma of achievement comparable to an NVQ Level 3.

The majority of students attending this course are successful in either starting up their own business or gaining employment in the industry. Accommodation is provided at the University of Sunderland halls of residence as part of the course fees.

One-Day Microbiology Workshop

Brewlab's dedicated Microbiology Workshop offers a comprehensive introduction to the use of microscopy and microbiology techniques. The course can be used to develop practical skills in laboratory analysis as well as to instigate a quality control programme for due diligence purposes. This is a one-day workshop where students can learn to use a light microscope to carry out basic microbiological techniques. Some understanding of the brewing process, along with basic maths and chemistry, would be beneficial but not essential.

By the end of the course attendees will have gained knowledge on how to set up and implement their own microbrewery hygiene and quality control procedures.

Advanced Craft Brewing Workshop

Advanced Brewing Workshops provide opportunities for brewers with amateur or small-scale commercial microbreweries to investigate their brewing operations in technical detail. The sessions run over an intensive weekend based at Brewlab's headquarters in Sunderland.

Full laboratory support is provided including technical staff, brewing facilities and a dedicated analytical laboratory. Participants are provided with opportunities to develop analytical skills including microscopy, basic chemical procedures and flavour evaluation. Some experimental work is conducted by Brewlab on relevant brewing issues. The sessions are intensive but rewarding and excellent value in helping to improve your products or to provide quality assurance.

Analytical Services

Brewlab provides extensive analytical and investigative services to the brewing industry, ranging from routine microbiological and chemical testing to detailed fault finding and product evaluation.

Microbiological Services
- Quality control and fault finding
- Analysis services

Chemical and Physical Analysis
- Due diligence analysis packages for legislative compliance

Yeast
- Yeast supply
- Yeast safe deposit service
- Yeast analysis and characterisation

Product Development

Brewlab can assist with recipe formulation, water analysis and product-specific liquor treatment advice, as well as providing access to pilot brewplants of 25 litres through 500 litres. The analytical/microbiological laboratories have access to a variety of instruments to analyse any new products:
- Gas and HPLC chromatography
- Mass spectrometry
- X-ray analysis and electron microscopy

Sensory analysis services include a panel of fully trained and experienced beer tasters. Where appropriate advice on how to conduct taste analysis on your site can be offered and Brewlab is pleased to work with breweries to develop quality assurance programmes involving both analysis and preparation.

Brewing Consultancy

If you require advice on simple recipe or raw material uses, through to a full turnkey project, Brewlab's technical staff can assist you through the process. Its brewers have extensive consultancy experience: contact mike@brewlab.co.uk.

Metal-Bashing

Learning to make beer is not the end of the skills you'll need as a full-time brewer. Where big breweries have their own engineering services departments, you'll have to be your own engineer, because brewing on a small scale is a very hands-on business. Assuming that you can't afford just to hire contractors and sit back and watch them work, you'll need both building and project management skills to prepare your premises even before the brewery equipment arrives.

Knowing one end of an oxyacetylene torch from another, unfortunately, doesn't form part of any known brewing course so some experience of practical fabrication will be a must when the plant is being installed and assembled. Your consultant, if you use one, will oversee the project; but you'll need to play an active part because once the contractors have left it will be up to you to run and service the plant. As there's a lot of pipework in a brewery, there's no better way of gaining the intimate knowledge of your plant that you'll need to keep it running smoothly than actually rolling up your sleeves and helping install it. Once it's installed, you'll need the skills and experience to make alterations and to carry out running repairs. Some people delight in metal-bashing and take to it naturally; others don't. Which category you fall into is something you'll only discover when a crucial valve springs a leak in the middle of the night...

The Institute of Brewing and Distilling (IBD)

Between the lofty academic heights of Heriot-Watt and the more workaday practicality of Brewlab stands the Institute of Brewing and Distilling (IBD). With more than 5,000 members in 100 countries, the IBD is the world's largest and undoubtedly the most prestigious members' organisation in the professions of brewing and distilling and is truly international.

The IBD's vision statement is "the advancement of education and professional development in the science and technology of brewing, distilling and related industries"; and while its most advanced professional qualification, the diploma, might be a little beyond the aspirations of most micro and craft brewers, the two more basic qualifications are more than suitable in both practical and theoretical applications. The IBD's professional qualifications are (in increasing level of standard):

- Fundamentals of Brewing and Packaging of Beer (FBPB)
- General Certificate in Brewing (GCB)
- General Certificate in Malting (GCM)
- General Certificate in Packaging (GCP)
- Diploma in Brewing (Dipl. B)
- Diploma in Packaging (Dipl. Pack)

Recognised as global standards, these exams are taken by thousands of candidates every year at centres around the world. The IBD also runs residential study courses, workshops, symposia and an annual major brewing convention, within either the IBD Africa or Asia Pacific Sections. *The Brewer & Distiller International* is a full-colour monthly members' magazine publishing technical, training and general interest articles, plus news and views. *The Journal of the Institute of Brewing* (*JIB*) is a quarterly scientific publication containing original research.

Specific IBD Qualifications for Brewers

Foundations of Brewing and Packaging

This qualification is suitable for all non-technical workers in the beer industry who would benefit from background knowledge in beer production (such as sales, marketing, finance or HR) and for those who have just commenced their technical or production careers. The FBPB takes the form of one multiple choice paper of two hours and has City & Guilds accreditation at Level 2 of the National Qualification Framework in the UK (or equivalent internationally recognised standards). A five-day residential course including brewery visit and practical experience is available and the exam may be taken on paper or online.

The full list of sections in the Foundations of Breewng and Packaging syllabus is:

1. Overview of Brewing and Packaging Practices
2. Brewing – Raw Materials for Sweet Wort Production
3. Brewing – Conversion of the Starch to Sugars
4. Brewing – Plant for Sweet Wort Production
5. Wort Boiling
6. Wort Clarification, Cooling and Oxygenation
7. The Basic Principles of Yeast Fermentation
8. Fermentation Practice
9. Beer Maturation and Storage
10a. Preparation of Chilled/Filtered Beer for Packaging
10b. Preparation of Cask Beer for Racking
11. Beer Packaging – General Topics
12a. Packaging of Chilled/Filtered Beer – Specialist Topics
12b. Racking of Cask Beer – Specialist Topics
13. Beer Quality – Process Control
14. Beer Quality – Flavour

15. Beer Quality – Microbiological Contamination
16. Beer Quality – Quality Management
17. Plant Cleaning
18. Engineering Maintenance
19. Brewing and the Environment

Note that kegged/bottled beer and cask beer are taught and examined as alternatives.

General Certificate in Brewing (GCB)

This qualification is suitable for all working brewers and production team members. The GCB takes the form of one multiple choice paper of two hours and has City & Guilds accreditation at Level 3 of the National Qualification Framework in the UK (or equivalent internationally recognised standards). The exam is taught through five full days of tutorials supported by online learning materials and assignments, or by a five-day residential course. There is also an examination fee.

The full list of sections in the GCB syllabus is as follows:

1. Introduction to Brewing
2. Raw Materials: Malt, Water, Hops, Yeast
3a. Wort Production – Milling, Mashing
3b. Wort Production – Separation, Boiling
3c. Wort Production – Clarification, Cooling, Oxygenation
4a. Fermentation Theory and Technology
4b. Yeast Management
5a. Maturation
5b. Cooling, Carbonation and Blending
5c. Filtration
6a. Quality – Process Control
6b. Quality – Management Systems
6c. Quality – Sensory Assessment
6d. Quality – Dissolved Oxygen
7a. Hygiene – Microbiological Contamination
7b. Plant Cleaning
8a. Engineering and Maintenance
8b. Environment and Utilities
8c. Effluent
8d. Co-Products
8e. Health and Safety

Note as above that keg/bottled beer and cask ale processing are taught and examined as alternatives.

Diploma in Brewing (Dipl. B)

The Diploma in Brewing is suitable for experienced operations managers and senior team leaders working in large plants. It might be considered by established microbrewers planning a large expansion or intending to diversify into high-level consultancy work. It is taught and examined at the IBD's London headquarters at a cost approaching £4,000, and demand for the course is always high. Some idea of the standard of the qualification might be derived from the first and last topics from the first and last of its three modules:

1.1.1 The structure and morphology of barley grains and plants – Structure of the grain: endosperm; aleurone layer; embryo; husk, pericarp and testa. Relevant differences between 2-row and 6-row barleys.

3.12.11 Control System Arrangements – Self-acting controllers (e.g. Spirax). Individual electronic analogue controls; PLC for multiple sequence controls of batch processes; small local computer control, to control multiple process control loops; large digital systems with distributed data highways, incorporating Supervisory Control and Data Acquisition (SCADA). Management Information Systems (MIS) for management data. Interlinking of systems. Advantages and disadvantages of each. Comparative costs (i.e. cost per loop).

The syllabus alone is 53 pages long, and the Diploma is examined by essay rather than multiple choice.

Membership of the IBD carries many advantages both to individual members and to their employers. Association with an internationally recognised professional body enhances a member's professional standing and provides opportunities for contact with professional colleagues in brewing, distilling, fermentation and allied industries. Apart from training and qualifications, member benefits include access to IBD publications, members' rates at industry events, access to the industry information carried on the IBD website, visits to industry and academic establishments and industry networking opportunities and contact strategies.

For more details on the Institute of Brewing and Distilling's qualifications or training, or for details on how to become a member, visit **www.ibd.org.uk**.

Chapter Two
Where to Brew

O ne of the first, most important, and in some ways most
difficult tasks you are going to face is finding a home for
your brewery. In some cases it won't be such a problem
because the premises will have come first. You might
be a publican installing a brewery in an outbuilding, for instance, or
you might even have been inspired to start brewing commercially
because the ideal site has come up. But whichever direction you
decide on, finding a home is the first major practical step.

And once you've found the premises, there's a long road ahead
before the first brew is loaded on to the dray. Not only does
the building have to be converted and equipped, but there are
more regulations to satisfy and procedures to go through than
you can shake a stick at. More of these later, though; for now,
let's stick with finding the right place to make your brewing
dream a reality.

The first new brewery in post-war Britain, as we have seen,
was founded in a Scottish baronial pile, Traquair House, when
the laird restored the 18th-century brewhouse that had originally
kept the castle's many inhabitants and visitors supplied with
ale. By a strange coincidence, the first new brewery in Northern
Ireland was also founded in the outbuildings of a grand country
house. Hilden Brewery was set up by Ann and Seamus Scullion
in 1981 in the stables at Hilden House, which was built in 1837
by the owners of Barbour Threads in nearby Lisburn, one of the
biggest thread mills in the world. The immediate advantage was
the instant availability of a suitable building; but Hilden House
also had plenty of room for a bar and restaurant and for an
annual beer and music festival, which becomes more popular
every year.

Few would-be local brewers have a Traquair or a Hilden House to
base themselves in, and the vast majority find homes on industrial
estates. But there's an important question to answer here, because
your first brewery may have to last you for years. Do you see brewing
as purely an industrial activity, something you just want to get on
with as efficiently as possible? Or is there more to it than that? Is
the brewery itself part of the retail strategy with tours, a shop, a bar,
maybe a restaurant?

Both strategies have their pros and cons. Making the brewing
process as efficient as possible, without the distraction of tour
parties and retailing, will hold your costs down and give you more
time to spend out on the road selling your beer. On the other

hand, welcoming people into the brewery generates cash and can also be a useful marketing device. But whichever model you choose, you will be bound by it for some time. If the former, you will opt for a unit on an industrial estate which no tourist will ever see. If the latter, you need to find a site that is attractive in itself thanks to its location, or to its architectural and historical value, or even both.

Historic Properties

The local brewing revolutions in mainland Britain and Northern Ireland started in grand country houses, as we have seen, and historic properties have proved popular sites for small breweries ever since. But by historic properties, I don't only mean grand country houses like Traquair and Hilden, but also units in regenerated industrial areas – 18th-century canal wharves, 19th-century cotton mills – and one-off conversion opportunities such as watermills, railway sheds, smithies, bakeries and so on. What these have in common is that they make the brewery itself a focus of interest, with the potential to generate considerable income from shoppers and tourists. This category could also be extended, therefore, to cover breweries in caravan parks, garden centres and other locations that attract paying customers.

Country Houses

Let's deal with country houses first. Ironically, perhaps the most ideally sited country house brewery remains resolutely off the tourist trail. Stanway House, near Winchcombe in the Cotswolds, is a fabulous confection of late Elizabethan and Jacobean stone with a baroque water garden that boasts the world's highest gravity-fed fountain and, for good measure, a 14t-century tithe barn. But the house is no museum, and the family that still lives in it after nearly 500 years only opens it to the public on Tuesday and Thursday afternoons in June, July and August. The brewery founded by Alex Pennycook in 1993 in Stanway's original brewhouse doesn't even unbend that far: if you want to see it and its two ancient wood-fired coppers, content yourself with a virtual tour on Alex's website.

Another country house brewery; another wood-fired boiler. With the help of Keith Bott of Titanic Brewery of Burslem, Staffordshire, the National Trust has restored the old brewhouse at Shugborough

Hall near Cannock. Keith oversees the brewing there, and says he has a lot of fun with that boiler. Getting the temperatures right can be a nightmare: on calm days it's a struggle to get it to boil at all, he says, while on windy ones it's a struggle to get it to stop!

Then there's North Yorkshire Brewery which, like Hilden, makes good use of its very stately home. Pinchinthorpe Hall near Guisborough is also a bistro, restaurant and hotel. Mention might also be made here of St Peter's Brewery, tucked away deep in the Suffolk countryside. It's not quite a stately home, but a Tudor moated manor house that was built using medieval gothic stone doorcases and huge ecclesiastical windows salvaged from the nearest dissolved monastery. The brewery is housed in former farm buildings in the grounds; St Peter's Hall itself, decorated with the owner's collection of French medieval ecclesiastical artwork and other antiques, is surely the most unusual and beautiful restaurant and functions room in the country.

Another country-house-based brewery is Elveden, set up in the old stableyard at Lord Iveagh's stately home near Thetford, Norfolk as part of a larger development of visitor attractions. Although these are exceptional cases, it might still be worth your while knocking on the doors of country houses in your district and asking if all their old stables, coach-houses, kennels and so forth are in use. After all, the worst they can say is, "'Fraid so, old boy."

Restored Industrial Areas

A better bet, if you have decided on a visitor-based "heritage" dimension to your business, is a unit in a restored industrial quarter. Rents in these kinds of development are likely to be high, but they attract shoppers and tourists, they ought to be well suited to the purpose, and planning permission should be fairly straightforward – either they're designated as light industrial land and will already have all the utilities and access you need, or they're unsuitable, in which case you'll be told at the outset.

The list of local breweries that have found themselves a home in some gem of industrial archaeology is a long one. Grainstore is in a Victorian railway granary in Oakham. Stonehenge is in the turbine-house of a hydroelectric power station that originally supplied the Royal Flying Corps aerodrome in Netheravon, Wiltshire. Big Lamp occupies a former steam-powered pumping station in Newburn,

Tyneside. Archers, Atlas, Beckstones, Empire, Howard Town, Millstone, Old Mill, Saltaire, Shardlow, Slaughterhouse, Stirling, Strathaven – the list goes on.

Surprisingly often, the old industrial buildings in question were once breweries, maltings or hop kilns themselves. Exmoor of Wiveliscombe, Somerset, Wickwar Brewery of Wickwar, Gloucestershire, Wychwood of Witney, Oxfordshire, Tower Brewery of Burton on Trent, Uley Brewery of Uley, Gloucestershire, and the Ram Brewery in Wandsworth, London, all occupy former breweries. Frog Island of Northampton and Black Sheep of Masham, North Yorkshire, are both housed in former maltings, while Wild Boars' home is a luxury Lake District hotel in Cumbria. This kind of location adds general interest to any brewery lucky enough to find one, and sometimes makes a quirky and attractive shop, brewery tap and/or visitors' centre too.

As well as stately homes and historic industrial buildings, local breweries are to be found in a wide range of often bizarre locations. New Plassey and Haywood Bad Ram are on caravan parks whose bars sell their beers. Bell's is in a garden centre. Nelson is in the historic dockyards at Chatham, Kent. Country Life is in the Big Sheep visitor attraction near Bideford, Devon. Bartrams in Suffolk is housed in a building, on an aerodrome, where parachutes were one packed. Bank Top occupies a Grade II-listed tennis pavilion in Bolton. Locations like this are one-offs, and finding one depends on your local knowledge. If your business model involves retailing from the brewery though, finding a site that already has a substantial footfall of people who come prepared to part with cash could be well worth the effort.

Farm Buildings

Farm buildings have always been popular locations for new breweries, and, in fact, well over 100 local breweries are sited on farms or vineyards.

Usually, these are straightforward commercial arrangements where new brewers looking for sites have found farmers trying to get a rent out of older buildings that don't suit modern agricultural needs. In many cases, farmers with surplus buildings and homeless would-be brewers have been brought together by good fortune, sound local knowledge and a wide network of contacts. In others, old farm or estate buildings have been converted into straightforward industrial units for rent just like any other. This accounts for the location of Oldershaw's on the Harrowby Hall estate near Grantham, and Loddon was originally a grainstore in Dunsden, Oxfordshire.

Often there's a conservation aspect to these arrangements. Old brick or stone dairies, cowsheds, hay barns, granaries and the like may be picturesque, and may even be listed; but if they're to be preserved, they need a commercial raison d'être, and brewing is in many cases the ideal use. Two such breweries are sited in redundant farm buildings owned by the National Trust. Branscombe Vale was founded in 1992 in two former cowsheds on the quaintly named Great Seaside Farm at Branscombe, Devon, while Westerham was founded in barns at Grange Farm, Great Cockham, Kent, in 2004. An increasing number of new brewers are finding derelict farm buildings to renovate, and in some cases the farmers themselves are converting their disused buildings into breweries on their own account. For many, though, it's more than just a sideline aimed at making some additional profit out of disused buildings; it's actually a way of giving some life and purpose to an economic activity that has become almost marginal.

Farm-Based Breweries

Making the leap from growing the ingredients to brewing the beer is nothing new. Paine's of St Neots and Ridley's of Chelmsford, two old-established regional brewers that have disappeared within the last two decades, started as farmers; a branch of the Paine family is still in the flour-milling business. Following their lead, Larkins Brewery was set up by the Dockerty family on their hop farm at Edenbridge in Kent in 1986; while Rother Valley Brewery was set up on a Sussex hop farm in 1993.

Recently this tendency has gained new impetus. Many growers are not only fed up with the rock-bottom prices paid for top-quality produce – premium malting barley, for instance, has sold at little more than feed prices in recent years – they are also keen to join the environmental movement. So we have farm-based breweries such as Atlantic in Cornwall, High House in Tyne and Wear, Wagtail in Norfolk and Wold Top in East Yorkshire growing organic barley and having it specially malted for them to reduce food miles; disposing of waste water in natural reedbeds; generating electricity to power the breweries with wind turbines; feeding livestock with spent grains; and using spent hops as mulch. If you see yourself and your brewery as part of this movement, you could do a lot worse than seek out a like-minded farmer to team up with. In commercial terms, environmental awareness is no longer a fad but an important aspect of the market; and of course there is satisfaction to be derived from doing your bit.

The attractions of life on the farm are many. But, realistically, for most would-be local brewers there are two alternatives: an industrial estate or a pub.

Pub Breweries

Once upon a time almost all pubs brewed their own ale, and in many parts of the country pub breweries were still relatively common until the late 19th century. By the early 1970s, though, there were just four left: the Three Tuns at Bishop's Castle and the All Nations at Madeley, both in Shropshire; the Old Swan at Netherton, West Midlands, universally known as Ma Pardoes; and the Blue Anchor at Helston, Cornwall. (All four are still brewing, although Ma Pardoes did actually close for quite a long while but has recently started brewing again.) Reviving the tradition of pub brewing has been one of the driving forces of the real ale revolution, and not for romantic reasons alone. With most of the pub trade firmly closed to the new brewers, ownership of the means of retail has seemed a sine qua non to many, and buying a brewery tap has been an important goal. There have even been some cases where the brewer has bought a pub expressly as a base for the brewery: Wensleydale Brewery in North Yorkshire, for example, won awards for its Rowley Mild when it was Lidstone's, based in Cambridgeshire. The owner then decided to move north, and spent a long time looking for a suitable pub to base production in before settling on the Foresters Arms in the Yorkshire Dales National Park. It was a bold move that paid off, and within a year the brewery was forced to relocate for a second time to a farm near Bellerby.

Buying a pub expressly as a home for a brewery is probably a bit extreme for most start-ups, though, especially if you have no experience in the licensed trade; but before moving on, mention should be made of the most extreme variant of this type of venture: the boutique brewery.

Boutique Breweries

Boutique breweries were much more common in America and on the Continent than in Britain, but they are growing in popularity. Essentially, the boutique brewery is a bar or beer café where the brewing equipment itself occupies centre stage, normally behind a huge sheet of glass.

Big vessels and pipework of gleaming brass make a spectacular backdrop for an evening's drinking; not surprisingly, the few boutique breweries in Britain are all urban and often very chic. In London there's the Camden Brewery, Camden, Beavertown in Tottenham Hale, Brewhouse & Kitchen, Angel, and Zerodegrees in Blackheath (branches also in Bristol and Reading); in Glasgow there's Clockwork Beer Co; and in Peterborough there's Oakham Ales' Brewery Tap in a converted 1930s dole office opposite the railway station. They were all founded by people with seriously deep pockets, which is perhaps why there are so few.

More commonly, breweries have been installed in cellars or barns by publicans who feel that the wholesale price of beer is simply too high, and to whom brewing on their own account looks like cutting out the middleman and pocketing the extra profit. It also adds a unique selling point to the pub and attracts real ale fans from all over the country, and there's more money to be made by selling ale to beer festivals and other pubs. The success of the best-known figure in the history of microbrewing in Britain, David Bruce, who chose pubs as the sites for his Firkin breweries, merely proves the point. He put his first brewery into the cellars of the Duke of York in Southwark in 1979. Renamed the Goose & Firkin, it was the first in a chain of brewpubs that eventually (and under different ownership) covered the country.

Actually, it's something of an illusion that you need to own a pub or pubs in order to make a go of a microbrewery. Many of the best-known survivors from the earliest days – Chiltern, Larkins, Cotleigh, Exmoor and others – have done perfectly well without trying their hand at retail. Conversely, many of the casualties – Trough, Hull and very nearly Banks & Taylor, which went into receivership but was bought by a white knight and is thankfully still with us – only got into difficulties through ownership of pubs. For the truth is that running pubs demands a completely different set of skills from running a brewery; and possessing the latter doesn't necessarily mean you possess the former.

Brewing on the Premises

Be that as it may, surplus space at a pub is an obvious location for a brewery; and about a quarter of the total give their address as a pub (or in one case a workingmen's club, and in a couple more a restaurant). Many more of today's crop of local brewers started out in pubs but have since had to move to larger premises. There are dozens of highly successful publicans turned brewers, some of whom have gone on to sell their pubs to concentrate on wholesale brewing. Many small pub breweries, on the other hand, brew pretty much exclusively for their own use, and quite often their breweries are squeezed into the tiniest of spaces – at the Tynllidiart Arms in Capel Bangor, Ceredigion, the brewing equipment is housed in the old outdoor loos. They might let the odd firkin out for beer festivals, but given the price of casks and the difficulty of getting their empties back, they have decided to supply their own pubs but not the wider free trade. Some of these pub breweries have achieved cult status, perhaps thanks to the very fact that their beers are so hard to find. The Railway Tavern at Brightlingsea, Essex, is a fine example: its Crab & Winkle Mild regularly wins awards at beer festivals, and although one or two favoured stockists might have it, to be absolutely sure of getting any you have to go to Brightlingsea. As indeed many beer-lovers do.

Partnerships

Less common are partnerships between publicans with spare space to let and would-be brewers looking for homes. This is a very good option for the brewery, since the host pub invariably stocks some or all of its products. Perhaps the best-known example is Hesket Newmarket in the Cumbrian village of the same name, where the brewery and its host pub, the Old Crown, are owned by two entirely separate cooperatives of villagers (many of whom, though, are members of both). The miniature tower brewery at the famous Three Tuns at Bishops Castle, Shropshire, is also now under separate ownership from the pub across the yard, and there would be a national outcry if the pub didn't stock the brewery's beers.

Other similar examples include the Alexandra Arms in Rugby, whose plant is shared between two local CAMRA members going under the name Atomic Brewery and the landlord, who brews his own ales under the pub's name. If you're looking for a home for your brewery, sounding out local free trade licensees (although not the tenants of tied houses, of course!) is a very good first step.

CASE STUDY

Brewing Services
Brewing off the beaten track:
Farm diversification in rural Wales with the Old
Farmhouse Brewery

What do you do with a half-collapsed old stone farmhouse, complete with a tree growing up through the roof, and no services? Turn it into a brewery, visitor centre and shop of course! This is exactly what Mark and Emma Evans did to a tumble-down building on their farm near St Davids in Pembrokeshire.

Mark has long had a passion for home brewing and, along with the derelict farmhouse, the farm has its own borehole water supply and already grows malting barley. It seemed a natural step to build a six-barrel (10 hectolitre) brewhouse on the site, producing a range of beer styles from lagers to bitters to NEPAs. These are sold in draft and small pack formats, both on site through their shop and to local outlets. The couple also rear their own cattle to produce beef for sale alongside the beer and so have no difficulty getting rid of the spent grain while, after treatment, any effluent is returned to the land. While not entirely a closed loop, it all adds up to a very sustainable business model.

The project was aided by a farm diversification grant from the Welsh Development Agency, which meant going through a few extra hoops during the planning stages, and the building was completely refurbished from top to bottom in early 2020. After a six-month build, brewing commenced in November 2020.

As with any project, it was important that the planning of both the building and the brewery was right from the start to avoid wasting both time and money, which was why Mark and Emma contacted Brewing Services Ltd in early 2019 when they first had the idea for the project. The aim was to work through all the requirements of turning this redundant building into a modern brewery, whilst still retaining as many of the farmhouse's original features as possible.

The first stage was to stabilise what remained of the old farmhouse, before starting the rebuild programme using local natural materials to fit in with the existing building. Next was to bring in the necessary services required to operate the brewery, before finally installing and commissioning the brewing equipment. To satisfy the grant application three quotes were required for all the brewing equipment; Brewing Services Ltd drew up the brewplant requirements before putting this out to tender, then worked with Mark and Emma to select the eventual brewplant suppliers.

Whilst the building work was going on and the brewery was being fabricated, Brewing Services helped the brewery to obtain the necessary consents, certification and licences and worked with Mark to adapt his existing home-brew recipes for the new equipment. Being UK farmers themselves and wanting to keep to an ethic of supporting home-grown businesses, Mark and Emma were keen to use UK suppliers for their raw materials. UK-grown hops go into many of their beers, alongside their own water, farm-grown malting barley and honey from their beehives.

Being off the beaten path can often be an issue for services and the Old Farmhouse Brewery was no exception; this meant extra treatment for the borehole water, installing an effluent treatment system with the agreement and collaboration of National Resource Wales and putting in a new three-phase power supply to the building. With sustainability in mind, Mark and Emma installed an air source heat pump system, aided by a green energy grant, which both chills the fermenting vessels and cold liquor tank and provides hot water and underfloor heating in the visitor centre with the heat recovered.

Starting with only a derelict farmhouse and a passion for brewing, and with the aid of farm diversification grants, a new farm-based Welsh craft brewery has emerged and is now going from strength to strength.

Brewing Services: www.brewingservices.co.uk
Old Farmhouse Brewery: www.oldfarmhousebrewery.co.uk

Industrial Estates

If your hopes of brewing in the stables of a stately home, or in a converted woollen mill, or a former dairy or cowshed, or in the yard of a friendly pub come to nothing, there is always the industrial estate; and the fact that maybe half of all new brewers operate from units on industrial estates speaks volumes.

The advantages are many and obvious. They're often fairly cheap to rent; there's little conversion work to do; and they're comparatively easy to find. Considerations such as adequate access for delivery vehicles, industrial-grade flooring, three-phase electricity and proper drainage can pretty much be taken for granted (in theory, at least), while all the necessary planning permissions ought to come with the lease. Often too, a base on an industrial estate offers the option of quick and easy expansion into neighbouring units – Hop Back Brewery of Salisbury, for instance, now occupies almost the entire industrial estate it moved on to 25-odd years ago. (It was actually founded in a pub.)

But although they are usually both well equipped and cost-effective, industrial estates do have their disadvantages. They are never going to figure on the local tourist trail, for instance; and an integral brewery shop or tap is pretty much out of the question too. So choosing a home on an industrial estate is not just a question of cost and convenience but has longer-term implications for how you plan to run your business. Unless you decide to relocate, you will inevitably remain first and foremost a manufacturer.

Size and Services

The choice of premises will not only be one of the first decisions you make, but also the hardest to go back on; and in large part the style and scope of your future operations will be determined by what you find now. So having made the choice between an industrial estate and something more characterful and picturesque, start your hunt for premises with a clear idea of where you'd like to be in five or ten years' time.

Size, especially, is going to matter. You can brew in a broom cupboard if you have to, but it's difficult and uncomfortable and leaves no room for expansion when your beers become a cult hit, as they undoubtedly will. Many's the brewery that has chugged along quite happily in a cramped and crowded basement until a major award came along, and with it a deluge of orders. Three such breweries, Mordue, Kelham Island and Coniston, found that winning the Champion Beer of Britain competition – held every August at the Great British Beer Festival – brought as many headaches as it did joys. They all had to farm out part of their production, and two of them then moved into bigger premises.

Although the brewing itself can be made ergonomically efficient almost to the point of absurdity – a 2.5 barrel brewery should be small enough to fit into most buildings and beer cellars – other activities, notably cask storage and washing, can't. So although you may be impressed, on your brewery visits, by miracles of compact engineering such as Green Jack in Lowestoft, do get as much space as your budget allows. Even if the building itself is small, a good-sized yard can always be partly covered over to shelter a cask-washer – and additional fermenters, when you need them.

If you're looking at older premises for conversion, be sure to keep a project manager's eye out for practical pitfalls. Brewing in a largely residential area is possible, but some people object to the smell and getting your plans past them can be difficult. While the fabric of the building itself may be sound or, at least, not unfeasibly unsound, you also have to think about things like flooring, drainage and water treatment (essential – you can't just pour waste water down the drain), and ventilation (equally essential: you're going to be filling the place up with CO_2 which, believe me, you don't want to breathe in). Can your building be adapted, within your budget, to meet all these needs?

Planning Permission

Having found the perfect building – picturesque, perhaps; on a well-trodden tourist trail; in reasonable condition; suitable for adaptation; with space for future expansion, yet still miraculously within your budget – you have to discover whether you're actually going to be allowed to brew there.

Getting planning permission can be drawn-out, time-consuming, complicated and expensive. But it's not half as drawn-out, time-consuming, complicated and expensive as not getting it. Councils vary in their attitude to enforcement, some being absolutely rigorous and others more flexible, but the last thing you want is to have to undo work you've already done. If you don't have planning permission, or if you do have it but then breach the terms and conditions set by the council, enforcement is a very real danger.

Class B2 Planning

If you've gone for the industrial estate option, getting permission to brew in your unit should be relatively straightforward. The site will already have permission for general industrial use – or use class B2, in planning jargon. However, there will still be some issues to settle with the local council – city, borough or district – before you start grinding your grist. If B2 use exists – and your solicitor should check this with the vendor or landlord of the site before you exchange – then the exact details of what you propose to do will be classed as "reserved matters" (another useful piece of planning jargon!), which you will need to agree with the council's Development Control department.

Other necessary compliances involving building regulations, health and safety matters, and waste water disposal will be dealt with in Chapter Four. However, you may find that the council won't give you the final go-ahead unless these compliances, especially health and safety and waste water disposal, are fully dealt with in your application.

Change of Use Permission

If you propose to brew in a historic property of some sort – or a farm or pub, that isn't already classed as B2, you will need change of use permission. You may very well need another, more difficult, permission, too: older buildings are frequently protected by statutory listing and need listed building consent before any alterations, however minor, can be made. Strictly speaking, this is not part of your change of use application as it's covered by different laws; but in practice the two applications can be submitted at the same time. They remain separate applications, though, and the outcome of one doesn't affect the outcome of the other. You can be granted listed building consent on the grounds that your proposals don't affect the building's character, but still be refused change of use permission on the grounds that, say, vehicle access is inadequate.

Refusal of either application can be challenged, so if you're knocked back on the one but get through on the other, the game's not necessarily up.

Planning Applications

Getting your planning application under way will involve you in two processes: evaluating your building itself and evaluating its surroundings. Obviously, it's wise to carry out this exercise as thoroughly as possible before signing a lease or making a purchase – you don't want to be stuck with premises you can't brew in, or face a long, hard battle to get your application through before you can start trading.

As far as the building is concerned, there's quite a long list of questions to answer:

- If it's an older property, is it listed? (The local council will give you this information.)
- Can it jump through all the relevant health and safety hoops?
- How good is the vehicle access?
- Is there room on the site for all employees, visitors and deliveries to park off-street and for vehicles to manoeuvre, i.e. for articulated lorries to reverse?

As for its surroundings, is it in an area where general industrial use is permitted by the Local Development Framework (LDF)? While you're at the town or city hall or on the council's website checking the LDF, ask yourself the following questions:

- Will you in future be likely to require a shop (use class A1) or a bar (use class A3)?
- Are permissions for these uses likely to be granted, or does the LDF frown on the volume of traffic a shop and bar are likely to generate?
- Is the premises in a conservation area, an Area of Outstanding Natural Beauty or a National Park?
- How many traffic movements on and off site do you envisage?
- Can you control noise and emissions to the satisfaction of local residents, if there are any?

Getting planning permission is – supposedly – somewhat more straightforward these days; and thanks to the web, it's easier to get the information you need. At **www.planningportal.gov.uk** you'll find a pretty exhaustive guide to planning matters; it enables you to apply online and includes a fee calculator to work out roughly how much the council will charge you. It has links to other sites detailing, for instance, national policy on converting surplus agricultural buildings to other employment-related uses (Public Planning Guidance note or PPG 7). Since 2002 there has been a presumption that councils should approve "well-conceived farm diversification proposals, particularly involving the re-use of existing buildings for business purposes". The Royal Town Planning Institute's website, **www.rtpi.org.uk**, includes a list of planning and development consultants. Hopefully you won't need one, but if your application is any less than perfectly straightforward, you might!

Councils have to determine your application within eight weeks of receiving it; but they have the power to extend the period under certain circumstances. You can appeal to the Secretary of State, but it's rather self-defeating as the appeal will almost certainly take longer than the council would. So if you want your application to be determined as quickly as possible – and to be sure of getting the right result – then everything hinges on thorough preparation and good communication. In effect, the planning process will take longer – a lot longer – than eight weeks (eight months, more like) but the bulk will be done before your application goes in.

Preparing the Planning Application

The important thing is not to be afraid. Some people are: they think the council is there to frustrate them or tie them up in red tape, and the only sure way to get an application through is to sneak it under the town hall's radar somehow. While it's true that councils can be awkward if they want to, and that there are more formalities to go through than at the State Opening of Parliament, in essence the council is there to help you and even has an obligation to make suitable provision for industrial developments such as yours. The grounds on which applications can be refused or substantially varied are finite; and if you discover in advance what they are, you shouldn't find it too hard to put together an application that is more or less bound to succeed.

First, check the relevant sections of the LDF thoroughly. This is available from the city, borough or district council, or on its website. Unfortunately, it's not a single document, but a collection of them; however, the site should be fairly easy to navigate. In the case of my local district council, South Cambridgeshire, the home page has a link to "planning", which has a further link to "district planning policy". Finally, there's a link to "Local Plan

2004" (as this book goes to press, old-style local plans are being replaced by new-fangled LDFs, but in most cases the old plan is still in force). The Local Plan is divided into two sections: general policy across the whole district, and more specific policies location by location. Armed with this information, you should at least be able to tell whether the building you have your eye on is likely to be acceptable for B2 use. Other council websites I have checked are less clear than South Cambridgeshire's, but still far from impenetrable; and by and large I have found that, once all the documents are located, LDFs are fairly straightforward and easy to understand.

However, the Planning Portal site and LDFs are very general documents and paint rather a rosy picture of the planning process. Things can and do go wrong. It took Oakham Ales two frustrating and interminable years to get permission to move from its original home in Rutland and convert the former DSS office in Peterborough it inhabited until only recently. It later transpired that discussions aimed at razing the whole area to extend the neighbouring shopping mall had been opened, but the project hadn't made it as far as the Local Plan when Oakham put in its application. Two years later the Brewery Tap had a compulsory purchase order slapped on it, and has lived under the shadow of demolition ever since. (At the time of writing it's still trading, and indeed still brewing, although the company has found a new and much bigger production base on an industrial estate.)

Other breweries could doubtless tell planning horror-stories just as hair-raising, but in the main, where applicants have run into really serious planning delays the premises have been in urban centres where there is strong competition for development sites. (Often, councils can't reveal details of negotiations such as those in Peterborough because of commercial confidentiality.) On other occasions, applicants have tried to get their putative breweries approved as B1, which covers light industrial use in residential areas and imposes stricter conditions than B2 on noise, fumes and traffic movements. Then again, attempts to install breweries in quirky or unusual premises have often run into problems with planning officers who argue that the use is unsuited to the building. Another big stumbling block that has faced pub breweries in the past has been the thorny question of mixed use. A lot of local planners have simply been unable to get their heads round the concept that a single business premises might want A4 use for part of the site and B1 or B2 for another. This was part of the problem that caused so much delay for Oakham, but with the huge increase in the number of pub breweries round the country, local planners seem to be getting less resistant to the idea than previously. If mixed use does seem to be presenting a problem, you can usually overcome it by arming yourself with a good number of precedents, preferably fairly local.

The Planning Officer

There is no way of guaranteeing that these kind of problems won't arise; but one way of reducing the risk is to open a good channel of communications with the planning officer working on your proposal. You will have to pay an administration fee to cover the costs of your application anyway, but some councils will charge extra for an initial consultation with your planning officer.

However, as it's this very officer who will recommend acceptance or rejection of your plan to the council's Development Control Committee, the extra charge is probably money well spent. Involving this officer in the evolution of your brewery makes it almost as much his or her baby as yours; in fact, one planning officer I spoke to while researching this chapter told me, "We always like getting a brewery to work on – it's a lot more interesting than most of the cases we get!" So by the time the application is ready to be formally considered, the two of you should have made it almost watertight. Of course, this process may itself have its ups and downs but remember, if your planning officer flatly vetoes an idea of yours, it's not out of bloody-mindedness (probably not, anyway) but out of a deep knowledge of local policies and a very shrewd understanding of what will or won't get through. The planning officer's main concern, after the suitability of the building itself, will be the impact of your business on its neighbours, especially if there are any residents in the immediate area. This concern is partly met by the LDF's approved uses for the locality. But the officer will also be interested in noise, smells and other emissions, waste discharge and any changes you propose to the appearance of the building, particularly if you will need equipment such as extractors, flues and tanks.

CASE STUDY

Brewing Services
Where to find the formal training

The obvious answer is that you'll get all the information you need from an experienced brewer, but choosing the right person to teach you the best brewing practice can be as difficult as finding the right brewing equipment. What you need is a person with a good practical brewing pedigree and knowledge, with decades of experience in designing and installing breweries. One of the UK's leading brewers and microbrewery designers is David Smith of Brewing Services Ltd (**www.brewingservices.co.uk**). David spent over 20 years working for Samuel Smith's in Tadcaster, first as a production brewer and then in a quality assurance role, before leaving to set up his brewing consultancy in 1988. This was just as the microbrewing industry was starting to gain traction and people with a good brewing knowledge were in high demand. Since then he has designed and installed many breweries but never lost sight of the fact that the equipment isn't much use without the know-how. Having initially set up his consultancy to provide technical assistance and quality assurance services to brewers, it soon became apparent there was a significant skills shortage.

With this in mind, David set up his own training course: The Fundamentals of Mini-Brewing. Billed as "the course designed by brewers for brewers", The Fundamentals of Mini-Brewing started out in 1989 as the first training course dedicated to those working, or wanting to work, in microbreweries. David, together with his son Rob who joined the company after many years working with Dartmoor, Freedom and Meantime breweries, runs this highly successful four-day course twice yearly.

It is firmly rooted in the experience that David, Rob and their guest lecturers have gained in their working lives. The aim of the course is to pass on that practical knowledge and provides the essential first step for anyone planning a microbrewery. It combines lectures by brewers and industry specialists with visits to a local maltings, other microbreweries and packagers. For those with little practical experience there is also the opportunity to help with a complete brew at York Brewery before the course begins. Topics discussed encompass the whole brewing process, from the importance of the correct brewing equipment and good brewery design to selecting the right raw materials and recipe formulation, from mashing in through to packaging and dispense of the finished product on the bar. The purpose of the course is to instil a greater insight into the art and science of brewing, all the while emphasising the need for consistently high quality and good brewing practice.

Following on from The Fundamentals of Mini-Brewing and once your brewery is up and running, Brewing Services Ltd offers tailored on-site training for brewery staff of all levels, as well as mentoring for other exams. The demand for experienced brewers is high and training novice brewers is a great way to ensure that each brewery's training needs are met.

www.brewingservices.co.uk

Microbrewer's Checklist

Before your brewery can be operational you will need to:
- Seek permission to brew from HM Revenues & Customs (HMRC). It should be a formality, but it can take some time.
- Register with HMRC for The Alcohol Wholesaler Registration Scheme.
- Seek permission to brew from environmental health. It's not usually a problem, but the environmental health officer will need to assess the brewery's external environmental impact and the building specification.
- Seek permission to dispose of trade effluent, usually provided by your water suppliers.
- Seek consent from planning authorities.
- Ensure adequate single-phase electricity supplies and points, preferably with waterproof sockets that must be protected with RCDs. An RCD, or residual current device, is a life-saving device which is designed to prevent people from getting a fatal electric shock.
- Install, a three-phase electricity supply if your output is going to be more than four barrels.
- Ensure that you have adequate site drainage to mains.
- Ensure adequate access to atmosphere for an exhaust chimney for fumes and steam.
- Ensure adequate (volume and quality) mains water supply.
- Ensure suitable collection of spent malt (some farmers will buy this as a feed).
- Ensure suitable collection of spent hops (these can usually be biodegraded for plant mulch).
- Ensure adequate ventilation of the brewery, especially where CO_2 might accumulate.
- Ensure completely sealed and/or drainable floors and adequately sealed walls. This could cost you as much as your capital expenditure on brewing vessels.
- Ensure that you have reliable people to brew and package the beer.

What You Will Need to Buy/Source

- Additional hydrometers/ sacchrometers (they will break with annoying regularity)
- Stock of malt and hops
- Clarification agents

- Casks and a device for cleaning them
- Cask closures
- A good yeast supply
- Sterilising solutions
- A qualified electrician to prepare the brewery site and be there for the first day of installation – all electrical appliances are supplied without wiring
- Safety equipment for you and/or your brewer – this includes chemical-proof gloves, goggles, eye-wash station and safety boots

Chapter Three
Planning Your Business

So you've done your training and you've found your premises. Your next step is to move in and install your brewery. But not just yet. First, you've got to make sure you have enough money not just to set yourself up but also to keep yourself afloat until the business starts paying its way.

This is not the place to tell you how or where to raise the money you'll need. You've doubtless got some capital already: the proceeds of the sale of your house, perhaps, or a redundancy cheque, or your life savings, or a bequest. You'll probably need more, though, and the obvious place to go is the bank. But before it parts with any money, the bank is going to ask some searching questions and will expect to see a detailed business plan.

The Business Plan

A business plan, as you undoubtedly already know, is far more than just a rosily optimistic cash-flow projection cobbled together to lull the bank into underwriting a daydream. If carried out thoroughly, it will confront you with the mathematics of your project coldly and in stark detail. If it doesn't make you run away screaming, it will help ensure that your newborn business will be a sturdy infant capable of making it through to adulthood.

An useful web resource is the government site Business is Great (**www.greatbusiness.gov.uk**) which has access to a wealth of free information for any person wanting to set up their own business.

When you are growing your business, there are always new challenges. From finding the right staff to accessing the right type of finance, from breaking into new markets to developing your people and your ideas, there will be times when you will really want advice, support and information.

Writing a business plan is a vital first step when starting a business, in order to set out your proposition, your market, customers and competitors. The business planning process will give you a feel for the various elements that will determine your success, from cash flow, to sales forecasting to your personnel structure. A good business plan will let you structure your finances efficiently, show potential investors the strength of your business, and focus your efforts on developing your business. A business plan isn't written once; it's a living document that you return to periodically to help you spot potential pitfalls before they happen.

Go to **www.gov.uk/write-business-plan** for lots of useful links on writing business plans.

CASE STUDY

Thomas Fawcett & Sons
The art of malt

Thomas Fawcett & Sons (the company) is an eighth-generation family business. The company was established in 1809 and is now in its 212th year of supplying top-quality malts to the brewing, food and distilling industries in the UK and into many export markets.

Over the years the company has supplied malts to practically every brewery in Britain. Today the company is best known for supplying the finest ale and coloured malts to brewers who specialise in cask-conditioned ales, especially small regionals, family and a whole host of smaller breweries that have emerged since the implementation of the 1989 Beer Orders. The company's roasted and crystal malts are used by some of the major brewing groups who still see value in achieving consistent natural colours and flavours in their beers.

The key ingredient to making good malt is the barley. The UK is blessed with a climate that, more often than not, produces the world's finest samples of malting barley, and the company goes out of its way to procure the best samples from the UK crop each harvest. Over the years pressure has built on farmers to produce ever greater yields at the expense of malting quality. Many new varieties that have emerged at low nitrogen make acceptable malt, but Fawcett prefers to focus on proven heritage malting varieties such as Maris Otter, Halcyon, Pearl and Golden Promise, paying the necessary premiums to the farmer to guarantee consistent supply. In the end it is consistency that matters to brewers, especially those that wish to build brands on customer loyalty through recognition and those that lack the resources to blend away inconsistencies or rely on adjuncts to tweak beers back into shape. Consistency of mash tun performance, flavour and colour remains Fawcett's key mantra.

One of the award-winning breweries that Thomas Fawcett & Sons has been supplying for more than 20 years is Church End Brewery in Nuneaton. Managing director Stewart Elliott again emphasises the key component when brewing an excellent beer is using the finest ale and coloured malts. With the brewery's Goat's Milk being awarded Supreme Champion Beer of Britain at the Great British Beer Festival Champion Beer of Britain Awards, and an award win for Fallen Angel, Stewart believes that the flavour and the quality of malts are a main factor. Thomas Fawcett & Sons has always delivered these ingredients together with an excellent personal service.

A while ago, local author Mark Wright approached Church End Brewery to make a beer to celebrate his new book, published in September, *A Traitor to His Blood*. The team at Church End Brewery are set to launch a new beer of the same name and Thomas Fawcett & Sons has been tasked with supplying a blend of coloured malts to give the beer the colour of blood red. This beer will be available shortly (visit **www.churchendbrewery.co.uk** to find out more).

Thomas Fawcett & Sons produces more than 30 different malts to help brewers, such as Church End Brewery, make innovative beers with which to excite and inspire the ever-changing tastes of beer lovers. As we come out of the pandemic, Thomas Fawcett & Sons is here to help all brewers create delicious beers.

www.fawcett-maltsters.co.uk

Capital Expenditure (Capex)

Your financial planning should fall under two headings; capital expenditure and running costs. Let's start with the capital you'll need.

By the time you get round to writing your business plan, you will know the exact purchase price (or premium, if leased) of your premises. But making your new home ready to receive your brewing equipment will, as we saw in the last chapter, entail costs that other businesses might not have to bear. Breweries use water, lots of it, not just to brew with, but to heat up and cool down the various vats and vessels and, of course, to keep everything squeaky clean. In terms of capital, using so much water means you must have adequate drainage including sloping floors (which you may have to lay at your own cost even in a brand-new unit on an industrial estate) and washable surfaces. It may also mean you will have to treat effluent before disposal, another capital item to consider. The cost of non-slip flooring, essential on safety grounds, should also be built into your capital estimates; and, again on safety grounds, so should adequate ventilation. Carbon dioxide, one of the products of fermentation, is deadly not only to the microbes that would otherwise colonise your beer, but also to you and your staff. Your council's environmental health department will insist on the prevention of concentrations of CO_2; so – and especially if you plan to use traditional open fermenters – you will have to factor in the cost of whatever ventilation and/or extraction measures (as well as monitoring equipment) it stipulates.

Casks

After your premises, your equipment will be your largest item of capital expenditure, and it can be anything from £10,000 (plus installation costs) to – well, the sky's the limit. One item of capex that is frequently and sometimes disastrously underestimated in brewery start-ups, though, is the stock (or population, to lapse into jargon) of casks that you will need. The most common size in use today is the nine-gallon firkin, and orthodoxy has it that a free trade brewer whose beers are distributed widely and whose empties trickle home with agonising slowness needs around 30 firkins for every bulk barrel, or 163 litres, of production capacity. A five-barrel brewery should therefore own a stock of at least 150 firkins, which cost around £80 each new; so put down at least £12,000 in your capital estimates for casks.

The temptation to skimp on casks is almost irresistible, especially if you're on a tight budget and other costs are running above your estimates. But you really will need that many; it's easy to be caught short by even a modest surge in demand and disappointed customers tend not to come back. Buy new: there are cheap second-hand casks around, but ask yourself why they're being sold. Unless they are the stock of a brewery that has closed, the answer, very probably, is that they're "leakers", and therefore worth only their scrap value. No publican or wholesaler likes to have to deal with a leaker, nor has any affection for the brewery that sends them one.

A vital note regarding casks is that they're extremely vulnerable to theft. After use they tend to be stacked at the pub's back door until the owner comes to collect them; so if you're talking about an irregular account that only orders every month or two, your expensive firkin could be sitting out in the open for weeks. The temptation to swipe it soon becomes irresistible to the more light-fingered of the local inhabitants (casks do have a scrap value), or alternatively it might be "uplifted" by another brewery collecting its own empties. For this reason the British Beer & Pub Association (**www.beerandpub.com**) allocates a unique colour band to any brewer, whether a BBPA or SIBA member or not the joining kind, who cares to apply for one. The banding consists of three hoops chosen from ten colours, normally painted round the middle of the cask between the rolling rings. For more details of the scheme, visit the website and follow links to its colour band register. The BBPA register is free to join and is an entirely voluntary scheme, so brewers are at liberty to pick their own colours if they prefer. However, if you're unregistered and your banding duplicates that of a registered brewer, you may find that helpful people keep sending your casks back to the wrong place. So you can either register, or choose a colour scheme of your own that's so unusual it's bound to be unique. And your unique identifying mark doesn't have to be in the form of bands, either. Some brewers I know paint both ends of their casks; one paints the entire vessel pale pink! It's also a good idea to stamp your name indelibly on the cask end.

The Delivery Van

Another vital piece of equipment that's easy to get wrong is the delivery van. A full firkin of beer doesn't take up much space but weighs about 50kg, so unless you don't mind being done for overloading your van from time to time, you need to choose with an eye to axle-weight rather than capacity. You also need to think about what sort of licence and tax-disc you will need. An ordinary Transit-style van should carry 20–30 full firkins without straying into the "Larger Goods Vehicle" vehicle excise licence category (TC55), and you will be able to drive it on your ordinary driving licence. This should be perfectly adequate for local deliveries; if you're planning anything more ambitious, you may need a vehicle whose total laden weight or maximum authorised mass exceeds 3.5 tonnes. Visit **www.gov.uk** and follow the links to "motoring" for more details.

Fees and Charges

Finally, managing the start-up will not be cost-free. For instance, there are the administration fees referred to in the previous chapter, payable to the local council merely for the privilege of applying for planning permission. Your consultant will also want paying: factor that fee into your financial plan. Find out in advance when these payments, as well as those due to builders and fabricators, will fall due. Knowing when you need to have funds available gives you two benefits: you won't be caught short when tradespeople demand payment; and you can organise one of those loans which you only draw on (and start paying interest on) when necessary.

Running Costs

Your brewery will have to bear many of the same general running costs as other businesses: utilities, insurance, business rates, rent or mortgage repayments, repayments on other borrowings, wages (if any) and associated costs, marketing and advertising, and deliveries. The information you will need to compute all these should be available from your bank or accountant, from one of the agencies listed above, or even from the websites of the relevant government departments.

However, as with any business sector, brewing has its peculiarities. One, in particular, might just help you with your business rates.

Your business rates, which are the property tax levied by your local council, are perhaps the easiest of your regular outgoings to calculate. They are based on a valuation carried out in 2017 aimed at establishing the rent your premises would command on the open market – exactly the same system, in fact, that used to be used to calculate domestic rates. This notional rent is known as the property's rateable value (RV), and what you actually pay is calculated as a percentage of it. The difference between modern business rates and old-fashioned domestic rates is that the council doesn't decide what percentage of your RV it may levy. Instead, the government sets it each year: for 2021–22 the standard percentage, or "multiplier", has been set at 51.2p in the pound, or 49.9p for businesses with an RV of £15,000 or less (£21,500 or less in Greater London). So make it a priority to find out the RV of your premises before you move in – if you find a site with a lower RV, it could save you quite a bit. Another relief that may help you with your business rates is that any part of your premises that is empty and unused can be rated separately, with a 50 per cent reduction. For up-to-date information, visit **www.gov.uk/calculate-your-business-rates**.

Finally there's a third, rather complicated, relief aimed at protecting threatened village amenities, which you might just be able to benefit from. The only pub in a village of 3,000 inhabitants or fewer is entitled to a business rates rebate of at least 50 per cent (or up to 100 per cent at the council's discretion) provided its RV is less than £14,000. If you base your brewery at a qualifying pub, and it doesn't push the RV over the £14,000 ceiling, you'll still get the full rebate. Even if it does, you might be able to have the brewery and the pub rated separately; in which case the pub will still qualify for its 50 per cent relief, while the brewery might qualify for the small business multiplier.

Excise Duty

When you pay your excise duty, and how much you'll pay, are explained in detail in the Appendix. To give you some idea, though, duty is calculated by percentage point of alcohol by volume per hundred litres or hectolitre (a 36-gallon barrel is 1.63hl). The current rate is £19.08 per hl per cent; so the full rate of duty on a barrel of a 4% ABV session bitter would be £124.40. However, if you're a small brewer producing up to 3,000 barrels a year, you're entitled to 50 per cent relief and would only pay £62.20. (Beers above 7.5% ABV are charged an additional £5.69 per hl per cent, and there is no Small Brewer Relief on these stronger beers.)

For lower-strength beers exceeding 1.2% but not exceeding 2.8% it is £8.42hl. There is no small brewer relief on this. There is also a sliding scale of relief for brewers producing more than 3,000 barrels a year; the complicated equations by which this is calculated are set out in the Appendix. Duty must be paid by direct debit on the

25th of the following month – again, details are can be found in the Appendix. Duty must be paid by direct debit on the 25th of the following month.

This leaves your ingredients – malt and hops – which are not going to be the biggest items on your list of outgoings. In fact, and to many people's amazement, they could well amount to less than £10 per firkin of standard-strength bitter.

Hops

The amount of hops you will need depends on your recipes, but a very rough guide for budgeting purposes is a maximum of 500g of aroma and a slightly lesser quantity of bittering varieties per barrel of a pretty hoppy beer. A five-barrel brewlength would therefore require about 2–2.5kg of each or 4–5kg all told. Hoppy beers, using American or Australian hops, are currently very much the thing, though, and that combined with the huge expansion in the number of brewers in the last couple of years has driven prices up dramatically. The exact price, of course, varies from harvest to harvest and according to the type of hops you use, but is now usually in the range of £10–15 per kilo. However, US or other hops could cost much more; some are £35 per kilo.

The cost of hops for an English-style ale is likely to be in the region of £48 to £70 per five-barrel brew. You will need to be more precise than this when making the cash flow projections for your business plan.

However, most hop suppliers do have online tools for working out costs based on the bitterness of the beer you want to brew and the hop varieties you plan to use. Because of crop shortages some suppliers are only offering some varieties on forward contracts rather than off the shelf.

Malt

Calculating the amount of malt you will use is more complicated, but a rough rule of thumb (again, very rough) is that a tonne will make 40 barrels of 4% ABV bitter. A tonne of floor-malted premium pale ale malt, at time of writing, is upwards of £750 – although, of course, you can get industrially made malt instead for £150 to £200 less. So that's about 125kg costing £95 per five-barrel brew; 25kg costing £18.75 per barrel; or 6.25kg costing £4.65 per firkin. So your ingredients, excepting the liquor, will have cost only £7-8.50 for 72 pints of best bitter. The duty, with the 50 per cent Small Brewer

Relief, will be £15.27 for a 4% ABV beer – a total, then, of less than £25 a firkin. Throw in the cost of your utilities, and you should be able to produce a five-barrel brewlength for about £550; which is £110 a barrel or £27.50 a firkin.

You may have to pay a delivery charge, but even that is only about £45 for a one-tonne pallet – enough for eight five-barrel brews – carried by Palletline, Palletways, or a similar group haulier. (Most merchants will make up a mixed pallet for you, so you don't have to buy the crystal and other specialist malts you will only use in small quantities in one-tonne lots: they come in 25kg bags. Many malt suppliers will also deliver packs of hops on the same pallet.)

These are, as I have said, very rough costings intended only to give you an overall picture of what you are likely to spend. Your brewing consultant will go into more detail with you, but before you reach that stage I strongly recommend you to visit **www.murphyandson.co.uk**. Murphy's is a very old, established firm of brewers' suppliers in Nottingham, which stocks all the consumables and process additives you will ever need from liquor treatment to finings. More than that, though, its site is an absolute treasure-trove of highly detailed technical and other information including extraction tables for all varieties of malt. In fact, Chris Garrett of Warminster Maltings in Wiltshire recommends the Murphy's site not only to start-up brewers planning their first year's outgoings, but also to more established brewers working out hop and malt grists for new recipes.

Pricing

So much for your outgoings. Now we come to the more pleasant side of the equation – namely, your likely income.

The most important thing you'll want to know is the price you can expect to charge per firkin – the nine-gallon barrel in which most cask beer is delivered these days. This should be determined based on your costs of production plus the profit margin you need to stay in business. There is an old industry adage which states, "Any fool can give beer away, a wise brewer sells beer at a profit."

Many brewers swap beer, which enables brewers to swap different-strength beers with the minimum of fuss. Instead of invoicing and paying each other in full every time, the brewer of the weaker of the beers being swapped simply pays the other brewer the strength-difference. It is important to remember that if you work on reduced margins swapping beer, you need to make that margin when you sell the other brewers' beers. There are many different formulas in use but most multiply the ABV by a set factor (no lower than 25) and then add a set amount per barrel (often £100); so a barrel (36 gallons) of a 4% ABV beer would cost £200.00 (4% x 25 + £100) or £50 per firkin.

Note, although brewers who use a formula almost always add a margin of their own when selling the beer into trade, wholesale prices have actually been declining recently thanks to the number of new breweries opening, and there are brewers who will indeed sell at the formula price or even lower. A great deal depends on how efficient your brewery is, and how much of your beer you retail yourself. If you produced 2,999 barrels a year at an average of 4% ABV and got the Bristol formula for all of it, your annual turnover would be £570,000. Your ingredients and duty would account for £300,000 or thereabouts; only you know, having totted up your rent, rates, repayments, utilities, wages, marketing costs and so on whether there would be enough change out of the remaining £270,000 for you to live on. Probably not, so you'll doubtless be looking to charge your own margin on top of the formula price.

SIBA's Beerflex

A good idea of how big a margin you can reasonably expect is provided by the prices agreed with pubcos and supermarkets by SIBA's Beerflex, which was formerly known as Direct Delivery Scheme (DDS). Back in 2002 when the service was launched there were just 200 beers available through the service, a number that has now increased to over 3,500 thanks to the craft-brewing boom that the UK has seen in recent years.

Beerflex has been a hit with many pub companies as it allows them a simple, cost-effective way to gain access to a huge range of beers brewed within a short distance of their pubs, which means they can offer their customers genuinely local, fresh-tasting draught beers. On top of that, consumers are happy as they're being given greater choice and brewers are happy as their beers are getting into pubs which were previously a closed door to small scale producers.

Beerflex will now enable brewers to price their beers based on beer styles and ingredients rather than being constrained by ABV, and the scheme is evolving to include a service which is integrated with pub companies' central distribution and consolidated deliveries as well as, for the first time, including craft keg beers alongside cask ales.

As a craft brewer, the quality of your beer is your greatest strength, and if it's no good, no one will buy a second bottle or pint. The problem is, though, that thanks to the recent proliferation of brewers and the introduction of new tiers of middleman in the form of wholesalers and non-brewing pubcos, the brewer's slice of the cake is actually dwindling. A pub in south-eastern England will charge, at time of writing, around £4 including VAT per pint of session-strength bitter – call it £3.20 net. Publicans typically add 100 per cent to the wholesale price to cover their own not inconsiderable overheads, which suggests that they're paying at least £115 a firkin for a beer of 4% ABV. That price comes, typically, from a pubco or a wholesaler; you can bet the brewer isn't getting much more than 60 per cent of it.

Tied tenants are famously the only people in the pub trade who pay list-price for their beer: anyone with any bargaining power at all gets a discount. Often, small brewers deliberately ramp up their price-lists so they can appear to be generous with discounts. What's important in all your price negotiations, though, is that you should keep a firm idea in your head of what your lowest economical prices are, and should never give in to the temptation to take less for the sake of volume.

The thought of all that extra margin has lured many small brewers down the path of pub ownership. Whether you should think of owning a pub or pubs yourself will be explored in Chapter Eight.

Cash Flow

Keeping the Cash Flowing

No matter whether you have agreed comparatively low prices for bulk orders, or are charging a premium for single-firkin orders of ales that have just won major awards (always a good opportunity for a temporary price uplift), actually getting paid can be a nightmare. I have even heard stories of small, and generally new, breweries that went under because their credit with their suppliers had run out, their overdraft facilities had been exhausted, and they were missing loan repayments.

Invoice promptly – making your beer is the easy bit. Many small brewers concentrate on making their beer and delivering it to customer and then forget to invoice for it. Or they then take their time to raise an invoice. There are too many brewers who have done

someone a favour, delivered the beer and then forgotto
for it. Most customers are not going to remind you tha
charged them for a delivery of beer.

With today's electronic invoicing using online apps, an invoice
can be raised wherever you are. As soon as the beer is delivered an
invoice can be sent. It is a sad fact that the older a debt, the harder
and costlier it becomes to chase and get it paid.

It is always helpful to offer alternative ways of payment. Cash
is good and there are some brewers who will only sell beer to a
pub or festival if they pay cash. Some prefer to pay by cheque.
But the reality of today's world is that many would rather not use
either system. So, offer alternatives. Invoices can be paid using
online banking. Or low-cost credit card payment such as Stripe.
Physical card payments can also be made via low-cost services
such as iZettle which connects a customer's card to a phone, tablet
or laptop.

It is important to keep in touch with debtors. Don't just send
an invoice and expect it to be paid. Sadly, there are too many
stories of brewers delivering beer to pubs for months on end then
the customer goes bust. Speak to your customers and make sure
they can give you a payment date. This is particularly important
if you are dealing with a larger customer with large finance
departments who are well versed at holding on to your money for
a long as they can.

Money will seem to go out faster than it comes in, so manage
payments. Keep on top of all costs, especially tax – VAT,
corporation tax, PAYEs and pension liabilities. HMRC will have
no trouble in chasing you. Likewise, your suppliers will expect
prompt payment on their agreed terms, just as you should off
yours. Delayed payments to your suppliers means you run the
risk of reduced credit and/or higher prices, or worse still, no credit
at all.

There are, of course, other providers such as Worldpay, and you
can spend many a happy hour trawling the net to find the provider
that suits you best. None of them, though, can help you with big
customers – supermarkets and pubcos – whose alleged credit
periods of 60 or 90 days are honoured more in the breach than
the observance.

Finally, it is important to forecast. Plan with your finances. Use
an accounting software or a spreadsheet to forecast future sales,
purchases and tax liabilities.

CASE STUDY

Fulton Boilers
Transitioning from steam to thermal fluid with Rebellion Beer Company

In 2015, with business improving but original process equipment reaching end-of-life, Rebellion Beer Company bucked the trend and, with impartial advice from heat transfer specialist Fulton, replaced its ageing steam boiler with a thermal fluid system. Now, six years on, we approached Rebellion's Mark Gloyens to update us on how brewery life has coped with the switch.

Anyone running a brewery will tell you just how critical the boil phase of the brewing process is, and when Rebellion set out on its journey from steam to thermal, it was warned that it would never succeed in getting that clean flavour achieved from a steam-driven rolling boil.

"The move from steam to thermal was a leap of faith on our part, but the warnings received from other breweries have been proven to be incorrect!" says Mark. "Product quality has improved because we now have more control over temperature for the wort boiling process than ever before. We're getting a very good-quality boil that is controllable and we have achieved everything we wanted from the move from steam to thermal fluid."

Thanks to the control and flexibility that the thermal system affords Rebellion, the brewery has had the ability to achieve various size batches as and when required. Until recently, this has enabled it to process research and development batches and has been especially useful throughout the pandemic when, at the beginning, throughput was decimated because pubs were forced to close. However, as lockdowns came and went, Rebellion successfully pivoted its business and started selling direct to the consumer via a home delivery service, which meant throughput very quickly returned to pre-pandemic levels.

"The beauty of the thermal fluid installation is its flexibility and ability to very easily adapt to our changing brewing strategies," says Mark. "Historically we would have been doing two brews per day to achieve maximum output, but because of its flexibility, we are now able to shut the thermal fluid heater down for a day per week to deep clean the brewhouse and increase output to three brews per day for the remainder of the week."

Mark explains that there have been further benefits: "A steam boiler is essentially a pressure vessel, and regulations state that pressurised systems must undergo an annual insurance inspection. This inspection would often take the steam boiler offline and mean our brewing processes were down for a day or more, with disruption from the downtime potentially being felt for several days after. Additionally, with even the best water treatment programme in place, steam at pressure can be very corrosive, leading to problems with steam traps, flanges and pipework, which we always seemed to be maintaining."

Six years on from the installation of Rebellion's thermal fluid system, Mark estimates that the savings made compared with maintaining the old steam system – and despite the thermal fluid installation being a more expensive capital outlay initially – have contributed significantly to the return on investment, with the investment now fully paid for.

Expanding on the flexibilities of the thermal fluid system, Mark has also announced that Rebellion is about to tap into the existing brewhouse line to create a small-batch development brewery and yeast propagation plant on the site. "It's been such an easy expansion to achieve. We've just been able to tap into the existing thermal fluid line and use the system for another duty without impacting on everything else," says Mark.

The new development line is capable of brewing five hectolitre (500 litre) batches and will enable development of commercial batches – such as strong beers or one-off batches that may not appeal to the wider consumer – to be processed without having to invest in a full 4,000 litre brew.

Summarising, Mark says that whenever he's asked if Rebellion is happy with the thermal fluid installation from Fulton, he simply tells them to come and take a look because it speaks for itself.

"You obviously need to consult the experts as we did when we approached Fulton over six years ago. They were completely unbiased because they manufacture both steam and thermal fluid solutions," he says. "But for Rebellion Beer Company, a thermal fluid solution was a no-brainer. It's more cost-effective, more reliable, relatively maintenance free and a much neater, more compact system that still provides the quality of heating needed for brewing."

www.fulton.co.uk

Exit Strategy

At some point in the future, the likelihood is that you'll want to sell up. You might fall ill, you might fall out with your partners (a very common cause of the closure of small breweries), or you might just want to retire. It may, when you're planning to get started, seem a bad omen to be planning your brewery's demise as well. But remember, this is not only your living but your pension. The question you'll want to ask then is, how much is my brewery worth? The simple answer is that it's worth what somebody will pay for it.

The actual value, however, is not the same thing as reaching a valuation, which depends very much on what you're selling. If you boil the brewery down to its constituent parts, there's the site, the equipment, and the brands and goodwill. The valuation of the site depends on whether it's freehold or leasehold and is something that only you can determine. A freehold you can have valued by any commercial property broker. A lease may or may not be "heritable" – that is, it may revert to the landlord, or you may be able to sell on its unexpired term. If the latter, the same commercial property broker will determine it for you. Your equipment undoubtedly has a second-hand price, which will depend on its condition and fluctuate according to market conditions; any brewing consultant can assess it for you. The valuation of the brands and goodwill will depend on how well you're trading, but a figure of three times net profit is often mentioned in valuing businesses without assets.

The same could be said of the value of your business as a going concern. It's such a rare occurrence in the small brewing world that there are no reliable guidelines: whether you can sell it as a business at all depends very much on whether there's someone willing to buy, and also on the nature of the sales. One brewery that I know sold recently for 2½ times its gross profit of £60,000. It had a turnover of £200,000 but was in leased premises, and sold relatively easily because it had top-class, fairly new equipment and a good steady trade with plenty of repeat custom. Use an established consultant.

Chapter Four
Equipping Your Brewery

There's many a good tune, my father used to remark, played on an old fiddle. And although he didn't actually have brewing equipment in mind, he might as well have. For a brewery doesn't have to be brand spanking new, all gleaming steel and copper and costing a small fortune to produce perfectly good beer. It can equally well be second-hand or even – if you really know what you're doing – cobbled up from scrap. Indeed in the early days of small brewing, it had to be.

There were, of course, long-established firms of brewers' engineers, mostly based in Burton-on-Trent, which could design and install a world-class brewery for you at the drop of a blueprint – provided, that is, that you wanted to brew a hundred barrels at a time. But if you only wanted to brew five, you had to forage for your vessels.

In fact, many small brewing pioneers – especially Peter Austin, founder of Hampshire's Ringwood Brewery – were just as well known for helping other start-ups as they were for their own. I well remember a visit as late as 1993 to Central Bottling International (CBI) of Doncaster, which originally specialised in selling reconditioned second-hand bottling lines, but found a new lease of life once the real ale revolution started. Microbrewers used to swarm all over its huge yard looking for usable vessels and pipework, and my visit coincided with Scottish & Newcastle's decision to take the old-fashioned cellar tanks out of its big managed houses and workingmen's clubs and replace them with conventional keg dispense. There they all stood in rows, fully insulated freestanding five-barrel tanks with pipe-stubs at their tops and bottoms and even little viewing panels so you could see what was going on inside – 1,800 of them. They made absolutely perfect fermenters and/or conditioning tanks, and CBI sold the lot within a few weeks of getting them in.

Constructing Your Own Equipment

You could, if you had to, follow the example of those pioneers and cobble up your brewery from scrap, and not just out of parsimony, either. Tim Dunford of Green Jack Brewery of Lowestoft did just that back in 2003, but only because he had to. Green Jack occupies the back part of a house that was, rather weirdly, left standing when the front was demolished for road-widening, and it's such an odd shape that he couldn't get what he needed off the peg and had to fabricate his own. His tanks were all originally used to make onion flavouring for the crisps and snacks industry, and when he first got them they stank of it. They all had to be altered in various ways, but Tim sought the aid of a local fabricator who instructed him in the finer arts of the angle-grinder and the oxyacetylene torch, and he did a brilliant job – as the rows of award certificates decorating one wall of his pub, the Triangle, demonstrate.

A word of caution here, though. The pioneers of the 1970s were able to make their Heath Robinson breweries work because, almost to a man, they were themselves refugees from the mainstream brewing industry. They'd been working with mash tuns and hop backs and paraflows since their teens and they knew everything there was to know about brewing equipment. Similarly Tim Dunford, although he has never worked for a mainstream brewery, had run another micro for a long time before founding Green Jack. He too knew from workaday experience what vessels he needed, what was going to be expected of them, and how to connect them all up. You, even if you're a veteran home brewer, are probably not quite so intimately familiar with the hardware you're going to need; and you're also not going to be quite as expert in keeping the whole rig running once it's actually set up.

A wise maxim here then, is that you should spend as much as you can on your equipment, even if it means skimping elsewhere. Once you're up and running you're going to be more than grateful for well-designed and well-built plant that works smoothly and efficiently, using up a minimum of energy and a minimum of labour and never breaking down. Something you can take for granted, really. That, for most mortals, is going to mean a purpose-built brewery from one of the main consultants – people like ABUK, Mossbrew, David Porter, David Smith and Brewing Design Services.

Brewing Consultants

Most start-up brewers these days will use the services of the brewing consultancy sector, which has evolved as the small brewing industry has grown over the years. In fact, given today's regulatory complexities it's a brave would-be brewer who doesn't exploit the vast expertise that is available from the various consultants, most of whom have huge experience and access to a network of other support services that you will find indispensable. However, they all have different specialities and ranges of services, so shop around!

Below are listed details of some of the best-known of them.

AB UK: The full name of AB UK, based in Misterton, Lincolnshire, is Advanced Bottling, and it supplies and installs bottling equipment as well as breweries. Specialises in reconditioned equipment.
Tel: +44 (0)1427 890 099
www.abuk.co.uk

Brewery Services: Brewery Services offers training and general consultancy for the microbrewing industry. Chris Holliland has particular experience with small-scale bottling machines and water management and has spent some years writing and teaching brewing courses when not making beer at a commercial brewery.
Tel: +44 (0) 1777 703 074
www.breweryservices.co.uk

Brewing Design Services: Founded as Inn Brewing by former Whitbread senior brewer David Shardlow in 1982, the company changed its name 10 years later to broaden its appeal beyond the brewpub and is now run by David's son Richard, who also runs Tring Brewery. BDS specialises in larger projects such as Butcombe's brand-new 60-barrel brewery in Somerset.
Tel: +44 (0) 1442 890 721
www.tringbrewery.co.uk

Iceni Brewery: Iceni is owned and run by Brendan Moore, founder of the East Anglian Brewers cooperative. Brendan also installs both brewing and bottling equipment and advises on marketing techniques.
Tel: +44(0) 1842 878 922
www.icenibrewery.co.uk

Johnson Brewing & Engineering Ltd: Vincent Johnson set up Johnson Brewing & Engineering in 2003. He graduated from Heriot-Watt in 1997 and spent a year working for S&N as a project engineer. Then followed five years working for Brendan Dobbin, installing brewplant all over Europe and the UK. Since 2003 he has concentrated mainly on the UK market and has supplied and installed many new breweries from 4–50 barrels in size.
Tel: +44 (0) 1204 887 754
www.johnsonbrewing.co.uk

Mossbrew: As well as running Mossbrew, Graham Moss owns the Ministry of Ale brewpub in Burnley. A biochemist by training, he also holds Master's degrees in Malting and Brewing Technology and Business Adminstration. He founded Mossbrew in 1994 and supplies everything from half-barrel pilot breweries upwards, with full installation, training and consultancy services thrown in.
Tel: +44 (0) 1142 492 309
www.mossbrew.co.uk

David Porter: Founder of Porter Brewing based at the Griffin Inn at Haslingden, Lancashire, David once owned a chain of five pubs but slimmed down this side of the business to concentrate on his installation and consultancy business. David has installed over 250 breweries in Britain and many overseas, and runs a full service including training and troubleshooting.
Tel: +44 (0)7976 845 705
www.pbcbreweryinstallations.com

Brewing Services

Brewing Services Ltd is run by David and Rob Smith, with offices in both Yorkshire and Essex. David worked at Sam Smith's Brewery in Tadcaster for more than 20 years before establishing his own brewing consultancy business in 1988. He quickly branched into training and subsequently into brewery design and has worked with more than 250 breweries across the UK and further afield. Rob joined Brewing Services Ltd in 2015. He started his brewing career at Dartmoor Brewery before becoming second brewer at Freedom Brewery, the UK's first dedicated craft lager brewery. He then spent three years as QA Brewer at Meantime Brewery, at the time London's second largest independent brewery and the largest craft brewer in the UK.

Brewery Startup Service

Brewing Services Ltd can help with producing better beer before you ever brew your first pint. Beginning with an on-site survey and project feasibility review, the team's expertise is available at every stage of the development of your brewery, from planning to completion and beyond. The Brewery Start-up Service provides advice on planning and building requirements, assessing utilities, selecting and fitting out premises and sourcing the right equipment at the right price. With more than 30 years' experience of site planning and equipment design, along with recipe formulation and training, Brewing Services Ltd has helped many brewers, in the UK and abroad, produce thousands of award-winning beers including several Champion Beers of Britain.

Brewing & QA Consultancy

David and Rob both strongly believe the secret to making great beer is sound brewing knowledge, good brewing technique and optimum efficiency and that a long-term relationship with brewers is the key to tackling day-to-day issues. They offer an annual Brewing & QA Survey package which includes regular on- and off-site technical support, microbiological and analytical checks and training. Their expertise in continually reviewing brewing procedures and solving long-term production problems has helped numerous breweries maintain and improve product quality and integrity.

David and Rob's aim is always to help breweries achieve maximum efficiency and produce the highest possible quality products, whether in cask, bottle, keg or can, and they would always encourage brewers to call for an informal chat.

Rob: +44 (0) 7966 693097
David: +44 (0) 7970 629552
Email: enquiries@brewingservices.co.uk
www.brewingservices.co.uk

If your budget isn't big, you may at this point be getting a bit nervous about how much you're likely to have to spend on your all-singing, all-dancing, cutting-edge, computer-controlled brewery.

Well, it depends on who you talk to. Some consultants can do the job for less than £30,000. Then there are others who would advise you to spend not less than £100,000. That doesn't mean that the former are cheapskates and the latter are con artists, though. All it means is that there's a broad spectrum of people coming into the industry, all with different philosophies, ambitions and levels of resource, and the various consultants specialise in catering for different segments of the market.

They will all, by and large, do you proud; just make sure, though, that you talk to three or more of them before deciding which you want to hire. Whichever of the consultants you opt to put your business with, however, you will soon discover one unexpected fact: at bottom, the equipment you will need is surprisingly simple, and the actual pieces of kit are surprisingly few.

Opting for purpose-built brewing equipment rather than improvised kit made from vats with former lives in other industries (and one brewery has vessels originally used to mix lipstick!) doesn't necessarily mean buying new, though. There's a lively trade in second-hand kit too. The attrition of mid-size breweries such as Gale's and Ridley's, which both closed in 2006–2007, seems to have run its course, and the source of large second-hand vessels has therefore pretty much dried up. However, many successful microbrewers have grown out of their original plant and swapped it for bigger vessels. Much of the kit that comes on the market as a result is fairly well worn, but then stainless steel and copper vats and tuns are pretty durable items provided they're well looked after.

Let us now pretend that we're walking through a classic tower brewery – that is, one where the malt and water are hoisted or pumped to the top, and all the subsequent processes are on successively lower floors to allow gravity to do the work. We are in the company of Richard Shardlow of Brewing Design Services of Tring, to whom I am indebted for this virtual tour. As we go, you can tick off what you're going to need piece by piece. First though, let's deal with the utilities and services you are certain to need.

Utilities and Services

Water

Beer is mostly water, and you're going to use an awful lot of it. What with cooling (and automatic temperature control at every stage of the process means a more consistent product and a less exhausting life) and cleaning, in fact, you're going to use about five times as much water as you will actually brew with. So if you produce 3,000 barrels of beer at 36 gallons per barrel, you're actually going to get through more than 1.8 million litres a year. This will put you on your water company's industrial tariff, details of which you will need anyway for your business plan.

If you are lucky enough to have your own well or borehole, however, your water will be free. The Environment Agency allows the abstraction of up to 20m³ or about 20,000 litres of groundwater per day from wells and boreholes without a licence. That's more than 17.3 million litres a year, or nearly four times what a 3,000-

barrel brewer is likely to need. You can even have your own well sunk: numerous commercial borehole diggers can be found by surfing the web. The water company doesn't just supply water; it also takes it away. However, to take advantage of this service you will need trade effluent consent, of which more below.

Electricity

As well as water you will also need energy to move it around, heat it up and cool it down. You can have a gas-fired copper, if you like, but even if you do, you are still going to use electricity on a literally industrial scale. You are therefore recommended to install a three-phase supply, even in a five-barrel plant, both as an economy measure (a single-phase supply, will draw 120–130 amps to generate 36kw of heat, whereas a three-phase supply will draw only 63 amps) and so that you don't keep blowing fuses.

Laboratory Tests

A key heading under services is the laboratory. The number and sophistication of tests and checks required these days places a fully functional lab beyond the resources or expertise of the smaller brewery. But there are plenty of contractors who will undertake them for you; your consultant will provide some of these services and will be pleased to put you in touch with a specialist such as Brewlab who can do the rest. Before you start brewing, you'll need to have your liquors analysed, and it's a good idea to carry out regular checks in case of changes to the water supply. Your consultant can arrange these.

The regulations concerning sampling for alcoholic strength are set out in the Appendix; again, a specialist such as Brewlab can carry these out, but nearer to home there are many commercial providers of laboratory services. If your consultant hasn't recommended one, check in Yellow Pages under "chemists – analytical and research" or "laboratory facilities".

Local laboratories can also carry out the regular microbiology tests recommended in the Society of Independent Brewers' code of conduct. If you sell beer to large retailers such as supermarkets, you will also be required to check regularly for heavy metals such as lead and arsenic, aflatoxins produced by fungi and toxins from nitrites in the water supply.

Pipework

Finally, not exactly a utility or service, but an essential part of the brewery that won't fit under the heading of any particular vessel, is the pipework. This is something you will become intimately familiar with very quickly, and Richard's advice is not to cut corners by choosing flexible hoses over solid pipes. There are two reasons for this: hoses won't last and will have to be replaced; and there will be an irresistible temptation to tuck them away where you won't see them. Actually, you're better off with highly conspicuous pipes in places where they can easily be inspected, cleaned and, if necessary, repaired or replaced.

Brewing Vessels

Malt Mill and Hot Liquor Tank

The brewing process starts when you fill your mash tun, so up in the very attic of our tower we find our malt mill and hopper and our hot liquor tank. Only Richard's advice is: don't bother with the malt mill. Years ago, maltsters expected their customers to grind their malt to their own specification and were rarely called on to do it themselves; and when they did, the grists they came up with weren't necessarily exactly what the brewers wanted. Nowadays though, with so many micros not possessing mills of their own, grinding is all part of the service; so why spend good money on kit you don't need? (You'll still need the hopper, though.)

The other constituent of the mash is, of course, hot liquor. A fairly plain insulated stainless steel tank with everyday immersion heater elements will do the trick, says Richard. It needs to heat the liquor to 72°C but can be allowed to do so overnight; an energy-saving thermostat and a timer switch (so you don't have to slip back to the brewery last thing at night to turn it on) might be useful extras.

Also in the attic we're likely to find the cold water tank. This is going to supply the four-fifths of your water requirement that you don't actually brew with, and it's got to be both refrigerated and well insulated. This is because the hopped wort, hot from the kettle, is going to have to be cooled rapidly to 18–19°C before it can be pitched with yeast. Given that the cold water tank is right up there in the attic where the sun can beat down on it uninterrupted, it will need refrigerating down to about 12°C before it can do the job.

CASE STUDY

Harbour Brewing
Canning line increases sales

For Rhys Powell and Eddie Lofthouse, co-founders of Harbour Brewing, the decision in 2011 to set up a brewery was made over a few beers in a pub in the bustling foodies, harbour town of Padstow.

Through studying brewing and distilling at university, and as a brewer for Sharps Brewery, Rhys had already established a career in the brewing industry. Eddie was in hospitality, running a hotel and bar; however, with the business closing and the premises facing a new phase of development, the time felt right to make a complete career change and turn his passion for beer into a reality.

But potential sites for brewing in Padstow were limited and expensive. So, they decided to open a brewery inland, just outside Bodmin. Their concept was to install a brewery system which enabled the brewing to be as creative as possible, incorporating innovative techniques, whilst respecting traditional and proven methods.

A Hungarian brewery system, along with fermentation vessels, was installed, swiftly followed in 2014 by a fully automatic Cimec bottling line, which can fill 2,500 bottles per hour.

But the pair soon realised that the sales of their range of full-flavoured beers would benefit from being in cans.

In July 2015, they installed an American Beer Equipment (LinCan 30) fully automated canning line. The new line can produce up to 1,800 330ml cans of carbonated beer per hour, with the support of Vigo.

Eddie is strongly of the view that brewers who want to be successful should offer beer on draft, in bottles and cans. He said: "Flexibility of packaging is what the market dictates. Cans are convenient, they don't break – so they're ideal for the beach and festivals – and I love the fact that you can stick loads in the fridge.

"There are cost benefits too – cans are cheaper than bottles and we are able to pass these savings on to our customers. You can do anything you want with your beers (for canning) and you know that they (cans) won't affect the product."

The investment in the canning line has had a positive effect on production – it increased.

"Our sales have increased 30 per cent since introducing cans. We are also in the latter stages of negotiation with a number of multiples, due to our strong brand and as a result of using a canning line which is CE compliant," said Eddie.

Most multiples require CE compliance throughout the production process to pass their stringent audits. Vigo ensures that all equipment installed meets all relevant British and European H&S Directives and Standards.

www.harbourbrewing.com

Mash Tun

The mash tun is one of the most important vessels in the brewery, for it's where the malt is made to yield up its fermentable sugars to create the sweet wort that will, eventually, be beer. But it's also one of the simplest – basically, it's just an insulated stainless-steel cylinder with a tight-fitting lid on top and a sieve in its bottom.

To get the best extraction, your mash tun will need to be well insulated enough to hold the mash at 72°C for an hour or an hour and a half. It also needs a sparging arm built into the lid: this is rather like the spray arm in your dishwasher at home, and once the wort has been run off, it sprays the grains with hot water to get the last little bits of sugar out of them. The grains lie either on a stainless steel plate drilled with just the right number of right-sized holes to let the wort run through once mashing has been satisfactorily completed, or on a wedgewire mesh that does the same job.

Emptying the mash tun is quite a job: a five-barrel brew of session bitter requires something like 120kg of malt, which will by this stage be sodden and therefore even heavier. It all has to be dug out by hand, which is made more difficult by the fact that a five-barrel mash tun isn't actually all that big, so it's very awkward to get at its contents. There is a tilting mash tun on the market that makes the job easier, although digging out the mash tun is the brewing industry's time-honoured way of keeping apprentices and juniors fit, and it's certainly a good work-out.

Spent Grain

What do you do with all that spent grain? If you're brewing every day it mounts up, so it is best to sell it as animal feed. Since July 2005 though, thanks to swine vesicular disease and foot and mouth, British brewers have to conform to European feed hygiene legislation, as they affect "co-products". This means registering with the Brewing, Food & Beverage Industry Suppliers Association (BFBi) Feed Assurance Scheme, going on a one-day course and paying a fee of £150-£590 plus VAT, depending on how big a brewery you are. It may seem just another bit of bureaucratic nonsense, but given the devastation caused by foot and mouth it is perhaps a forgiveable precaution. The sale of co-products is so important for your cash-flow (the first payment you receive will almost certainly not be for the sale of beer, but for the sale of spent grains), and any other means of disposing of spent grains would be so difficult that registration is indispensable. Visit **www.bfbi.org.uk** for details.

The Copper and Hop Back

The next stop for your wort on its journey towards becoming beer is the copper, where it will be boiled up with hops. The wort will already be pretty hot when it is run into the copper, so a couple of thermostatically controlled immersion heater elements should suffice to bring it nicely to the boil and keep it there for as long as need be. But although this is the cheapest and easiest way to do the job, it's by no means the only way. A handful of breweries, notably Caledonian, have coppers fired directly by gas-jets, which is picturesque and produces caramel that gives the beer a highly distinctive taste, but there are health and safety issues. Another more expensive method is a gas immersion coil, which is highly efficient. Then there's steam, either in a coil or an external jacket, which is very expensive to install and highly dangerous if not assiduously maintained, but is both cheap to run and very flexible, since the same steam can also be used for cleaning. The copper needs to be vented externally to get rid of the steam it produces, and it can have a sprayball built into its lid to allow thorough cleaning with detergent and rinsing with boiling water after use (although you can just hose it out with boiling water, since it should already be sterile).

Perhaps the hop back should come under the same heading as the copper, although strictly speaking it's the next stage in the process. Essentially it's just a huge sieve, like the steel plate or wedgewire mesh in the mash tun, only in this case it's the "trub" or used hops that it's there to collect, so the hopped wort can run clean into the fermenters. Richard, who runs Tring Brewery as well as Brewing Design Services, actually uses the hop back for the last addition of hops. Instead of putting the late hops into the copper itself, he puts them in the hop back, dampens them a little and then lets the wort sit on them for a while before it drains through. Adding the late hops directly to the boil, he says, evaporates many of the aromatic resins. Doing it this way gives him more aroma from fewer hops. Be that as it may, the used hop litter or trub has to be got rid of. Pelletised hops, says Richard, tend to disintegrate in the boil to the extent where (with the water company's express approval) they can simply be hosed down the drain. Used whole hops have to be dug out by hand and make excellent mulch.

Fermentation

This is where your plentiful supply of refrigerated water comes in, since the hopped wort leaves the copper having just boiled and has to be rapidly cooled to 18–19°C (collection temperature) before it can be pitched with yeast. The wort therefore needs to be run through a heat exchanger, of which there are a number of types, into the fermenting vessel, whose temperature also needs to be controlled (preferably automatically, so you don't have to alter it manually every two hours day and night) by means of a cooling jacket. Fermentation is an exothermic reaction – that is, it generates its own heat – and the temperature of the fermenting wort will gradually creep up as the process goes on. Too hot a reaction will generate off-flavours, so the fermentation temperature needs to be kept down to about 21°C. Different shapes of fermentation vessel produce different temperatures, too; consult your installer as to which shape – cylindrical, cylindro-conical or square – will suit you best. The cooling jacket also needs to be efficient enough to bring the temperature of the wort down sharply to 8–12°C within 24 hours of fermentation ending.

Open Fermenters

There is some argument as to whether fermenters need lids or not. In some parts of the country, especially in the north of England, open square fermenters made of slate are traditional; and being able to peer into the fermenting vessel as the yeast begins to grow its thick, rocky head is perhaps the most aesthetically pleasing part of the whole operation – visitors love it. But there are drawbacks, says Richard. Open fermenters demand excellent ventilation and extraction equipment, since the CO_2 given off during fermentation is lethal even in fairly low doses. CO_2 in high concentrations burns the nose and eyes; but it will cause unconsciousness at much lower levels than that, and will then asphyxiate you. Your environmental health officer (EHO) will probably stipulate what monitoring and ventilation equipment you will need at the planning stage; some EHOs have been known to veto open fermenters altogether.

Closed Fermenters

Closed fermenters are also more hygienic, says Richard – which is vitally important, as this is the most delicate stage in the proceedings. Historically, it's infection when fermenting that is the brewer's biggest danger. Improved hygiene and handling

BREWING SERVICES LTD

EST. 1988

BREWERY START-UPS & EXPANSIONS

REGULAR ON-SITE Q.A. SURVEYS

TECHNICAL SUPPORT & TROUBLESHOOTING

ON-SITE TRAINING &

RESIDENTIAL TRAINING COURSES

Rob Smith or David Smith

Rob: 07966 693097 / David: 07970 629552

enquiries@brewingservices.co.uk

www.brewingservices.co.uk

PBC BREWERY SOLUTIONS LTD.

PBC BREWERY SOLUTIONS LTD
The number one installer and trainer in the UK.

BREWERY INSTALLATION
We have installed more than 400 breweries worldwide in over 20 countries and there are currently over 200 operational breweries in the UK alone who have entrusted us to design, supply and install their equipment. Between us our team has over 50 years' experience in breweries and making beer.

BREWERY TRAINING
As well as offering the best installation service, we also run a number of short courses every year at our purpose-built brewery in Salford. Share in our experience of running successful pubs, successful businesses, a comprehensive knowledge of the market, a passion for breweries and, above all, our ability to brew great beer.

If it's just a one-off vessel or spare part you require please don't hesitate to contact us!

Whatever your requirements in your brewing future, make sure you take a wide range of advice and sort the barley from the chaff.

We welcome all enquiries and try to help as much as we can, our website can be seen at www.pbcbrewerysolutions.com, or email us on info@pbcbrewerysolutions.com, if you want a chat ring Derek Eastwood on +44 (0) 7976 845 705 or Dave Carr on +44 (0) 7740 094 677

@VigoLtd
Exclusive UK supplier of
ABE
AMERICAN BEER EQUIPMENT
Crafted for you
Give us a call on
01404 892100.
Equipment
Service
Support
www.vigoltd.com
vigo
Equipping the Nation's Craft Breweries
ABE brewhouses (>2 BBL) & canning machines • Speidel Braumeister brewing systems (10-200 litre)
Bottle / keg / BiB fillers • Labellers • Tanks • Temperature control • Pumps • Filters • Cappers

RELIABLE CLOSURES THAT HELP SEAL, PROTECT AND ADD VALUE TO BRANDS
SPILES
CLIP CORKS
TAPS
KEYSTONES
SHIVES
RANKIN
Quality Stoppers and Closures
Since 1774
+44 (0)1844 203100 sales@rankincork.co.uk
rankincork.co.uk

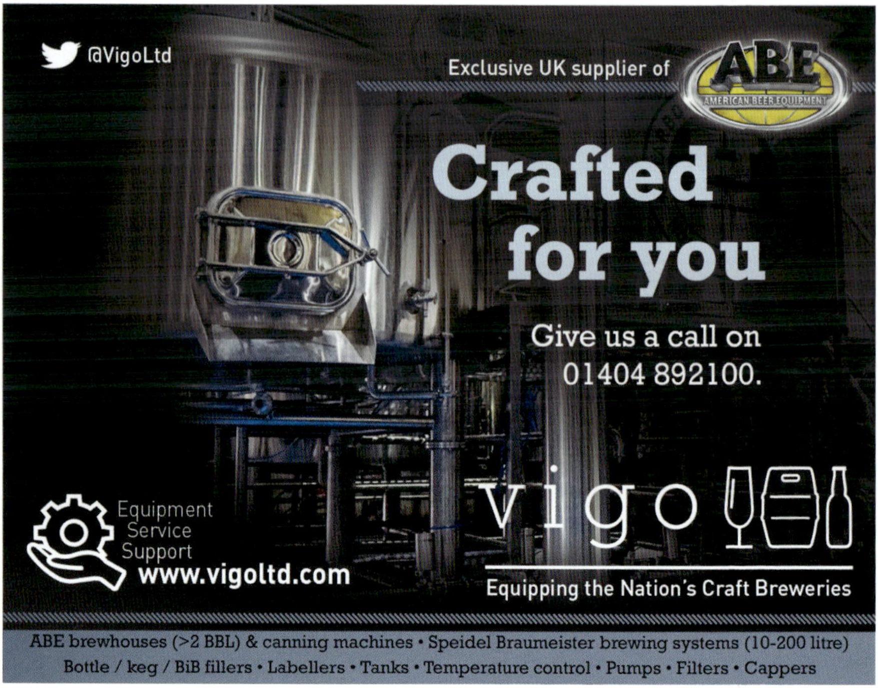

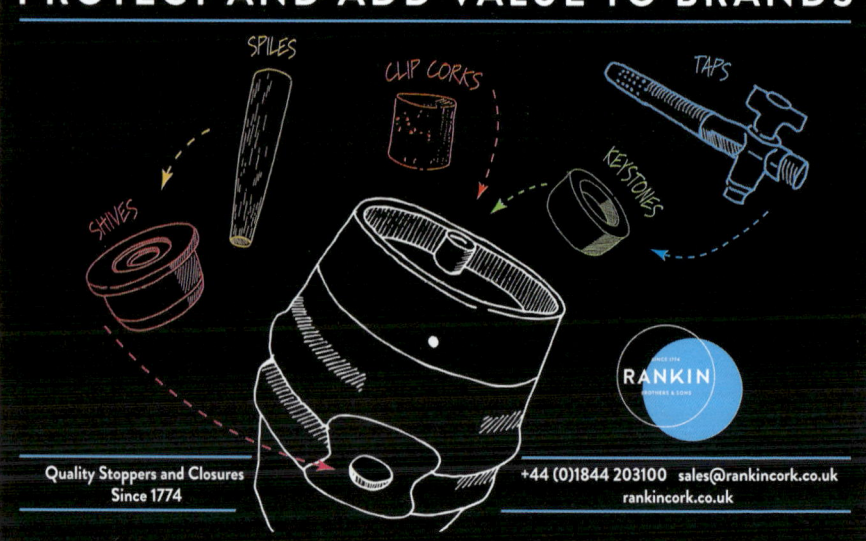

mean that spoilt brews due to yeast infection aren't as common these days as they were; nevertheless, you need to be ruthlessly disciplined in your hygiene procedures at this stage. Not only do closed fermenters mean there is no risk of birds, rodents or brewery visitors making unwelcome deposits in them, but they are less vulnerable to passing bacteria and spores and can have "cips" – cleaning in place systems – built in. Opting for closed fermenters means that your entire brewery is virtually a closed system from mash tun on. Almost the only time it needs to be opened during the process is for the addition of hops – which are, of course, added to the wort while it is boiling and therefore safe from infection.

Once fermentation is complete – and it can last for anything from a day to a week – there are really only two processes left for most microbrewers: collecting the yeast, and racking the beer into casks. Your yeast will grow by five or six times during fermentation; you can skim excess barm off the top of the wort with a sterile bucket, and there's a trap known as a thimble that fits into the base of the vessel to collect the clumped or "flocculated" yeast cells that sink down to the bottom. Once you've harvested enough yeast for your next brew, the rest will go as highly nutritious pig-feed – provided, of course, that you have signed up to the BFBi's Feed Assurance Scheme.

Casks

As we discovered in the previous chapter, most brewers reckon they need a ratio of seven casks for every one out in trade. The most common casks these days are nine-gallon firkins, either stainless steel or aluminium at around £80 each, so they're not cheap; and you might also want a handful of 4½-gallon "pins" for very strong beers or 18-gallon "kilderkins" for fast-selling beers.

The full 36-gallon barrel is almost obsolete as an actual cask and is really only used as a unit of account these days. That's not because few pubs or clubs can sell beer quickly enough to warrant such a large container: there are probably thousands whose throughput of lager would justify the use of full-sized barrels. But they are nightmares to handle, weighing 200kg or more when full. I do believe there are still a handful of 54 gallon hogsheads in circulation in the north-west, but I have never seen one. You may also come across metric barrels of 50–100 litres, which are commonly used for lager and keg beer, of which more below.

CASE STUDY

Hook Norton
170 years of beer

The Hook Norton Brewery is situated in the stunning Cotswold Hills, providing customers with well over a century of brewing expertise and its handcrafted brewing heritage.

The independent family business has moved with the times, taking all that it has learned over the years and incorporating that with a modern approach to the new brewing market it's operating in and subsequently creating a range of real ales for today's consumer to enjoy.

Today, Hook Norton is a rarity as one of 32 breweries that remain family owned. Not only does it create an outstanding range of award-winning beers, but it also provides visitors with a free museum, meeting rooms, the brewery shop and Malthouse Kitchen Café.

Not only does it have this great range of experiences located within the brewery itself, but Hook Norton also has a range of 36 pubs that have a home within many local communities, serving their customers a wide array of food and drink.

The team at Hook Norton have created an offering that is well recognised by those locally and further afield, with the chance to sample their beers in one of their numerous pubs, or alternatively in a brewery tour where customers can learn about the pivotally important history of the brand.

Over the years Hook Norton's beer range has expanded dramatically, now offering customers a selection from their core range, seasonal and keg range for all to enjoy.

Hook Norton's award-winning core beer range is available all year round for customers to enjoy, all of which are complemented by a new seasonal ale to provide a little variety as they year goes on.

Included in the range is Hooky, an amber bitter of 3.5% ABV, followed by Old Hooky, a stronger fruity beer at 4.6% ABV, and Hooky Gold, a very pale ale at 4.1% ABV.

The seasonal beer range is a collection of cask ale beers created throughout the year that are made in order to reflect the needs of their drinkers. Each beer uses ingredients that are specifically associated with the season, therefore creating something that is recognisably fit for that time of year.

Some of this year's included: Cold Turkey, Outside Half, Double Stout, Amarillo Gold, Sundial, Crafty Fox, Haymaker, Inspired, Autumn Ways, Flagship, Greedy Goose and Twelve Days.

Lastly the Hooky beer keg range, which provides customers with the same quality that would be found in a cask, includes Red Rye, Merula Stout and Cotswold Pale, all of which can be enjoyed all year round.

www.hooky.co.uk

Alternative Barrels and Casks

The price of new barrels may tempt you to investigate second-hand ones; but do be careful, especially if there are any visible mends, for a "leaker" will cost you dear. Not only does it have to be replaced, but if it fails dramatically all over a publican's cellar, it may well cost you their business.

Similarly, plastic casks have attracted considerable criticism. On paper, they're the answer to the small brewer's prayer – lightweight, rigid, durable and very cheap. But some say they're prone to sudden and dramatic failure, that they don't stand up to the stresses of frequent rough handling and that the plastic is degraded by washing at high temperatures. On the other hand, plastics technology has advanced considerably in recent years and many small brewers now swear by plastic. Visit **www.breweryplastics.biz** and make up your own mind.

Whatever casks you use, cleaning them to sterility is absolutely essential. Rinse them out thoroughly with a power-washer; use a sprayball with detergent; and then steam them. In fact, ease of cleaning is one reason why the brewing industry has resolutely refused to countenance cubic containers. Barrels are traditionally barrel-shaped so they can be rolled round the brewery yard and up and down the ramps in pub cellars quickly and easily. Cubic containers would be more efficient, stacking into a smaller space, and could easily be moved around on tail-lifts and pump-trucks. But the corners would be havens for bacteria, which single disadvantage outweighs the multitude of advantages. Let discipline in your cask-washing procedure slip even once and you risk sending out spoilt or infected beer, for which the retailer on the receiving end may never forgive you. Let it slip more than once and you risk being labelled as a dirty brewery, a reputation that is hard to shake off and that could kill your business.

Craft Beer

Not all your beer, of course, will go into casks. Depending on your business model, you might well sell as much in bottle as on draught. Bottled sales will almost certainly be very important to you, and the ramifications of bottling your beer will be dealt with in a later chapter. There's a growing band of brewers interested mainly in foreign beer styles whose draught volume is not cask-conditioned but keg, bottled or canned.

One of the biggest changes in the microbrewing sector since

the first edition of this book was published has been a growing affinity for keg. For many years – decades, in fact – microbrewers by and large stood shoulder to shoulder with the Campaign for Real Ale in loathing the stuff, remembering unfondly both the ghastly almost non-alcoholic national brands that prompted the consumer backlash of the 1970s (Watney's Starlight at 2% ABV!) and the second-generation "smooth" keg brands of the '90s (whatever happened to Boddingtons?).

But as long as 20 years ago there were those who broke ranks. Inspired more by the café culture of the Continent than by the British pub tradition, Freedom and Porterhouse breweries set up more or less all-keg boutique bars in the West End of London in the mid-1990s, and the Porterhouse in Covent Garden is still with us. Others followed, notably Meantime Brewing in Greenwich, West Brewing in Glasgow and Camden Town Brewery in north London.

The earliest micros to adopt keg did so in order to recreate the best beers from Europe and North America, where serving cold, filtered and sometimes pasteurised beer under CO_2 is too natural to be worthy of comment. Indeed the French don't even have a word for cask-conditioned beer: the idiomatic equivalent of "draught" is "sous pression"; its opposite, "sans pression", would be meaningless. And legions of British travellers to Belgium – even those who fancy themselves real ale diehards – have discovered to their delight that the method of dispense isn't really all that important: it's the quality of the liquid that counts.

But if keg beer can match cask for flavour, the word still carries a bad taste. So the new wave of brewers that has emerged in such numbers since the first edition of this book appeared (surely no coincidence!) started calling themselves "craft brewers" and their products "craft beers" in line with common American practice. The term had actually been considered by SIBA when it was founded in 1980 but was rejected on the grounds that it implied a degree of amateurism; and indeed both the Craft Brewing Association and the UK Craft Brewers Network page on Facebook concern themselves mostly with home brewing. The use of the term has been criticised more recently on the grounds that it doesn't have any intrinsic meaning, and that it's no more than a marketing expression that anyone can use – and indeed many big regional brewers have jumped on the craft bandwagon. Nevertheless the descriptor has stuck because it does have a meaning: it's associated with brewers who will try anything in terms of beer styles, in terms of ingredients, in terms of dispense methods, in terms of packaging – some of them are even having their beers contract-canned, which 10 years ago would have seemed almost blasphemous. These are the qualities that a new generation of beer-drinkers passionately demands, and that the craft brewers take great pleasure in supplying.

Craft beer may or may not be a fad. In five years the term might be completely obsolete. But there's another impetus that will probably drive more and more British microbrewers to look seriously at kegging their ales: mathematics.

Five or six years ago there were 500 independent brewers and 60,000 pubs, or 120 potential accounts per brewer. Today there are only 45,000 pubs and approaching 1,800 independent breweries, or 30 potential accounts per brewer; and the ratio is getting worse every day. Unanswerable maths dictates that the old-school pub trade can no longer sustain the number of brewers clamouring to supply it. And the bottled trade, monopolised as it is by the big supermarket chains, is for most independent brewers a marginal alternative at best. Few microbrewers make their living selling bottled beers to specialist off-licences and at farmers' markets!

But there are huge opportunities for keg beers which have no ullage, which are easy to handle and which will keep almost indefinitely: not just in the cocktail bars and gastropubs of the nouveau East End, but much further downmarket – in the very accounts, in fact, that keg beer was first designed for 80 years ago.

All over the country, thousands of licensed bars in village halls, leisure centres, sports clubs, theatres, arts centres and community centres can't stock cask beer but are intensely local in their outlook. Often owned by parish or district councils, they would willingly, were it possible, stock a beer from a brewery that employed local people and paid their business rates to the local town hall. In terms of overall annual barrelage many of these accounts might appear too small to bother with. But many of them, even the most modest of village halls, operate chiefly as function rooms that can shift impressive volumes per session.

There are other keg opportunities to exploit, too. Such workingmen's, comrades and social clubs as survive are in many cases already keg-only and their committees would stock locally produced beers if such were available. Breweries with intensely rural trading areas, especially in Scotland, are looking to kegging to give their beers the shelf-life that small isolated pubs with big seasonal fluctuations in throughput require. Keg can also be more convenient than cask for outside bars – no settling time, so no need to move on to the site 48 hours in advance of the event itself. And even dyed-in-the-wool real ale pubs will often stock a craft-brewed keg lager, stout or Belgian-style blonde ale to underline and enhance their support for microbreweries

But isn't kegging hugely expensive? Well, not necessarily. An expert tinkerer who already filters and carbonates beers for bottling can adapt the bottling line to keg short runs for individual accounts. But it's unbelievably time-consuming, and any microbrewer who is serious about the opportunity would probably want to install a keg washer and filler such as the trolley-mounted four-nozzle DME from ABUK of Misterton, Nottinghamshire, which would cost more than £8,000.

If keg sales take off, there are two alternative routes to expansion. One is to take the plunge and invest in in-line carbonation (much more reliable than carbonating in tank, according to ABUK), sterile filtration and a larger manual filler starting at around £20,000 the lot (depending on the strength of the pound: much of the equipment is imported from Germany or the Czech Republic). You pretty much have to filter, since the method of dispense rouses the beer; but there's no need to pasteurise: sterile-filtered and carbonated beers even of moderate ABV can have a six-month shelf-life without being boiled!

If, however, £20,000 is rather a large step, you might always consider contract-kegging as an intermediate phase. A number of new-wave contract-kegging operations have sprung up since craft beer became popular, among them Hambleton Ales of Melmerby, North Yorkshire; while older- established brewers such as Everard's of Leicester have been supplying the service for many years for the more traditional keg trade. Everard's has a minimum kegging run of 60 barrels (or about 200 11 gallon kegs), which is probably fairly typical. Expect to pay £3-4 per keg for filling, or up to £800 for a minimum run, to which you would have to add the cost of tanking your beer to the brewery. This could be in the region of £500 for a 180-barrel (600-keg) tanker, depending on the price of diesel this week; the cost is likely to be the same even if the tanker isn't full. If you don't have your own kegs and pallets, you'll have to hire at around £6 per keg. The total cost, therefore, of contract-filling 200 kegs will be around £2,300 or £11.50 a keg, so it might be just a stopgap while you consider your longer-term options.

There are other costs, too: temperature-controlled conditioning tanks, for instance, especially if you want to brew an authentic lager. Large ones cost a lot, but the German fabricator Speidel makes freestanding 240 litre chiller tanks at approaching £1,000 each (its UK agent is Vigo of Devon). Then there are the fonts themselves, and here the sky is the limit. But you don't have to include flashing lights and a brushed titanium finish: a modest font will cost no more than £70 (or visit **www.morepour.com** for a cheaper alternative) and if even that seems a lot, there is a hidden advantage. Once landlords have allowed them to be installed on their bars, it seems, they regard them as permanent fixtures (provided your beer sells, of course), which gets you off the guest ale rollercoaster.

To offset all these costs is the 50p a pint premium that keg lagers, stouts, Belgian-style blonde beers and even British-style golden ales can command at the bar (more if you describe them as craft beers!), which should translate into a premium of £20 a keg for the brewer. There's also the fact that new 11 gallon kegs from a company like Kammac of Burton-on-Trent cost marginally less than new nine-gallon firkins, which all adds up in the long run. There could be a sales advantage, too: real ale publicans who won't extend their range on grounds of throughput and ullage might very well consider adding a long-lived, waste-free keg beer to their offering.

To many microbrewers, of course, the very idea of keg is anathema. But these are hard times and getting harder, and there can be few microbrewers nowadays determined enough to dismiss a business opportunity on grounds of ideology. As for quality, anybody who has enjoyed a superb draught de Koninck in Antwerp or Gouden Carolus in Mechelen will surely agree that a squirt of CO_2 won't harm a good beer – even as being pulled through a handpump won't improve a bad one.

KeyKeg

An alternative to the metal container for dispensing draft beer is the plastic keg. The most widely used is the KeyKeg. The one-way, recyclable kegs are a cheaper option than metal counterparts and come in a number of sizes from 10 to 30 litres.

In proper storage conditions, beer stays fresh for as long as in a steel keg. Depending on the qualities, the type of beer and the alcohol content, possibly longer. Other factors that play a role are pasteurisation and the quality of the filling procedure. After tapping, beer will stay fresh in a KeyKeg for 3-4 weeks on average. The shelf life of the beer naturally depends on the type of beer, storage conditions and cleanliness of the draft system.

Any style of beer can be filled into a plastic container. Some even age lambics, imperial stouts and other beers in a KeyKeg with great results. Forced carbonation of the beer is not possible in a KeyKeg. However, under the right conditions, secondary fermentation is possible, but it is important that the CO_2 content does not rise too far.

Canning

Canned beers once regarded as an inferior product to be piled high and sold cheaply in supermarkets have become as must-have as the latest Apple iPhone. Many craft brewers are making expensive investments installing a canning line. Others are buying canning time in other people's breweries or taking advantage of one of the mobile canning companies which are opening.

The debate over draught beer or in bottles versus cans is as old as the introduction of the first canned beer in the 1920s in the US. Once canned beer was said to taint the flavour of beer. Today, host brewers agree the modern aluminium can preserves beer from the demons of oxygen and light, which can change the flavour of the brew chemically. Beer from a can is fresher and more environmentally friendly.

One of London's newest and hippest breweries is Hop Stuff. They are one of many brewers venturing into canning and offering their brews in 330ml cans rather than the more traditional glass bottles. Hop Stuff founder James Yeomans said: "The move into can has been a long time coming for us – the can allows portability in a way no bottle could."

Martin Constable, Chairman of the Can Makers, said: "Cans are increasing in popularity as brewers recognise the role they play in maintaining the integrity of their beer and their recyclability. The drink is protected, kept fresh, sealed from light and air and is quick to chill. It is served in the exact state that the brewer intended.

"The improved accessibility of the canned craft beer means that brewers and consumers alike have fallen in love with it. It appears on the shelf in many independent stores and is increasingly listed in supermarkets. Plus, it is opening the craft beer market up to wider markets, attracting more females to what is often considered a male product."

Water Disposal

The last step in the brewing process is getting rid of the four-fifths of water you used but didn't brew with safely and hygienically. This water is going to be full of all sorts of pollutants, some of them organic – bits of hop-litter, protein, suspended solids – and some of them chemical, in particular, industrial-strength detergents. It may also have a low pH value.

You can't simply flush it down the drain – not, at any rate, without trade effluent consent from your water and sewerage provider. This comes with a detailed questionnaire about what sort of and how much effluent you propose to discharge; the advice is to be scrupulously honest, since if you breach the terms of your consent, the sewerage provider not only can but probably will revoke it altogether (it can fine you, too). Since sewerage providers continually monitor discharges, you won't get away unnoticed with craftily tipping it away, either. Especially as it's going to be in the region of 450,000 gallons a year!

If you don't have mains drainage, you might consider planting a reed bed, for which you will need discharge consent from the Environment Agency. It is becoming increasingly popular to dispose of pollutants by creating a reed bed as certain reeds can actually digest most if not all of the nasties a brewery generates, and the site itself will be a haven for wildlife and is therefore environmentally friendly. But there are drawbacks: you may not have enough space, and establishing a reed bed is a slow and expensive process. Most brewers who have done so seem satisfied with the result, though, and I have heard of only one instance where the reed bed's performance has been ruled inadequate by the Environment Agency. A good site where you'll find more information about reed beds is **www.oceans-esu.com**. The Environment Agency also has a helpline: Tel: +44 (0) 3708 506 506.

Chapter Five
What to Brew

Wine snobs like to be dismissive of beer. Wine, they say, has infinite variety: red, white, rosé, still, sparkling, dry, sweet, New World, Old World, grown on chalk, grown on flint, grown in a hot climate, grown in a cool climate, grown on a south-facing slope, grown on a west-facing slope – and as for grape varieties, why, the permutations are endless! But as for beer… well, it's just beer, isn't it?

If the big multinational brewers had their way, the wine snobs' scorn would be justified; 90 per cent of the world's beer is a pale (both in colour and in character) imitation of Czech or German pilsner, brewed (as one disgruntled ale brewer of my acquaintance once put it) from broken biscuits and old bus tickets, and served cold to mask the nasty tinny flavour that comes from too short a lagering period (which is the only flavour most of it has). It's made as cheaply as possible, using the lowest-grade ingredients available, taking every short cut in the brewing chemist's book and intended to be the same wherever you go, whatever the label. However, some 90 per cent of the world's wine is pretty ropy, too, if you think about it, but as a craft brewer you stand shoulder to shoulder with the makers of the best 10 per cent. That's the bracket you want to be in; it's only a pity that the best of beers can't command the same price premium as the best of wines!

Don't, whatever you do, let the winemakers command the high ground, or get you down or dent your self-esteem. Beer has just as many variations as wine – more, in fact – and you are setting out to master all of them. In so doing, you have picked a harder row to hoe than any winemaker, for most of their work is done for them. All their ingredients come in one juicy little package, the grape, the sweetest fruit of them all, with liquor, fermentable material and aromatics all contained in one skin. All they have to do is grow it – and in many cases they needn't even choose which variety to grow, so protected are they by regulation – press it and ferment it. If things go wrong, they can always blame the weather. Even the choices they do have to make – how to prune, whether and how long to macerate, what temperature to ferment at – are largely dictated by tradition and regulation. They don't have to make anything like the number of choices you will – how to treat your liquor, what grains to blend in your grist, in what proportions, which hops to use for bitterness and aroma, in what quantities, at what stage of the boil to add them, what strain of yeast to propagate and even what styles of beer to brew. For you, the choices are infinite, and you are going to have to make them yourself. Don't be daunted, though. For as a brewer you are free to make whatever you want.

Then for ingredients! There's pale malt, brown malt, amber malt, black malt, crystal malt, chocolate malt, unmalted roasted barley, malted wheat, unmalted wheat, torrefied wheat, oats, rye, rice (if you're American), sorghum (if you're African), buckwheat (if you're gluten intolerant), invert sugar, candy sugar, honey… and we haven't even started on the hops yet! As a home brewer, you may have played around with all of the above; you might also have experimented with flavourings such as ginger and other spices, various fruits, exotic sugars and even spirits. Some of your experiments may have been, frankly, mistakes; others may have been triumphant successes. But as someone whose livelihood now depends not so much on what you can brew as on what you can sell, you're going to have to think hard about the range of beers you can realistically put out there in the marketplace.

Being thoughtful and realistic, though, needn't mean being too cautious. Perhaps it's a foolhardy brewery that doesn't have a session bitter, a best bitter and perhaps a special bitter in its range (although perhaps less so these days). In order to compete effectively – with the established regionals in the early days and more recently with each other – small brewers have always had to offer something different. Part of the glory of being a micro is that you can create something completely off the wall that will break even at only two or three barrels a week, whereas for someone like Greene King or Marston's it would have to sell two or three hundred barrels a week to be worthwhile.

The ability to brew interesting beers in small quantities has always been one of the small brewing sector's key advantages over the older and larger brewers. By the time the small brewing revolution came along, regional and national breweries had been rationalising their ranges for years. It was the downside of economy of scale: any beer style they couldn't brew in economic quantities was doomed, even though there might still be some demand for it. The tied house system and the closed mentality that it engendered meant there was no chance of two or three brewers combining to continue to offer, say, a single old ale between them: if they couldn't sustain a brand of their own, they wouldn't buy in from another brewer. The exception to this rule was Guinness, which as it was Irish and had no tied estate wasn't regarded as dangerous. So old-established breweries that hadn't had a dry stout of their own for generations would happily stock Guinness; and Guinness got a very healthy trade out of it, commanding five per cent of the entire British beer market.

Even in the early 1970s, though, most regionals produced quite a wide selection of draught beer. Mostly there was a light mild, a dark mild, a session bitter, a best bitter, a special bitter and sometimes a strong Christmas special. On the bottled side, most brewers, even quite small ones, still had a light or pale and a brown ale of their own (often just the bitter and the mild pasteurised and bottled), a sweet stout and a barley wine. But these were dying out, and regional brewers were increasingly concentrating on their core ranges. It was years before they noticed that the micros were succeeding by experimenting and diversifying; ever since then they too have been experimenting and diversifying, but you can safely say, in terms of beer styles at least, that where the micros have led the regionals have tended to follow.

For having the motive, means and opportunity to experiment has always suited the temperament of microbrewers in general. Few of them turned to brewing for the money; and the love that drives most of them has always been evident not only in the quality of what they brew, but also in their enthusiasm for different styles and genres. There's also, sometimes, a strong sense of fun in evidence. Yes, these people are trying to make a living. But for many of them the conventional ways of making a living have been crushing disappointments, and they're out to enjoy their working hours as much as their leisure time. This is a wholly laudable urge (which you must share, or you wouldn't have picked this book up), and it has produced some wholly laudable, if somewhat eccentric, beers.

For instance, there was the Kitchen Brewery of West Yorkshire, now defunct, whose beers were all brewed with various vegetables. Then there was a hotly contested but strictly unofficial competition in the early 1990s between Parish of Leicestershire and Sheffield's Frog & Parrot brewpub to see who could brew the stronger version of their respective barley wines, Baz's Bonce Blower and Roger & Out. I can't remember who managed to keep their yeast alive and fermenting for longest, but the eventual victor was, as I recall, over 20 per cent alcohol. I never got to try either contender. I did, however, try the ginger wheat beer produced by Salopian, always an experimental brewery. It was a delight, and I wish it were still being produced.

I could mention Hanby's Cherry Bomb; I could mention Nethergate Umbel Ale. I could go on and on, indeed; but in a way it would be misleading. For where the microbrewing industry as a whole has really led the way has not been in the production of eccentric one-offs, fascinating though they are, but in the setting of trends that the rest of the industry has followed.

Themed Ranges and Unusual Ingredients

The creative drive that has allowed smaller brewers to get away with experimenting is based on the inversion of the law of economy of scale described above: micros can make an acceptable margin on volumes that would be loss-making even for the smallest of regionals. This has proved very useful in preserving beer styles, especially the darker styles such as mild, barley wine and old ale that would otherwise have vanished completely or, indeed, that already had. The first microbrewed beer to win CAMRA's Champion Beer of Britain Competition back in 1987 was Pitfield Brewery's Dark Star, a strong dark ale of a type not listed by a regional or national brewery within even the longest of living memories.

After Dark Star's triumph, Pitfield went on to recreate a whole raft of historic styles using recipes that are mostly more than 150 years and in one case over 200 years old. Its XXXX Stock Ale at 10 per cent alcohol is a comparative stripling, being made to a recipe dating from 1896. The London Porter recipe comes from 1850, the IPA from 1837, the Amber Ale from 1830, and the Imperial Stout from 1792. There are many frustrations in trying to recreate old recipes. The brewers of yore were often frustratingly inexact in recording quantities, boil times and so on; and the varieties, characteristics and methods of processing malt and hops have changed so much over the generations that we really can't know what sugars and acids the ingredients of a century ago contained, and what flavours they would yield. Nevertheless, Pitfield is only one small brewer that has looked to the past to inspire the present. The Teignworthy Brewery at Tucker's Maltings in Newton Abbot, Devon, produces a similar range under the Edwin Tucker brand. Although its recipes are undated, beers such as Empress Russian Stout, East India Pale Ale and Old Walnut Brown root it firmly in the glory days of British brewing history. Mention must also go to Williams Brothers of Alloa, Clackmannanshire, which for many years and under several names has specialised in researching and recreating historic Scottish beer styles remarkable for being flavoured with locally available alternatives to hops. Fraoch was the first and best-known and claims to recreate Pictish heather ale. Almost nothing is known about Pictish heather ale, as you might guess; it may even be that the heather was not actually used as a flavouring agent at all, but that its microfauna included wild yeasts and that sprigs of it were therefore used to ferment the beer. Be that as it may, Fraoch (pronounced "frook") is an excellent beer that has won friends around the world and is widely exported. Its stablemates – Alba, flavoured with spruce tips; Grozet, flavoured with gooseberries; and Ebulum, flavoured with elderberries – are not as big sellers as Fraoch but are just as… interesting.

Theming

Theming the range in this way is an enjoyable and effective way of creating a strong identity for the brewery, and of course the theme needn't be retro. In most cases it's only the beers' names that are themed, while the recipes themselves are unconnected. An outstanding example of this is Triple fff of Alton, Hampshire, whose beers are all named after classic rock singles and album tracks – hence a range that includes Witch's Promise, a 6% Christmas special; Moondance, a 4.2% best bitter; and Pressed Rat and Warthog, a 3.8% dark mild. (Bryncelyn of Swansea, another pop-pickin' micro, has a range themed entirely on Buddy Holly.) Abbeydale of Sheffield has a huge range of beers all on a monastic theme – Absolution, Matins and so forth, although what any God-fearing abbot or prior would make of a beer called Black Mass I leave to your imagination. More common are beers named after local landmarks or events, or even the locals themselves (not necessarily living ones, though: Wood's Local Heroes range commemorated South Shropshire worthies going all the way back to King Caractacus).

There are brewers for whom theming means more than just a common source of brand names: Rooster's of Harrogate (now of Knaresborough after founder Sean Franklin's retirement), for instance, pioneered the use of exotic American and other New World varieties and all its beers were astonishingly hoppy, long before being astonishingly hoppy was fashionable. Other brewers have also looked abroad to find a common identity for their ranges. In some ways this is counterintuitive, for the genesis of the new-wave brewers lies in the consumer revolt of the 1970s against keg dispense and dreadful British-brewed lagers (which in those days were often no more than very pale ales served ice-cold). In the cynical and exploitative hands of the big bad brewers of 30–40 years ago, both the "k" word and the "l" word became instantly recognisable signifiers of weak beer, brewed as cheaply as possible and as bland as the brewer's chemists could make it. But in time, more widely travelled beer lovers – both drinkers and brewers – came to realise three important truths: that not all foreign beer is "lager"; that not all foreign beer is bad; and that if beer is brewed well, it won't be ruined by being dispensed under CO2 pressure.

Continental Styles

These realisations have prompted many British microbrewers to experiment with continental styles, with varying degrees of authenticity and commercial success. The two don't always go hand in hand, mind: Pilgrim Brewery's excellent and extremely authentic Bavarian-style wheat beer, Springbock, is no longer brewed; while Harviestoun Brewery's lager, Schiehallion, although not nearly so authentic, has won prize after prize and goes from strength to strength. Many other microbreweries brew lagers and other German-style products with varying degrees of success, and thanks to the German influence, wheat, malted or not, has become a commonplace ingredient in British brewing.

Before the craft boom came along, though, only a handful of breweries had gone beyond producing one or two examples of foreign styles, and most of those that did were boutique breweries where the emphasis was as much on the style of retailing as on the beer itself. Mash in Great Portland Street, central London, was, until it closed in 2012, a US-style boutique brewery with a wheat beer, a Pils and a fruit beer on its list alongside a porter and an IPA. Meantime, in Greenwich, run by German-trained brewer Alastair Hook, produces authentic Kölsch and Altbier for Sainsbury's and a US-inspired range of specialities including chocolate- and coffee-flavoured beers. West Brewing in Glasgow lists a Hefeweisse or cloudy wheat beer; a Helles or everyday pale beer; a Dunkles or dark lager; and a Dunkel Hefeweisse, or dark wheat beer with yeast sediment. Zerodregrees, with branches in London, Bristol and Reading, brews German-style wheat beer, Pilsner and dark lager.

Interestingly, although many of these pioneers were prepared to try their hands at German beer styles, nobody dared have a go at anything Belgian. Were Belgian beers simply too idiosyncratic and too formidable to imitate? Perhaps the prize was so far out of reach that to make a grab for it and miss was to risk a nasty fall? Hwever, today's craft brewers, being American-inspired, cosmopolitan in outlook and fascinated by beer styles, have the chutzpah to go for it. The field is wide open for British-brewed abbey ales, strong blonde beers or even sour oud bruins and red beers. Are you up for it? Then why not!

Golden Ales

Earlier, I spoke about new brewers setting trends that regionals have followed. Would Fuller's, I wonder, have released its superb London Porter, or Marston's its authentic and stunning Old Empire IPA, if micros such as Pitfield had not delved into the brewing books of yesteryear in search of forgotten flavours? Would Badger (as Hall & Woodhouse likes to be known) have brought out its extraordinary peach-blossom beer if micros had not experimented with fruit flavours first? Would we have Young's Waggle Dance or Fuller's Organic Honeydew if Enville Ales had not pioneered the use of honey in brewing?

Regionals, though, are still pretty conservative in their attitude towards speciality beers. Mostly, given the downside of economy of scale already mentioned, their regular ranges only encompass the more popular styles; and when they do try something outrageous, it's normally as a seasonal special. But there are two trends established by microbrewers that regionals have followed enthusiastically: pretty much everybody now brews a "golden ale" of one sort or another; and regionals by and large are pursuing the green agenda as energetically as they can.

The emergence of golden ales over the past 20-odd years has been perhaps the climax of the shift away from dark beers in modern ale brewing. Porters died out in the First World War, thanks to malting restrictions; and stout would have gone the same way if the government hadn't been too nervous to impose curbs on Irish maltsters as well as mainland ones. Dark mild, once the country's leading beer style, was a casualty – although its death has been hideously long drawn-out – of post-Second World War prosperity. Bitter – or pale ale, as it used to be more widely called – was the toff's drink, expensive and aspirational, and only started outselling mild in the 1950s. Lager pretty much finished mild off in the 1970s, and today it is a minority style, brewed in significant volume only in Leeds and Manchester.

Golden ales as a definable beer style first emerged some 25 years ago, when Somerset's Exmoor Brewery produced Exmoor Gold and Hop Back of Salisbury came out with Summer Lightning. There had been very pale beers before then: Boddington's from Manchester was perhaps the best-known, but Wem Pale from north Shropshire was just as light-coloured, and so was the main beer from the famous Three Tuns brewpub in south Shropshire. Green's of Luton, Burt's on the Isle of Wight, and Holdens of Dudley were among the many brewers that had produced beer brands with the words "gold" or "golden" in their names in the preceding 30-odd years. But from the early 1990s onwards, ale brewers increasingly looked to much lighter-coloured and lighter-bodied beers, often with a hop aroma so pronounced as to be almost unbalanced, to challenge lager's strengthening grip on the market. (I'm proud to say that I was the first to identify golden ale as a separate beer style in print, in a 1994 issue of *Brewers Guardian* with a précis in the *Journal of the Institute of Brewing* May–June 1995.) The turning point for golden ales, though, came in 1996 when an extraordinarily hot summer plunged ale brewing into crisis. It wasn't just that ale drinkers turned to chilled lager as the temperature soared; it was also that the weather ruthlessly exposed weaknesses in the supply chain. Ale that had been virtually cooked in warehouses and drays arrived at the pub as an undrinkable soup; there were even tales of casks bursting in the heat.

Before then, micros had been more interested in recreating the stronger, darker styles of the past, and the listing sections of successive *Good Beer Guides* are packed with stouts, porters, barley wines and old ales. The 1996 Guide, compiled in spring that year, has only 22 microbrewers producing ales with the words "gold" or "golde" in their names, and just three regionals, Belhaven, Gale's and Timothy Taylor (although Elgood's, Fuller's and Wadworth had also brought out golden ales under different names: Barleymead, IPA and Summersault). After 1996 though, the balance began to change. Two years after that summer, the Guide listed 55 gold or golden beers from micros and 11 from regionals; the 2007 edition listed 134 and 16 respectively. Golden ales have won the Champion Beer of Britain title year after year since 2001, prompting CAMRA to recognise the style with a category of its own in 2005 (since when Crouch Vale Brewers Gold has won twice in a row). So golden ale is a style pretty much invented by microbrewers that has come to a position of huge importance in the ale market.

CASE STUDY

Lacons
The Great Yarmouth brewery

In May 2013, in front of a handful of onlookers from the brewing world and the local press, the first sack of malt was poured into the mash tun and Lacons officially recommenced brewing in Great Yarmouth after a break of 45 years.

The brewery of 2013 was a far cry from that of Lacons' heyday in the mid-19th century. Lacons Church Plain brewery site covered a vast area in Great Yarmouth and included its own maltings, cooper's works, bottling plant and garage. It employed over 150 people of various trades from brewer to electrician to drayman and was producing over 100,000 barrels per year prior to its closure by Whitbread in the late 1960s.

In sharp contrast to this, the new brewery was a small five-barrel kit sited in an old Victorian warehouse. The malt was bought in from a local maltings and the hops were from all corners of the earth.

At the helm of the new brewery was Wil Wood, previously of Fyne Ales and Oakham. Wil's aim for the new brewery was to create beer that lived up to the historic reputation of Lacons and to take it forward into a new generation.

A few years down the line and Lacons is once again a familiar sight on bars around East Anglia. With the multi-award-winning amber ale Encore as its flagship beer and the revived Audit Ale taking CAMRA's Champion Winter Beer of Britain 2019, the team couldn't be more pleased with how their beer has gone down.

In 2017 the company invested in a brand new 30-barrel kit and there has since been further expansion, with new vessels being installed and a new warehouse having been acquired next to the Falcon Brewery.

With Encore taking centre stage so often Lacons invested in new branding that would reflect its status as a contemporary bitter. The new pump clip was launched in May 2019 and features a reworked falcon icon on a circular motif. The new look is being well received in industry and plans are in motion to roll the new style out across its other core ales.

Head brewer, Wil, has worked on a number of collaborations in recent years, including a sour beer with South Norfolk's Ampersand

Brew Co. Available in limited quantities, Ambit heralded an exciting phase of development for Lacons as it continued to develop its range of small-batch craft ales.

Most excitingly, a Lacons ale was listed among the winners at the 2019 Champion Beer of Britain awards, which is an achievement that the team could have only dreamed of back in 2009, when reviving the brewery was an idea still in its infancy.

www.lacons.co.uk

The Range of Beers

So far we have concentrated on the huge diversity of beer styles available to you, and there are many microbrewers who have taken the fullest possible advantage of it. Bartrams of Bury St Edmunds, Suffolk, for instance, has 22 regular brews in its portfolio ranging from a 3.4 per cent alcohol dark mild to a 6.9 per cent stout and including a porter, a honey beer and a gooseberry beer. It also produces five seasonal specials and an entirely separate range under the Zodiac brand. At the other end of the alphabet, Weird Bear of Hanwell, London, brews an astonishing range of regular, occasional and collaboration beers. This is rather reminiscent of some Belgian brewers who produce literally dozens of different brews, although in many cases these are actually the same beers rebadged for individual customers.

Rebadging is not a practice that has caught on to any great extent in Britain, partly because there are fewer local wholesalers. But some UK brewers will either rebadge a beer as a favoured customer's house bitter, or even make a special blend of one or more of its regular beers for the same purpose. This may be a bit of a performance, but if it means guaranteeing a regular reorder, it may well be worth the slight additional effort.

There is, of course, the opposite approach of brewing one superb beer and focusing all your efforts on building it up as the leading brand in its region. Black Sheep of Masham, North Yorkshire, Butcombe of Bristol, and Abbey Ales of Bath are all outstanding examples of breweries that adopted this strategy, only starting to extend their ranges once their main brands became firmly established. A common factor linking these three is that their founders – Paul Theakston of Black Sheep, Simon Whitmore of Butcombe and Alan Morgan of Abbey Ales – were all extremely well known and senior personalities in the brewing industries in their districts before they struck out on their own. They knew the free trade and the free trade knew them – and trusted them. They knew what the free trade needed and how to tackle it. They didn't need gimmicks or novelties to help them stand out from the rest of the pack: pinning all their faith on a single beer marked them out as serious players with a serious product. They generated a confidence in themselves and their single brands that turned out to be entirely justified. I can think of a handful of similar cases, but you have to be a very special person to succeed with the single-brand strategy; and anyway, for most small brewers the diversity is all part of the fun.

Few go the extremes that Bartrams do, but many approach double figures in their regular ranges and produce a long list of seasonals and one-offs as well. Seasonal beers in particular have a long and respectable history – or at least winter warmers and Christmas specials do. Generations of Londoners have eagerly awaited the arrival of winter, whose fogs and chills and long dark evenings are Nature's way of telling them that Young's Winter Warmer has arrived. Other regionals have also traditionally brewed strong ales for the season. Morrells' Varsity was legendary; McMullen's Stronghart was the first be lauded as "liquid Christmas pudding", although many others have hijacked the description since; and Greene King Strong Suffolk, occasionally allowed out on draught at the right time of year, is a fascinating and unique survival of the centuries-old practice of blending strong old ale with fresh pale.

Seasonal Specials

It was the regional brewers who first extended the idea of a seasonal special to cover spring, summer and autumn as well as winter. Harvey's of Lewes claims to have been the first to launch a seasonal special – Tom Paine, a summer ale named after Lewes's most famous son, appeared in 1991. The idea quickly spread. Seasonal ales not only gave the brewers' own tenants and direct-delivered free trade accounts some variety in response to the diversity offered by the micros, it also gave the brewers a palette of novelty beers to offer the wholesale trade, which was then a new opportunity for them. Some regionals, Bateman's for example, extended the idea beyond the merely seasonal and offered monthly specials, too. The frenzy has somewhat abated in recent years as the crisis in the pub trade made sustainable volumes harder and harder to achieve: some two-thirds of the regionals and just over half of all microbrewers still produce seasonal ranges, but in many case the "range" is a single beer, normally for Christmas.

Part of the problem is that without a definite tradition of different seasonal beers such as exists in many continental markets, brewers don't really have a clear idea of which style best suits which season. Winter ales have always tended to be strong and dark, although Young's Winter Warmer was originally the brewer's stab at a Burton-style pale ale and is only 5% ABV. Most brewers have substantially reduced both the strength and darkness of their winter beers in recent years: they may be delicious, they may keep out the cold, but most people can only manage one pint, and where's the profit in that? Summer beers are another no-brainer that turn out on inspection to be more problematic: originally, they were in the main straightforward competitors to lager, very pale, quite aromatic and best served cold. But they failed to woo lager drinkers, and as golden ales became a mainstream style they lost any claim to seasonality.

As for spring and autumn, they have no seasonal styles; so with no traditional template as a guide, brewers simply produce whatever seems most suitable to them. One of the best spring beers is Harvey's Knots of May, a light mild which coincides handily with CAMRA's Mild Month campaign every May; and Shepherd Neame's Late Red is a splendid consolation for the shortening days of autumn. But no ancient tradition makes the one a spring beer and the other an autumn beer. If you are going to produce a seasonal range, therefore, you have carte blanche as to what to brew when, and no limits but your own imagination.

One-offs, especially in aid of good causes, are an altogether more straightforward business and well worth investigating. However, they tend in the main to be bottled and will therefore be considered in the relevant chapter. One exception to this is the CAMRA Festival Special. CAMRA branches like to have one, two or in odd cases even more exclusive ales brewed for the annual beer festivals. Often the chairman and other branch committee worthies will descend on the brewery or breweries lucky enough to be chosen as the provider, and "help" with the mashing. Often too, by a mysterious and undoubtedly psychic process, the specials will emerge as medal-winners in the Beer of the Festival competition. On the whole, therefore, and despite any irritation that might be occasioned by the local branch's "help", it's well worth accepting an invitation to brew a festival special. Whatever you send to the festival will sell out, and any surplus you brew is likely to be accepted by the local free trade – especially if it wins a medal.

Pursuing the Green Agenda

Not surprisingly, microbrewers have also been keen to pursue the green agenda with all its various headings: vegetarian, low-impact, organic – they're all values that can be applied to brewing.

Finding beers, particularly cask ales, that are suitable for vegans and vegetarians is surprisingly difficult. This is because the most effective substance for clearing or fining beer is isinglass, a collagen derived from various species of fish. Isinglass is a gel that, when added to the finished beer, flocculates the live yeast into a spongy mass that sinks; the beer can be strained off it. Of course, none of it remains in the beer – that's the whole point, after all. But vegetarians still object, correctly, that a living creature has had to die merely in order to clarify a beer. Ironically, isinglass is more rarely used in keg or bottled beer, which is filtered and therefore shouldn't need fining; and a yeasty sediment is an expected feature of bottle-conditioned beer, so that shouldn't really need fining either. But cask ale does; and while there are alternatives, they're not as effective. Filtration agents such as kieselguhr and bentonite, widely used in the wine industry, operate in a different way and can affect the character of the beer; while carrageenan or Irish moss effectively removes protein that would cause a haze, but isn't so effective at dealing with yeast. Still, they are used with some success by many brewers, so if you want to appeal to vegans and vegetarians, give them a try.

Keeping it Local

There are many ways in which you can reduce the overall environmental impact of your brewery. Brewing uses a lot of energy, both to move liquids around and to heat them up and cool them down. In your brewery design you can incorporate the same sort of energy-reduction measures that might be used in any other processing plant: good insulation, short pipe-runs, solar panels and wind turbines, which will reduce your electricity bill as well as your carbon footprint. But cutting your food miles will be much harder.

One way of reducing food miles is to concentrate your sales effort on as small an area as possible. Given the structure of the trade this isn't always easy: you have to sell where you can, and if that means long road trips, either on your own truck or on the wholesaler's, there's not a lot you can do about it. Sourcing your materials locally is another possibility, but equally problematic. There's a growing trend among brewers to buy their barley from local growers – and it's not just microbrewers who are doing it either. Shepherd Neame in Kent, Black Sheep in North Yorkshire and St Austell Brewery in Cornwall are all keenly developing local sources of supply. But wherever you buy your barley, it all has to go to the maltster to be processed, and as there are only three traditional floor maltings left – Warminster in Wiltshire, Crisp's in Norfolk and Fawcett's in North Yorkshire – the trip there and back can be a pretty long one.

Hops, too, can have a long journey. It's all very well for brewers in Kent or Hereford and Worcester to boast about their use of local hops, but they have Britain's last hop-growers right on their doorsteps, and everybody else has to buy further afield. But given the shortage of British hops and their substitution by European equivalents and the current fashion for using bushels and bushels of imported New World varieties, hops and localism aren't terribly compatible.

Going Organic

Another part of the green agenda that you can pursue is the use of organic ingredients. Organic beers are becoming more and more popular and widespread: many brewers, even quite big ones such as Fuller's, now have at least one organic beer in their range; others have gone over to organic ingredients entirely.

The first British organic beer that I know of was brewed by the now-defunct Ross Brew House of Bristol in the late 1980s; Golden Promise, launched in 1991 by Edinburgh's Caledonian Brewery, was the first to gain national distribution. Sourcing organic ingredients was not easy: the malt was made from a strain of barley also named Golden Promise and developed for the whisky industry, while the hops had to be imported from New Zealand. The dearth of suitable ingredients meant that others were slow to follow Caledonian's example, but more than 25 years on organic barley is easily available; and although supplies of British-grown organic hops have not kept pace with demand, they can always be eked out with imports. There are still only a handful of all-organic breweries in Britain, and a few more that are nearly there; but other brewers between them produce a couple of dozen brands at least, and several more are imported.

The demand for organic ingredients has imposed a new discipline on hop merchants and maltsters, who previously would process raw materials from different growers all mixed together. Now they have learnt to keep organic hops and barley separate from non-organic produce, a good habit that has had an equally valuable but perhaps unforeseen side-effect. For they have also learnt to process the produce of individual growers separately, so that full traceability is not only possible but commonplace these days. This means that if you only want to use malt and hops from growers in your locality, you can. Of course, they will still have had to travel to the oasts (or kilns in Hereford and Worcester) or maltings and then to your brewery, so the actual road miles involved will not have been reduced in the slightest. But discerning consumers these days put a considerable premium on traceability, and it may well be worth your while taking advantage of the fact. For although it's not easy being green, people will love you for it.

Since 1993, Britain has conformed to European Regulation 2092/91 regarding certification of organic producers. If you are brewing an all-organic beer as part of a wider range, it is not strictly necessary to be certified organic: you can get away – and many do – with simply stating on your labels that all your ingredients are from certified organic producers. However, to take full advantage of the possibilities offered by "going organic", it's probably best to get yourself certified. To contact any of the 10 certifying bodies (it's not a Soil Association monopoly!) approved by the Department for the Environment, Food and Rural Affairs (DEFRA), visit **www.defra.gov.uk** or **www.organicfarmers.org.uk**.

Ingredients: Malt

The malt is, of course, the heart of the beer, providing all the fermentable materials that create the alcohol (unless you're using brewing sugars as well), the residual sugars that create the mouthfeel and many of the flavour components.

In Britain we have always tended to think of malt as coming entirely from barley, except for the handful of oats used to give some stouts a smooth, silky texture. Until recently, that is. Wheat is now a widely used grain in British brewing, so widely used, in fact, that British wheat beer ranks as a fourth category in its own right alongside Belgian, Bavarian and Berliner. Typically, the British style doesn't use nearly as much wheat as its continental cousins because the desired effect is a lighter body rather than the clove, vanilla, banana and bubblegum flavours that tend to come with higher proportions.

Malt is made, as we have discovered, by tricking barley into beginning to germinate and thereby starting the process of converting the starch in the grain into fermentable sugar. The process involves a lot of soaking and drying, and traditionally the drying was done by heaping the damp grain in rows on a floor for two or three weeks before drying it over a fire. The rows of grain would be turned by a man plodding up and down pulling a device like a cross between a wheelbarrow and a rake; and as is the way of things, this method of "floor-malting" has been mechanised almost out of existence.

Most small brewers, though, like to get their malt from the country's few surviving floor maltings, not because the quality of the beer made from traditionally malted barley is necessarily better than beer brewed from machine-made malt, but because they say it's easier to work with. What's true is that the remaining floor maltings are comparatively small concerns and therefore buy in smaller batches, which they can ipso facto inspect more thoroughly, and that the man plodding up and down turning the malt is simultaneously conducting a continuous quality check. Some Scottish brewers, at the time of writing, were even approaching the few distilleries that still floor malt their own barley to see whether they'd care to try producing ale malts alongside their whisky malts. Unfortunately, most of these distilleries are owned by global corporations which still tend to concentrate production on a handful of huge sites; perhaps the modest extra profits generated by making and selling ale malt on the side might keep some of these traditional little whisky maltings open for a few years more?

Types of Malt

Pale malts of various types, principally lager malt, pale ale malt and wheat malt, kilned at low temperature to preserve the golden colour of the grain, are the base on which nearly all modern beers are founded. The grists of even the blackest of beers generally have pale malts as their main constituents, the colour being supplied by surprisingly small doses of dark malt. These are the malts that, in the late 18th and early 19th centuries, changed the world of beer forever. Previously, malt had been dried over peat, straw, dried furze or broom, wood or charcoal and tended to be dark, smoked and, thanks to the difficulty of controlling the temperature of such fires, uneven in colour, flavour and moisture content. When in the middle of the 17th century the maltsters of Derbyshire started exhausting local sources of timber, they found that the locally mined hard coal produced a low-sulphur smokeless coke, ideal for malting. By the end of the century malt was being dried over coke in neighbouring counties and also in parts of Scotland (although peat remained the preferred fuel there). Coke gave an even and controllable heat and worked at lower temperatures than wood or charcoal, making it possible to kiln malts that were pale, clean-tasting and uniform, and produced crystal-clear golden or amber beers. Daniel Defoe was an early supporter of strong Derby pale ales; and Burton brewers were exporting pale ales to the Baltic before the Napoleonic War and to the East Indies after it. In the early 1840s the brewers of Pilsen, in what is now the Czech Republic, also discovered the potential of pale malt kilned over coke; lager as we know it was born.

Low-temperature kilning preserves the saccharifying enzymes in the malt, as well as its original colour. This means that the malt can be used with other unmalted grains such as wheat, corn and rice.

You will probably learn all you need to know about all the different types of malt and how to handle them during your training. Here, though, is a brief reminder of the wonderful variety of malts available to you, listed for convenience only by degrees lovibond, the scale used to measure the malt's colour:

- **Lager malt (2°L):** The malt that produces the world's most popular beer style – pale gold, mid-flavoured, pilsner derivatives – can also be used as the base malt for other beers, even dark ales. Its diastatic capability makes it ideal for use with low-enzyme speciality malts or unmalted grains.

- **Wheat malt (2°L):** Has a high protein content, causing wheat beer's characteristic haze. It also has good head-retention qualities: torrefied wheat is often used in small quantities for this purpose. Low in polyphenols, it is often used in modest quantities by British brewers to lighten the body of their golden ales. It has to be mashed with grains that supply a husk bed (lager malt is ideal).

- **Pale ale malt (3°L):** The malt most associated with British ale is kilned at a slightly higher temperature than lager malt for a fuller flavour and darker colour. It also tends to have fewer enzymes than lager malt, although enough to allow the use of adjuncts in the mash.

- **Rye malt (3°L):** Can be used in small quantities for its spicy flavour.

- **Vienna malt (3–7°L):** Produces the full-bodied amber or reddish beers that were once popular in Austria, but survive mainly in Mexico, Dos Equis and Negra Modelo being noted modern examples.

- **Mild ale malt (4°L):** Although most surviving milds are dark, the base malt isn't, creating an amber- or copper-coloured wort and producing a dry, full-flavoured beer, with brown, chocolate and/or black malts used sparingly to give the characteristic colour. Mild ale malt is also a good base for stronger ales, whether coloured or not.

- **Carapils malt (7°L):** Kilned at low temperature, it adds sweetness, smoothness and body to pale ales and lagers without affecting the colour or adding caramel notes. Also aids head retention.
- **Crystal malt (10–20°L):** Produced in such a way that most of the starch is not saccharified and is then caramelised during kilning, crystal malts are very widely used in small additions in ales and lagers to give extra sweetness and flavour ranging in character from delicate light honey to rich toffee flavours. Crystal malts also thicken the mouthfeel, and create an attractive bronze colour.
- **Munich malt (10–20°L):** An aromatic lager malt that yields a dark reddish-orange wort and a slightly sweet caramel flavour. Munich malt comes in two grades, light and dark.
- **Biscuit malt (25°L):** A base malt toasted and roasted to give the beer a biscuity flavour and a deep amber colour.
- **Victory malt (25°L):** A roasted malt similar to biscuit malt but with a nuttier taste. Also adds orange highlights to the colour.
- **Amber malt (30°L):** Similar to mild ale or Vienna malt, but with more colour and a biscuity flavour. Used mainly in old and brown ales.
- **Brown malt (65°L):** Traditionally kilned over a wood fire for a smoky flavour; used very sparingly in stouts and porters.
- **Special Belgian malt (220°L):** A rare malt with a nutty, roasted sweetness that in small quantities enriches brown ales and porters, and in larger proportions adds a plummy, vinous quality to barley wines and strong winter beers.
- **Chocolate malt (350–400°L):** Its smooth roasted flavour and brownish-black colour with ruby highlights make chocolate malt irreplaceable in dark ales such as milds, stouts and porters; it can also be used in dark lagers.
- **Black malt (500–600°L):** Even darker than chocolate malt, with a sharp, burnt, acidic flavour that can take the sweet edge off some stronger beers.

Unmalted Grains

Malting is the process of artificially stimulating the enzymes that in nature convert the grain's starch content into soluble sugar that the yeast can get at. Not all brewing grains need to be malted, though. Up to 50 per cent of the grist of most Belgian witbier is unmalted wheat, but the malted barley that makes up the other half has enough enzymes to convert the whole mash. Unmalted oats are added to some beers, especially stout, not for their negligible fermentable material but for their husky roughness, which "scrubs" microscopic particles out of the wort for a silky-smooth finish.

Maize and rice are almost flavourless, but are high in convertible starch. They have no enzymes of their own, but as with Belgian wheat beer, the barley malts they are mashed with have enough surplus enzymes for the whole mash. They are also very cheap, which is why they are so common in beers from the poorer Latin American countries (and in many mainstream US lagers, but that's another story). Finally, there's roasted barley, which is virtually burnt to an inky-black 550°L and has an acrid charred-wood flavour. It's the signature flavour of Guinness and, to a lesser extent, Murphy's and Beamish as well.

Brewing Sugars

The use of sugar in brewing has been legal in Britain since 1847 and is now widespread throughout the world. Some brewers oppose the practice completely, because they say sugar is only used as a cheap source of fermentable material to pad out the more expensive malt; and in some cases this is true. American beers in particular use large amounts of rice or corn-based syrups, and are characteristically light-bodied (or indeed bland) as a result.

However, there are other more legitimate and indeed time-honoured uses for various types of sugar in judicious quantities. Corn-derived sugars are often used to boost the strength of the final product without significantly affecting its flavour, or to adjust from mash to mash to achieve consistent alcoholic strength. In northern Europe a derivative of beet sugar was traditionally used for the same purpose, but beet sugar created an undesirable flavour that could be avoided by inverting it – boiling it slowly with a little water and citric acid to produce a highly concentrated syrup, which was then crystallised to form sugar "diamonds". This sort of sugar is still used in Belgium, where it is called "candi". Corn-derived sugars are also used in small quantities to "prime" beer before it is bottled or put into cask. Priming sugars prompt a slight secondary fermentation to give the beer a bit of fizz and create a head.

Finally, sugars of various sorts are used for their particular flavour characteristics. A dry beer can be sweetened by the use of non-fermentable lactose. Maltodextrin is a soluble starch that creates a heavier body and richer mouthfeel. Honey is an increasingly popular adjunct and retains its distinctive taste throughout the brewing process. And black treacle or molasses is sometimes added to dark beers for its density and depth of flavour.

Maltsters

Bairds Malt Ltd
Station Maltings, Witham, Essex, CM8 2DU
Tel: +44 (0)1376 513 566;
www.bairds-malt.co.uk

Crisp Malting Group Ltd
Great Ryburgh, Fakenham, Norfolk, NR21 7AS
Tel: +44 (0)1328 829 391;
www.crispmalt.co.uk

French and Jupps Ltd
Stanstead Abbotts, Ware, Herts, SG12 8HG
Tel: +44 (0)1920 870 015;
www.frenchandjupps.com

JP Simpson & Co (Alnwick) Ltd
Tweed Valley Maltings, Tweedside Trading Estate,
Berwick upon Tweed, TD15 2UZ
Tel: +44 (0)1289 330 033
www.simpsonsmalt.co.uk

Muntons plc
Cedars Maltings, Stowmarket, Suffolk, IP14 2AG
Tel: +44 (0)1449 618 300;
www.muntons.com

Thomas Fawcett & Sons Ltd
Eastfield Lane, Castleford, W Yorks, WF10 4LE
Tel: +44 (0)1977 552 490;
www.fawcett-maltsters.co.uk

Warminster Maltings Ltd
39 Pound Street, Warminster, Wilts, BA12 8NN
Tel: +44 (0)1985 212 014;
www.warminster-malt.co.uk

Ingredients: Hops

Hops, whether used as whole flowers (or "cones"), dried pellets or extracts, contain the acids that will protect your beer from bacterial infection and provide its bitterness as well as the oils and resins that will produce much of its aroma and flavour.

A cousin of both cannabis and the common nettle, hops were used throughout the medieval period as a dyestuff and a herbal remedy for a variety of ailments (they are still used to treat insomnia). The young shoots are a spring delicacy rather like asparagus, still much eaten in Belgium, and the leaves are a good salad vegetable, while the stems yield a strong fibre suitable for both clothing and ropemaking.

Hops are first recorded as being used in brewing in Germany in the 9th century, and until recently it was thought that they didn't come to Britain until the end of the Middle Ages – as some versions of the rhyme have it, "turkey and carp, pickerel and beer [hopped ale] came into England all in one year" (1492). Modern research however, suggests that even if they weren't commonly used by British brewers until the later Middle Ages, they were far from unknown. They may have been used by monastic brewers in Kent even before the Conquest; although if that is indeed the case, it was as a purely local version of the herb grist used in different regions.

Hopped beer seems to have started arriving in significant quantities in the 14th century as imports to satisfy the thirst of growing communities of Flemish, Dutch, Danish and German merchants and craftsmen for a taste of home. The first English hop garden now seems to have been planted not in Kent in the early 16th century, as used to be thought, but in Suffolk two centuries earlier. Certainly London brewers were commonly using hops in the early 15th century and over the next 200 years their use became pretty much universal (although unhopped ale held out in the more remote parts of the Pennines until the 18th century and, of course, whisky is made from "wash" or unhopped ale).

Hops are now only grown on any scale in two regions, Herefordshire/Worcestershire and Kent/Sussex, although in the 19th Century there were commercial hop gardens or yards in almost every county in Great Britain. And indeed there is no inherent reason why they can't be grown just about anywhere. The hedges around my home in Cambridgeshire abound with wild hops, descendants of plants that escaped from the county's hop gardens over 100 years ago.

One achievement of small independent brewers as a body in the last 35-odd years has been to reawaken interest in different hop varieties. Before that, hops had been prized chiefly for their bittering quality, and most of the efforts of researchers and growers had been devoted to developing high-alpha strains and finding new ways of extracting the prized bittering agents.

Pioneers like Sean Franklin of Rooster's Brewery of Knaresborough and Brendan Dobbin (who briefly had his own brewery in Manchester but is best known in the industry as an installer and consultant) began working with imported varieties, mainly from the USA and New Zealand, in the 1980s. Before then, hop grists were almost universally blended from different native types, with consistent performance in mind rather than the flavour and aroma characteristics of individual varieties. These innovators and the many microbrewers who took their lead opened the way for the importation of foreign varieties in commercial quantities; thanks to them, today's craft brewers, who have an almost fetishistic obsession with hops, have a rich and varied palette to experiment with.

Native Hop Varieties

Traditional English strains have been somewhat eclipsed among small brewers by the plethora of highly aromatic continental, North American and New World varieties now on the market. I have heard even the venerable Fuggle dismissed as "brown and boring". It hasn't helped that as the English hop-growing industry has struggled somewhat in recent years, prices of some native varieties are significantly higher than those of many imported ones. But there's more to English hops than Fuggles and Goldings, and the industry has advanced a great deal in recent decades. Dwarf or hedgerow hops, for instance, were first developed at Wye College in Kent in the 1980s. But of more interest to craft brewers would be new English aroma varieties.

The blackcurrant-scented Bramling Cross has been with us for almost a century; more recent strains worth investigating are the spicy First Gold, the high-alpha dual-purpose Herald, the oily Wye Northdown and the floral Wye Target. These and other native varieties are still, by and large, higher in alpha acids than the North American types that are so sexy at the moment, but try them as late or even dry hops and you will be surprised at the intense aromas they can give to your beers.

CASE STUDY

OPM Group
Choosing your printer

As a new brewer, your focus on entering the brewing industry is to work hard to develop unique products that taste and look great, with competition in craft brewing increasing steadily as more small and individual companies are entering the fray.

As a result, there is even greater need to have a unique beer label design to draw attention and enable you to build a brand identity around your beers and their taste.

Your beer label design is not just any other visual. It stands for your brand values and message, and therefore, the design and printing of your label requires careful planning.

As a label printer, OPM understands that it is the label that has the customer choosing your brand because of what they see, and the company likes to say, "The label may sell the customer on your product the first time, the taste is what will have them coming back for more."

It is important to choose your printer with care. A considerate printer that truly wants to partner with you in the success of your business should have a desire to share information, empowering you to make the best purchasing decisions.

You will also need to consider all aspects of the label's form and function – not only that it meets the legal obligation for government information, including alcohol warning and capacity.

The function of your label raises crucial questions, for example, what environments will your label face? Be sure to consider the real-world scenarios your labels need to perform in, including how they are stored and transported.

With an amazing variety of choices, from colours, to label materials, adhesives, protection options and embellishments, there are numerous ways to build the best label. Knowing what you want and what you have budgeted for will help your printer find creative solutions that look great, work well, and stay within budget.

Your deadline for delivery of labels is vitally important to planning the printing process, since there are several stages to ordering, proofs and approvals, and printing your labels. It is wise begin the order process early.

After agreeing all design and print specifications it is good practice to create a shared timeline based on the bottling date and approve proofs quickly to avoid delays.

Utilising specialty printing techniques like foil stamping, sculpted embossing, screen and die cutting can offer many creative and personal dimensions of touch to labels – tactile effects that help make the vital difference between products left on the shelf and those that make it home with the customer.

With an innovative approach to enhancing your brand, OPM has the perfect technology to produce eye-catching beverage labels. It offers new and unique label treatment combinations without compromising your label performance requirements throughout the lifecycle.

www.opmgroup.co.uk

Imported Hops

The sheer profusion of exotic varieties now available to British brewers makes it impossible to provide anything like a comprehensive list, and doubtless you will already be eagerly experimenting with them, and with various blends of them, by brewing up hop teas. Kings of the heap at time of writing are the North American varieties, and in particular the all-conquering Citra. But since it's not only the varieties you use that matters but how you use them, don't neglect the European classics! You could, after all, be about to stumble across the Next Big Thing.

Czech Republic

Possibly the world's finest aroma variety – certainly as far as lagers are concerned – the Saaz is a "noble" hop that has been growing around the Bohemian towns of Žatec and Louny for centuries. Saaz is very low in alpha acids, which means you have to use an awful lot of it if it's your main bittering hop; on the other hand, it's high in polyphenols, which helps extend shelf life. Its real attraction, though, is its balance of volatile oils. It's especially high in farnesene, whose aromas of magnolia, lavender and lemon make it as prized in the cosmetics industry as it is in brewing. Saaz is still grown in its native Bohemia – in huge quantities, despite its low yield, susceptibility to mildew and small cones – but there are also extensive plantations in Belgium, Poland, New Zealand and the US. The US variety is higher in alphas than the European.

Germany

Lager as we know it may have been invented in Bohemia, but the Germans weren't slow to catch on and the long-established Bavarian native or "noble" aromatic varieties proved ideal. Hallertauer from the Holledau region in central Bavaria was badly hit by disease in the 1970s and '80s and was largely replaced by Hersbrucker. Tettnang, a dual-use variety often blended with Hallertau, comes from Baden-Württemberg and is produced in great quantities for export around the world. Less well-known outside Germany is Spalt, a hop whose aroma has been described as "woody", from the Nuremburg region. All of these varieties are low in alpha acids, with content typically ranging from 3.5-5.5 per cent, but high in aromatic oil and should produce soft citrusy aromas that balance the often sweetish European malts perfectly.

Plant varieties, however noble, eventually get tired and

vulnerable to mites, mildews, and diseases. In the last 30 years
or so German plant-breeders have been busy conjuring up
replacements for the older strains, especially the Hallertauer,
some of which have been loaded with extra acid for improved
bittering. Among these are the Hallertau Herkules, Magnum,
Merkur and Taurus, of which the Magnum is perhaps the most
aromatic. Polaris is another new strain with excellent bittering
qualities. Among the more aromatic newcomers are Opal and
Saphir, while Perle is a mid-alpha variety much prized as dual-
purpose hop.

North America
American beer drinkers love their aroma hops but don't go in
much for bitterness, which for the English beer drinker often
means disappointingly short, characterless finishes. Cascade is a
case in point. Developed at Oregon State University as a resistant
alternative to the susceptible Cluster variety, Cascade was ready
for release by 1967. But US brewers were slow to take it up until
their regular supplies of German Hallertau were disrupted by an
outbreak of mildew in 1971. Today it's North America's top variety by
a country mile. It's perfectly suited to its market – it has just enough
alpha acid to qualify as a bittering hop, but not enough to produce
the long, bitter finish that US drinkers seem to dislike. But its volatile
component is quite high in the richly scented farnesene with its
aroma of magnolias and especially high in the peach-scented
myrcene, which makes it a veritable Southern Comfort of a hop.

Even more heavily loaded with myrcene is Citra, which was
only released in 2007 but has become immensely popular thanks
to its heady scents of peach, orange and lemon. With 11-13
per cent alpha acid, it counts as a dual-purpose variety and alongside
the exotic aroma has that smack of bitterness that British drinkers
prefer. It's one of a host of American dual-purpose hops that are
heavy on aroma – Amarillo, Galena, Mount Rainier and Willamette
are a few others – and which have really led the charge for US
hops worldwide!

Australia
Australian beers, rather like Australians themselves, are sunny and
rarely bitter. Even their high-alpha hops, like Topaz and Faux Coeur
(originally a French variety) are quite aromatic. The best-known
dual-purpose variety, Galaxy, has an 11-16 per cent alpha acid

content, but is very high in hop oil, making it potentially explosive if used very late in the boil. Australian aromatics such as Ella are bred to be both floral and full of citrus flavours.

New Zealand

One of the first "exotic" hops to enliven the British microbrewing scene back in the late 1990s, Green Bullet has since become an established favourite with British brewers and has also found popularity in the US. Developed from the Styrian Golding, it's a bittering variety high in alphas but also in oils, which makes it very versatile – not only can it be used as the main aroma hop, it also delivers a torrent of spice if added very late. Much the same could be said of other NZ bittering hops such as Pacific Gem and Pacific Jade. The dual-purpose Nelson Sauvin is noted for its rounded fruitiness, while aromatics such as Hallertau Aroma and Motueka are packed with fresh citrus zest.

Getting the Most Out of Hops

- Buy in a pack size as close to the brew length usage as you can. Aroma is lost once the pack is opened. For smaller needs buy in fresh packs or vacuum packs in double silver foil.
- Ask the age of the hops and buy from the latest harvest.
- Store in a deep freeze, refrigerator or cold room. Hop bitterness is lost faster at higher temperatures. Pellets are sometimes easier to store than whole hops.
- Learn to evaluate hops yourself. To assess or compare hop aroma, make a hop tea, cool it and then smell. Hop merchants rub and sniff hops every day, but there are two problems for the novice: hops may smell powerful when rubbed in the hand, yet may not be so powerful when in the beer; and minor differences in the rub can mean big differences in the beer.
- Test-brew with the new hop alone to see where it fits on the bitterness, aroma and intensity scales. Test it in a 100 per cent pale malt beer with a standard water treatment so that the hop aroma shows through clearly. Adjust the portion quantities by the alpha content of the new hop and start with a comparison of the flavour at about 28 International Bitterness Units (similar to commercial ales).
- Build a hop grist by looking at the grists of beers you like and experimenting. Track down recipes in home-brewing books and on the internet. Remember when mixing a grist that

aromas from different hops can sometimes "average out" and dilute the effect. Single-hop beers usually (but not always) have more aroma definition than mixed-varietal beers.

- Choose your alpha hop carefully. Some alphas have strong aromas in spite of their early addition to the boil that may alter the final hop character.

- Look closely at your yeast. The same hop can taste different when used with a different yeast. Make sure your yeast is compatible with the beer you are trying to make.

- Control your brewing process, or other aromas might hide the hop aroma. Higher alcohols, esters, diacetyl and hydrogen sulfide will all disguise or overlay your hop aroma.

All the above information and far, far more is available on the British Hop Association website, **www.britishhops.org.uk**.

Hop Merchants

Botanix
Hop Pocket Lane, Paddock Wood, Kent, TN12 6DQ
Tel: +44 (0)1892 833 415
www.barthhaasgroup.com/en/

Charles Faram
The Hopstore, Monksfield Lane, Newland, Worcs, WR13 5BB;
Tel: +44 (0)1905 830 734
www.charlesfaram.co.uk

Wealden Hops
Congelows, Benover Road, Yalding, Kent, ME18 6ET;
Tel: +44 (0)1622 817 175

Lupofresh Ltd
Benover Road, Yalding, Kent, ME18 6ET;
Tel: +44 (0)1622 815 720

Further merchants can be found via the British Hop Association at **www.britishhops.org.uk**.

Grow Your Own Hops

If you have any unused outdoor space – even if it's only a small patch – it's well worth considering planting a bine or two, particularly of the more expensive or harder-to-get varieties. The yield won't be much, but on the other hand they're not much trouble to grow and they do make an attractive feature. They're ornamental as well as fragrant, and a green-hop beer is a seasonal highlight that adds great interest to your list. Even if you don't actually brew with them, they make eye-catching and unusual merchandise. They're great in popourri, swags or wreaths of dried bines are very impressive traditional decorations, and dried and crushed hop cones stuffed into a pillow are a natural way of getting a good night's sleep.

Planting Hops

The hop is a hardy perennial climber grown from a rhizome and needs plenty of sun. Its bines can grow to 25ft high in a season, so a modern dwarf variety that grows no more than 10ft might be more suitable for you. Commercial growers build complexes of trellises with poles and wires, but if you have space you could put up a straightforward freestanding pergola in a sunny position (sheltered from the wind, though). Alternatively, train the bines on wirework or twine against a south- or west-facing wall that gets plenty of direct sun and will act as a storage heater at night. Plant a row of timber uprights 3-5ft apart and an inch or two proud of the wall to give the bines something to wrap themselves round. Secure them to the wall using wooden plates and long decking screws, and dot them liberally with wood-staples to attach your twine or wiring to.

Hops thrive in a well-drained loam with a pH of 6.5-8. They use lots of water but don't like to stand in wet soil, so water them little and often, conditioning soil (so the minerals won't leach out) with fertilisers high in potassium, phosphates and nitrogen.

They need at least 120 frost-free days before they produce cones, so plant them in mid to late March for a crop in July. Plant the rhizomes vertically with the buds facing upwards, or horizontally about two inches deep. Leave 5ft between each rhizome, or 3ft if they're the same variety. Use plenty of mulch – bark chip is ideal – to conserve water and keep weeds down. As the first shoots appear, start training them up your lattice of twine and keep them off the ground. Water them little but often in the first year as their infant root-systems can't deal with too much soaking – they won't take the water up, they'll just rot. New plants won't produce much in the way of cones either, although in subsequent years they can bear anything from 3.5-10kg if all goes well (500g-1.5kg dried weight).

Be Brutal with the Shoots

Your natural urge will be to let every shoot flourish, but be strong! Give in, and you'll end up with a tangle of shoots and stunted cones. When the bine is about 1ft tall select the two or three strongest-looking shoots and start wrapping them clockwise round your uprights. Trim any that appear right down at ground level – get them young and they make good eating. Lateral shoots will soon start sprouting: curl these around your twine or wire and keep untangling them as they grow.

Diseases and Bugs

Hops have many enemies. Downy mildew flourishes on moist shoots and leaves so be sure you're watering the soil, not the plant, and nip off any brittle shoots or curled leaves as soon as they appear. Once your bines are established pick off all leaves and shoots up to about 3-3.5ft from the ground. If the early leaves are very dull with yellow splotches you have wilt. Again, infected leaves must be ruthlessly removed.

Disease- and pest-free hop plants are grown mainly in East Anglian nurseries and cost £7.50 to £10 each: try **www.aplus-hops.co.uk** or **www.willingham-nurseries.co.uk**.

The Hop Harvest

If the cones look ripe, squeeze them. If there's any give, they're not ready. Wait until they feel dry and papery; the cones that have had most sunlight will be ready first. Don't pick them cone by cone, commercial growers cut down whole bines and take them to a shed for stripping. Take a pair of secateurs, cut off the topmost shoots and laterals and strip them in the kitchen. Then the sun can get at the next tier down and you can cut those too. Repeat until the whole bine is stripped.

As you strip each bine, pack the cones into a freezer bag – scrunch them in hard – tie the bag off and pop it into the freezer. At the end of the harvest you can either thaw them out and stick them into your green-hop brew, remembering that dried hops you buy are condensed from 70 per cent moisture to 10 per cent, or keep them until you need them. You can dry them, if you've the patience.

Chapter Six
Selling Draught Beer

Realistically, where can you sell your beer? You may be based in a pub, or at least have one that acts as your brewery tap, but these sales alone won't necessarily make you a living. To get your beers out into the trade, you therefore need to understand the structure of the market. This chapter will deal with the "on-trade" – pubs, clubs and so on – and will therefore be mainly concerned with sales of draught beer.

There are two contrasting points of view here. One says that an overcrowded small brewing sector and the iron grip of the tied system means that the traditional route to market – sales of draught beer to pubs – is dead and that new brewers have to seek alternative outlets. The opposing view is that the long-term health of the sector as a whole demands that the tied house system be cracked open. They are not mutually exclusive. You can continue to seek draught sales to pubs at the same time as seeking new opportunities. Let us look at both and, to start with, the draught beer opportunity.

There are around 180,000 on-licensed premises in Britain, not just pubs and clubs but restaurants, casinos, hotels, village halls, golf clubs, sports-centre bars, theatre bars, airport bars and all manner of other varieties of watering holes. Few of them will have any relevance to your business. Some may provide opportunities, but the ones that really matter are the country's 45,000 or so pubs (but still dwindling at a rate of around 30 a week) and 15,000-odd sports and social clubs. Be warned: not many of them will be buying beer from you.

As we have already seen, ownership in the pub trade has changed dramatically since the 1990 Beer Orders that followed the big Monopolies and Mergers Commission enquiry into the nation's beer supply. There used to be brewery-owned tied houses – some run by managers directly employed by the brewery, others by self-employed tenants – and owner-operated free houses, many of which had accepted low-interest loans from a brewery in return for stocking only its beers, the old-fashioned "loan tie". Not any more. It's not so simple now.

The Local Free Trade

When you first decided to investigate becoming a local brewer, part of the attraction may well have been the cheery relationships you saw yourself enjoying with your local publicans, and indeed their customers, as you turned up each week with your regular beer delivery. If that's the case, disabuse yourself now. It's extremely unlikely that you'll be able to generate enough sales to sustain your business through the local free trade alone.

Perhaps 12,000 of the country's pubs are genuinely owner-operated free houses with the discretion to stock your ales. Some of them, although perhaps not as many as in the past, will be restricted by a tied brewery loan. Others buy strictly on price, or are unadventurous and favour well-known national and big regional brands, or have clienteles that are just not interested in real ale. The few that are left will be besieged by people like you. Having said that, a guaranteed local sale, however limited, is an essential precursor to starting up. It creates awareness of your beers (and indeed of your existence) and for the first few weeks or months might be the only cash-flow you have. So even if you intend in the longer term to sell your beer much further afield, it's absolutely imperative that you research your local market thoroughly:

- How many genuine free houses are there within, say, a 20 mile radius?
- What sort of range do they stock currently – is it all from national and regional brewers, or are they apparently micro-friendly?
- How many handpumps do they have?
- Do they, or could they, stock changing guest ales, or might they stock a keg ale from you?
- How many of the local free traders who blithely agree to give your beers a whirl will actually, when it comes to it, place an order – and how often will such orders be repeated?

Most parts of the country have a cadre of free trade landlords whose pubs attract diehard beer aficionados and who love to stock as widely as they can, filling six, seven, eight or even more handpumps with a never-ending rotation of exotic guest ales. (Although not everywhere: in regions where the tie has always been strong, such as Greater London and Surrey, the free trade is negligible.) Pubs like this will invariably give your beer a try, and are a useful place to be seen, but part of their unique selling point is their rapid turnover of brands, and you'll be lucky to get more than infrequent orders from them.

In the early days of your brewing business, it is important to look to local outlets for your beers. It lowers distribution costs and enables any technical challenges to be easily dealt with. Also, there is increasing demand from consumers who want to shop local.

CASE STUDY

PBC Brewing Installations
Brewing installations

Paul Greetham, founder and managing director of microbrewery Beatnikz Republic Brewing Company, together with his team have been brewing daring, innovative and high-quality beer since 2017. You can taste these wonderful beers at the newly opened Beatnikz Republic Bar in Dale Street, Northern Quarter, Manchester.

Two years ago, Paul attended a training course hosted by PBC Brewing Installations and it was here that David Porter introduced Paul to the idea of increasing production at Beatnikz from 6,000 litres a week. Paul was looking for a robust kit that would be economical and enable him to increase beer production without employing more staff. PBC installed more tanks and fermenting vessels and now, two years on, it is installing an eight-barrel kit, allowing this microbrewery to produce 8,500 litres each week and expand its national distribution.

David Porter and his team at PBC have over 40 years of experience between them and Paul would strongly recommend attending one of the courses and allowing PBC to equip the brewery with exceptional quality kit. The course is outlined below. It covers subjects including barley types and malting together with other ingredients including hops; the brewing process; and the plant requirements.

Day one
Covering theory of barley production, malting, the various types of malt, lab analysis of malt, water, hops, yeast and the findings associated with that.

Day two
The brewing process in theory, which covers the process from preparing the malt, through mashing in, boiling, fermentation and packaging. The day includes a presentation as well as a practical demonstration of how to bottle real ale, from experts at the Leek Brewery.

Day three
This is your chance to get hands-on in the brewery and spend a full day making beer, using the commercial brewery to brew two beers at the same time.

Day four

This is your chance to analyse the beer in the fermenting vessels and then discuss the brewing equipment you have used. Also covered on this day are cleansing and sterilising, cask washing and filling, as well as effluent, planning, environmental health officers, HM Revenue & Customs, marketing and business analysis and costs.

Day five – optional

This day covers advanced theory and cold filtering, carbonating and back pressure, and filling ale or lager into kegs and bottles. Here, you will also be able to discuss craft beers in cans with a presentation on various filter technologies.

The team offers the only course in the world that can provide practical and theoretical insight into cold filtering, coarse filtering, kegging and bottling carbonated beers in a day.

Cost including lunch

Four days £400 + VAT
Five days £550 + VAT

www.pbcbreweryinstallations.com

Owner-Operators

Perhaps more important is the rather more numerous breed of owner-operators who like to stock a decent if not extravagant selection that will include a local product if at all possible. It's in pubs like this that you stand your best chance of building up the steady trade you'll need; and in many cases this kind of loyal regular account was only stocking better-known regional brands before a genuinely local brewer came along and wormed their way into a regular slot. So don't be deterred if your local free house only stocks the usual suspects – Adnams, Fuller's London Pride, Marston's Pedigree, that sort of thing; it could end up as your best outlet.

You may already know most of the qualifying licensees in your area; to meet more, join the local branch of CAMRA – you can sign up online at **www.camra.org.uk** – to share local knowledge with fellow members and get personal introductions to the right retailers. Do your groundwork thoroughly, and try to establish a coterie of two or three local free houses that will have one or more of your beers permanently on tap and maybe half-a-dozen more that will order regular guests from you. But always bear in mind that only a handful of small brewers – mainly those that operate in very rural counties such as Shropshire and Devon, where the tie has never been strong – can depend on enough business in the local free trade alone to make a living. As the number of local breweries continues to grow, the pressure on the genuine free trade increases. You will therefore, almost certainly, need to find other markets.

Brewery-Tied Estates

These days, and contrary to public belief, breweries actually own remarkably few pubs. Of the multinationals, only Heineken still has a retail division, which it is hoping to add to with the purchase of pubs from pubco Punch. Greene King and Marston's, the two "neo-national" brewers (that is, regional brewers whose estates have surpassed the old Monopolies and Mergers Commission ceiling of 2,000) have more than 5,000 pubs between them, while the smaller surviving regionals own another 4,500-odd between them. In these brewery-owned estates the tie is rigorously imposed; guest ales might be permitted, but only from the brewery's own list and any tenant buying outside the tie is liable to be evicted. So if there's a regional brewer's name on the pub sign, don't try and sell your beer there.

However, not all brewery-tied houses belong to regionals that won't stock other brewers' brands. Microbrewers themselves account for about 400 pubs. As we saw in Chapter Two, many small brewers are based in or associated with a pub, which in most cases stock a range of guest ales from other brewers too. These pubs are never going to shift huge amounts of your beer, but it's still worth trying to get the odd order out of them as a profile-raiser because they tend to attract enthusiasts who will take note of and seek out your beers in future. Similarly, some smaller breweries also have mini-estates of their own in which they usually stock not only their beers but also guests from other brewers. They don't do this out of charity – the sort of customer who seeks out their pub is going to want a good range of different ales to try, preferably including as large a number as feasible of changing guest ales.

You may very well find yourself knocking at open doors if you approach these brewers with ales of top quality; so worth a quick call, especially if they are local to you, are:

Banks & Taylor, Shefford, Beds
Tel: +44 (0) 1462 815 080
www.banksandtaylor.com

Bath Ales, Warmley, Bristol
Tel: +44 (0) 117 947 4797
www.bathales.com

Beartown Brewery, Congleton, Cheshire
Tel: +44 (0) 1260 299 964
www.beartownbrewery.co.uk

Burton Bridge, Burton upon Trent
Tel: +44 (0) 1283 510 573
www.burtonbridgebrewery.co.uk

Butcombe, Wrington, Bristol
Tel: +44(0) 1934 863 963
www.butcombe.com

Evan Evans, Llandeilo, Carmarthen
Tel: +44(0) 1558 824 455
www.evanevansbrewery.com

Hop Back, Downton, Wilts
Tel: +44 (0) 1725 510 986
www.hopback.co.uk

Milk Street, Frome, Somerset
Tel: +44 (0) 1373 467 766
Web: www.milkstreetbrewery.co.uk

Milton Brewery, Milton, Cambs
Tel: +44 (0) 1223 862 067
www.miltonbrewery.co.uk

Oakham Ales, Peterborough, Cambs
Tel: +44 (0) 1733 370 500
www.oakhamales.com

Ossett Brewery, Ossett, W Yorks
Tel: +44 (0) 1924 261 333
www.ossett-brewery.co.uk

Vale Brewery, Haddenham, Bucks
Tel: +44 (0) 1884 239 237
www.valebrewery.co.uk

Whitstable Brewery, Grafty Green, Kent
Tel: +44 (0) 1622 851 007
www.whitstablebrewery.co.uk

Wickwar Brewery, Wickwar, Glos
Tel: +44 (0) 1454 292 000
www.wickwarbrewing.co.uk

Non-brewing Pub Chains

But if fewer than a quarter of Britain's pubs still fit the traditional "vertical integration" model of brewery ownership and exclusive supply, that doesn't mean the tied house system is dead, or even feeling a little unwell. The non-brewing pub companies that between them own well over 30,000 of Britain's pubs range from giants like Enterprise Inns with 4,500 down to local chains with four or five. The smallest chains are often very receptive to local micros, but like the brewery-owned estates of old, the big chains are operated either by directly employed managers or by lessees or tenants. Like the brewery-owned estates of old, they are firmly tied; so you can't just roll up at the door and try to talk the licensee into buying your beer.

As we shall see, there are ways of getting your beer on the bar in pubs owned by the various tenanted pubcos. But you can write off almost all the directly managed town-centre "style bar" operators. Their customers would rather fill the gutters with regurgitated shots, alcopops and the like – sugary, synthetic concoctions the chain buyers can procure for less than the price of bottled water, but for which they can charge the punter as much as château-bottled claret – than your ale. A handful of high street chains might have a solitary handpump lurking forlornly among the lager fonts, serving a musty sample of a national or leading regional brand. But by and large the high street is Budweiser territory (and I don't mean Budvar), and is barred to you and, indeed, pretty much all cask beer.

Big "family dining" managed house brands such as Harvester and Beefeater are equally unwelcoming to the craft brewer. They do, mostly, list a real ale; but inevitably it will be a cheap national brand that bears as much relation to the nectar you brew as their food does to… well, food.

JD Wetherspoon

Uniquely among big managed house chains, the JD Wetherspoon Organisation has always been a keen supporter of small brewers, but there's a limit to how many brewers' beers it can stock in its 900+ pubs.

Wetherspoon's was founded in the late 1970s by Tim Martin, a barrister who decided that running pubs would be more rewarding and more socially useful than practising law. Martin was one of a handful of radical entrepreneurs such as David Bruce of the Firkin chain and Michael Cannon of Inn Leisure who set out to challenge the stranglehold then exerted over the London pub scene by Allied, Watney's, Bass, Whitbread and Courage; and his legal training was to stand him in good stead.

His chosen route was not to buy run-down pubs and transform them, but to lease derelict shopfronts, filling stations and other high street properties, and turn them into comfortable bars where a good selection of real ale was on sale at a reasonable price. It was a bold strategy – in those days magistrates refused to grant new licences where other pubs were already operating. This attitude harked back to the temperance days of 50 years before and was intended to prevent "proliferation"; and the magistrates maintained that where there were already pubs, there was no "need" for new ones. Martin single-handedly overturned the policy, successfully arguing in court after court that the existing Big Six tenancies, run-down, restrictive and overpriced as they were, didn't answer the consumer's "need" for better pubs. His applications for new licences were invariably opposed by all vested interests – brewers and licensees afraid of the competition as well as anti-alcohol campaigners who opposed every application as a matter of principle. But he was always prepared to appeal when he was refused, and I can't think of a single case in those early days when he lost an appeal (although he has lost one or two since).

His formula worked, and in the 1980s and the first half of the 1990s Wetherspoon pubs appeared throughout London and then throughout Britain. There were even rumours of a venture in France at one stage. Wetherspoon's expansion slowed as other operators built on Martin's success at getting new licences and started competing aggressively for a finite number of suitable premises. You could even argue that Martin was personally responsible for the explosion of city-centre "drinking barns" of the last 25 years, and the company diversified out of its original music-free, TV-free, community-oriented pubs into more youthful bars (Lloyd's Number One) and even lodges. But it has always stuck to its principle of patronising local and regional brewers, sporting rows of six or more handpumps serving guest ales from all over Britain and Europe, and holding regular beer festivals.

Getting your beers into Wetherspoon's is harder now than it used to be, simply because there are more breweries competing for slots, but the company is still a great patron of local brewers. Its real ales are sourced by East-West Ales, an independent company based in Paddock Wood in Kent (Tel: +44 (0) 1892 725 617); the people you need to impress there are Dave Aucutt and Janet Cheeseman.

Leased and Tenanted Pubcos

The biggest of the modern chains though, run their pubs as quasi-traditional tenancies or leaseholds. These too, are tied; but in this case it's generally the bigger chains that allow their licensees the most freedom. Ted Tuppen, founder of Enterprise Inns, said in his early days that he would be happy for his tenants to stock whatever their customers would buy, provided it all came from one supplier and at the right price. For unlike the brewers of old, these pubcos have no supply chain of their own: all their beers are delivered by third-party distributors. The range that these companies can stock and distribute is pretty big: one of them has claimed in the past to carry 2,000 draught beers from 300 breweries. However, these are mostly the large or medium concerns that can keep up with the logistics and meet the prices demanded, and few of the newer brewers have geared themselves up to operate on the scale and in the manner necessary to penetrate the pubco market successfully unaided.

The bigger pubcos have regional lists featuring beers from local brewers as well as seasonal ales drawn from a wider supply base and they sometimes host promotions that they call beer festivals, during which they temporarily allow their tenants to stock from a wider list still. But generally speaking your best way of getting your beers into their pubs is via the Society of Independent Brewers' Beerflex scheme.

That accounts for the bigger pubcos. But there are many smaller ones as well. Some are run as property companies that squeeze as much rent as possible out of their tenants while buying the cheapest beer they can find. Not much opportunity for you in these cases – but on the other hand, some of the smaller locally based chains are extremely friendly to local brewers and indeed specialise in stocking their beers. Tynemill in the East Midlands, Ken Ryan's Barter Inns in London, Market Town Taverns in West Yorkshire, Brunning & Price in Cheshire and North Wales, and English Inns in Bedfordshire and Hertfordshire are all good examples. But they probably own fewer than 300 pubs between them and in trying to sell to them you are joining a very long queue.

Below is a selection of micro-friendly pub companies. There may well be other small chains of a similar bent in your area. If you know of any pubs that seem to serve a wider than usual range of ales and don't obviously belong to a brewery, ask the licensee who the owner is. It may be one of the national giant pubcos but it may well be a smaller local outfit that can be persuaded to stock your beer.

Brunning & Price
Yew Tree Farm Buildings, Saighton, Chester, CH3 6EG;
Tel: +44 (0) 1244 333 100
www.brunningandprice.co.uk
15 pubs in the North-West and north Wales.

Camelot Inns
PI House, 23 Clifton Road, Shefford, Beds, SG17 5AF
Tel: +44 (0) 1462 812 621
www.camelotinns.co.uk
Nine managed pubs in its estate.

Cascade Public House Management
5 Merlin Way, Bowerhill Trading Estate, Melksham,
Wilts, SN12 6TJ
Tel: +44 (0) 1225 704 734
www.cascadepubs.co.uk
14 pubs in the South-West; sister company of Moles Brewery.

Castle Rock Ltd
Queensbridge Road, Nottingham, NG2 1NB;
Tel: +44 (0) 1159 851 615
www.castlerockbrewery.co.uk
17 pubs in East Midlands; founded by former CAMRA National
Chairman Chris Holmes.

Market Town Taverns
6 Green Dragon Yard, Knaresborough, N Yorks, HG5 8AU
Tel: +44 (0) 1423 86610
www.markettowntaverns.co.uk
Eight pubs in Yorkshire.

Sir John Fitzgerald
Café Royal Buildings, 8 Nelson St, Newcastle upon Tyne, NE1 5AW
Tel: +44 (0) 1912 320 664
www.sjf.co.uk
28 pubs, mainly in the North-East.

The Peach Pub Company
Peach Barns, Somerton Road, North Aston, Bicester,
Oxfordshire, OX25 6HX
Tel: +44 (0) 1869 220 110
20 pubs in the Midlands and South-East of England.

The Wholesale Trade

Not all that long ago, cask ale brewers were deeply suspicious
of the wholesale trade. Brewers were understandably paranoid

about the way their beers – living, breathing products, after all – were being handled. How long did they take to work through the distribution chain? How many drops and pick-ups were there between brewery and pub? What temperature control, if any, was there in the supply chain? What state would the casks return in, and when? The wholesale trade did little to allay their suspicions.

But the way the market was changing left small brewers, and indeed many regional brewers, with little alternative but to trust the wholesale trade. The guest ale market that opened up in the 1990s was a truly national market; ales from Kent were called for in Cumbria and vice versa, and only the independent wholesale trade could handle the traffic.

It was at this time that independent wholesalers specialising in real ale such as The Beer Seller, Flying Firkin, East-West Ales, Small Beer, Little Ale Cart and many others set up in business. Some disappeared; others prospered – The Beer Seller, in particular, became a major national player, supplying not only small free traders but also the big pubcos. It was then snapped up by Scottish & Newcastle and renamed Waverley TBS, Waverley Vintners having been S&N's existing wholesale division, but collapsed with debts of more than £60 million in 2012. That left Flying Firkin – northern-based, but now with a much longer reach having acquired the non-Wetherspoon business of East-West Ales and its southern customer base – as by far the leading independent.

The new generation of specialist wholesalers did their best to speed up turnaround times so that the beer arrived at the retailer reasonably fresh and the casks got back to the brewery reasonably quickly. They also sought, mostly although by no means universally, to introduce refrigerated storage and transport so that the problem of beer-barrels exploding on wholesalers' lorries, which had actually happened during the very hot summer of 1996, occurred no more.

These new wave distributors existed alongside a big national network of well-established locally rooted general licensed trade wholesalers, some of them family firms several generations old who dealt in beer and lager as well as wines, spirits, soft drinks, bag-snacks and sundries. Many of these older companies still exist, and 26 of them with 53 depots in England and Wales between them are now members of a consortium called National Drink Distributors (NDD). They deal in a wider range of beers than they used to, running guest and seasonal ale programmes for their 25,000 regular accounts, and in many cases trying to stock at least some local products; so if they haven't traditionally been big players in the microbrewing world, they are well worth cultivating now.

Before tackling the wholesale trade, though, you have to ask what it will require of you. The answer, in a nutshell, is reliability. That's why most wholesalers won't handle your beers until you've been in business for a while; they don't want to go to all the effort and expense of offering their customers a beer that may very well not be available tomorrow, so they'll want to know that you're sound and solvent. They want reliable quality as well as reliable supply: nothing upsets them more, as you can imagine, than getting a load of returns from an angry licensee, because the beer tastes like vinegar. So even if, as often happens, your very first brew is enthusiastically greeted with a clutch of CAMRA Beer of the Festival awards, most wholesalers will want to be sure you're thoroughly bedded in before they commit resources and energy to pushing your beers.

Selling through wholesalers does have its drawbacks. You have no control over the quality of your beer as it passes through the supply chain. You have to share your margin, which may be slim enough already, with a middleman. You may have to wait quite a while to get your casks back. You will almost certainly have to wait to get paid, especially if you're dealing with some of the big national chains. They might claim to have a credit period of 60 days, but a glitch – carelessness, laziness or simply the inevitable cases of human error – can wreak havoc with your cash-flow. Marc Bartram tells a story of chasing his payments from the very biggest chain for month after month, only to find out entirely by accident that his cheques were being sent to a very bemused Buffy's Brewery, which, like him, could get no sense at all out of the bureaucrats in the wholesaler's accounts department. Glitches of this kind can take a lot of time and effort on your part to sort out. Marc is not the only brewer who swears he will never sell to a wholesaler again unless they pay upfront – which, of course, they don't. But there's a limit to how much effort you can put into sales yourself, and as your business grows you may well find the services of a wholesaler indispensable.

To meet reliable wholesalers, join SIBA. It has many of them among its associate membership, with full contact details given on its website; and Flying Firkin in particular is commendably eager to give beers from new breweries a go. But since the craft ale movement got going in 2010-2011, a great many small local wholesalers have sprung up, as knowledgeable and enthusiastic as the brewers whose beers they distribute and the publicans they supply. To compile an exhaustive list would be impossible since the situation is still fluid, but here is a sample recommended to me by craft brewers themselves:

Big Beer Distribution, Bristol
www.thebigbeerco.com

Jolly Good Beer, Cambridge
www.jollygoodbeer.co.uk

New Wave, Edinburgh
www.anewwave.co.uk

Pig's Ears, Richmond, Surrey
www.pigs-ears.co.uk

Pivovar, York
www.pivovarorders.co.uk

The Brewers Wholesale, Stourbridge
www.thebrewerswholsale.co.uk

Two other recommendations without websites are Forest Wholesale of Tolpuddle, Dorset, and Paul Duke of Stafford. Both have Facebook pages.

A last word on the wholesale trade concerns brewery swaps. Many small breweries try to vary the repertoire of beers they can offer their customers and, at the same time, to get their beers more widely known by swapping beers with other breweries. This isn't quite the same thing as straightforward wholesale distribution, and it doesn't in itself increase your sales volume. But it's a trading model that has worked very well for very many small brewers for very many years; a little further down the line, perhaps when you're more established, it could prove a handy boost for you too.

Niche Opportunities

One of the very first new breweries to be established, way back in the early 1970s, was the Miners Arms at Priddy, Somerset. It wasn't a pub though; despite the name, it was a restaurant. You'd think, wouldn't you, that hotels and restaurants would be keen to offer tourists and diners craft-made local products? Well, in 99 per cent of cases, they're not, and on the rare occasions when they are, they tend to be more interested in bottled beer than draught, so perhaps we'll deal with them in the next chapter alongside the tourist gift shops and other miscellaneous outlets.

The Club Trade

One large part of the on-trade that hasn't really been penetrated by local brewers, though, is the club trade. Not nightclubs, but Britain's 15,000-odd traditional sports and social clubs.

In theory, your local workingmen's club ought to be the ideal home for your ales. You're a local outfit, maybe employing local people, which should appeal to the committee that decides what beers to stock. You should be able to offer an attractive price; if you brew less than 3,000 barrels you qualify for 50 per cent duty relief, which you can share with a big, steady customer such as a club. The club is big, and usually busy, and full of thirsty working-class drinkers who like their ale; so your beer will turn over quickly enough to ensure that it's always in excellent condition.

Workingmen's clubs, though, have remained stubbornly resistant to the advances of local brewers. Many are still loan- tied, for a start; and even if they're not, committees tend to remain loyal to traditional suppliers who often offer not inconsiderable inducements. An all-expenses-paid annual day out at the races, complete with Champagne buffet and executive marquee for the entire club committee including spouses may not actually qualify as bribery, but it's not the sort of jaunt the average working family would indulge in if the brewery wasn't paying. The wholesale price clubs have to pay is one you would find hard to match, even with your duty relief. Finally, they may be big, busy and full of good, steady drinkers, but the drink they drink these days tends to be lager rather than ale. The ale they do sell tends to be keg rather than cask, for ease of handling.

Even at the traditional end of the club trade, though, this resistance is beginning to crack. The truth is that membership of workingmen's clubs, Royal British Legions and the like, is tumbling, despite the cheap beer, because their offering is simply not up-to-date. Leatherette banquettes, scruffy lino floors, keg ale, bad singers with obvious comb-overs, and bingo are just not attractive any more, and clubs are having to raise their game to stay alive. Some of them are now offering equal rights to women. There is no reason why real ale shouldn't be part of the equation, especially if it's locally brewed. So it's up to you to go to see your local club steward and secretary, demonstrate that stocking real ale is perfectly possible (even if there isn't a proper cellar, there's bound to be a cold room) and persuade them that well-priced and properly promoted cask beer will attract members. They'll give you a hearing, and the worst they can say is no. Then you go back next year and see if they've changed their minds yet.

You will probably have less trouble getting a sympathetic hearing at sports clubs. There are two sorts here, though; those whose bars are only busy – or in some cases only open at all – on match days aren't going to stock cask ale, even from a local brewer. But the larger, busier and – though I hardly dare utter the words – more middle-class establishments such as golf clubs are proving fruitful territory for those cask ale brewers who actually try to tackle them. Middle-class men tend to drink real ale rather than lager, it's a fact. They also tend to be more appreciative of lesser-known and local brewers whose products have the cachet of, if not exclusivity, certainly rarity. So, don't ignore the club trade. Clubs may not be easy accounts to crack, and they may not pay top dollar, but they are in general a growth area for real ale, and listing one or two local sporting or social clubs among your regular outlets will pay off in terms of long-term, reliable, regular business.

Outside Bars

Running outside bars at events private and public is an opportunity that more and more small breweries are learning to exploit. It's an area that offers two main advantages: the overheads are comparatively low and the margins are comparatively high. It also has its drawbacks, as we shall see. Even at public events such as village shows, your overheads are likely to be minimal. In capital terms, you need a strong trestle table, an awning of some sort, a stillage system on which to mount your casks, some cooling jackets and a biscuit-tin for the cash. If you're selling ale racked off bright into polypins rather than from the cask, you can even dispense with the stillage, although a reliable cooling system is still indispensable. These will all involve from you a modest one-off outlay. You may need some paid assistance. To offset the expenses you get the full retail price of the beer – £180 a firkin rather than the £50-£60 you get wholesale – and if you can't make a nice margin on that, you're doing something wrong.

There are drawbacks. You will need a personal licence (see Chapter Eight), but then you should get one of those anyway. It takes time to set up and take down. There will be the occasional disaster when only half the predicted numbers turn up; and if you've racked beer off specially then the unsold surplus will, unless you have another outside bar the very next day, be spoiled (you can get duty drawback on it, but that's not much help). (I have heard of brewers sneaking very small quantities of freshly racked ale back into the system, but it's risky. You never know what infections are lurking in the sort of barns where ceilidhs are often held and you certainly wouldn't want them in your brewery. If you really can't overcome the temptation to spread unsold bright beer among a few casks, make sure it's from unbroached containers only. It's safer just to stand the loss, though.)

As well as the cash they generate, though, outside bars have a promotional value. In brewing as in life, you can never have too many friends; outside bars spread your name around in the neighbourhood. So: hard work; chancy; but a good sales opportunity and an equally good profile raiser.

Marketing

Naturally, your first efforts in marketing are going to be concentrated on finding outlets for your beers. But equally important, and in some ways more difficult, is making an impression on the beer-drinking public. Getting repeat orders from your trade customers will depend on how much of your beer they can sell to their patrons and although you might say that they're the retailers and it's up to them to promote themselves, there's a great deal you can do to help.

Your marketing effort starts at the simplest possible level – with the names of your beers, and the design of your pump-clips. In most of the pubs where your beer is on sale, your pump-clip is likely to be the only way you have of communicating directly with the public and the only chance you will get to persuade people who have never heard of you to buy your beer. What sort of people are they likely to be, and what sort of message are they most likely to respond to?

CASE STUDY

Pillars Brewery
Craft lager – the un-traditional way

When the partners at Pillars Brewery and taproom in Walthamstow, London, embarked on their craft lager brewing enterprise, they knew it was imperative to "plough their own furrow". With so many breweries in the London area producing good ales, Pillars Brewery wanted to make its mark and it has certainly achieved this by producing its "untraditional lager".

After three years of investigation with visits to many breweries specialising in pils-type lager and many test brews at home, Pillars Brewery was ready to take its product to the next stage. The partners Gavin, Eamonn, Samie and Omar knew that a traditional British mash conversion system would not be the optimum solution to achieve their aims, so they started a dialogue and ultimately ordered a turnkey plant from Enterprise Tondelli and its manufacturing partners in Italy, Simatec.

This dialogue with the supplier partnership has been ongoing, resulting in continual improvement of the product. One recent example is the trend for dry hopping, which can cause some challenges for both costings and tank hygiene.

The supplier developed the isobaric hop injector or IHI for short. This unit, utilised with the conditioning vessel, reduces hop consumption by around 50-60 per cent, can reduce tank time by two days and results in a conditioning tank easier to clean.

Pillar Untraditional Lager is 4.5% ABV and described as a session IPL hoppy lager with a clean finish. The lager is produced adhering to German purity laws, but has a mix of four hops coupled with dry hopping in the later stages. Three other lagers are produced for sale in the brewery's taproom. The taproom specials comprise of a 4.5% Czech-style pilsner called Pillars Pilsner, a 6.2% amber IPL and Citralicious Lager, an unfiltered, dry hopped 4.8% lager using lots of Citra hops.

The beers are available in kegs within the local area of the brewery and in stainless steel growlers from the brewery for that ultimate fresh taste, unless you drink straight out of the conditioning tank.

Growlers are refillable containers filled from the taps in the taproom. It's a way to take home freshly poured beer from the range served on any given day. Pillars' growlers have an excellent closure mechanism with a replaceable seal which protects against oxygen ingress.

Kegs were selected for local distribution and the high carbonation enhances the hoppy aroma for fresh tasting beers. The keg filler is a purpose-built keg washer and racker with an on-board hot caustic tank for internal cleaning at both high and low pressures, cleaning both the outside of the spear and the internals of the keg to ensure no contamination. Sterility is enhanced by steam sterilisation.

To reduce the hot oxidation, the wort is transferred as few times as possible. At Pillars the wort is only transferred twice. One vessel is a multipurpose vessel that acts as the mash tun, copper and whirlpool, whilst the other vessel is a lauter which helps increase the extract efficiency, thereby saving costs on every brew.

In London, mains water is very hard, so Pillars invested in a water treatment plant by Enterprise Tondelli. The plant is equipped with reverse osmosis so water can be made suitable for lager brewing by adding the required salts. A steam boiler, along with hot and cold liquor tanks, plus a mains water buffer tank due to the restricted site supply mains, were also included.

Conscious of the environmental responsibility of a modern brewery, Pillars installed a refrigeration system coupled with an externally located chiller. Traditionally a large chiller would be used on demand, but the system supplied generates the "cold" charge over 24 hours using a smaller refrigeration compressor with lower running costs. This is then stored in an ice bank for use over the 30 minutes or so required to cool the hot wort after the boiling cycle.

The ice bank has an outlet for the fermenting and conditioning vessels, making a common system, which reduces running costs. Eyeing innovation, the brewery opted for a type of food-grade glycol commonly used in aviation. The benefit is that the glycol is less viscous and thus uses less energy, benefiting its carbon footprint.

Equipment is only part of the story, Pillars says. After fermentation many breweries condition beers for a couple of weeks. Pillars conditions its beers at temperatures close to freezing for a minimum of five weeks in tanks. Why? "This improves the quality of the beer. The long conditioning creates a crisp, clean finish and removes nasty off-flavours found in beer that has been rushed," says the brewery.

The beer is then dry hopped, adding a burst of hop aroma.

www.pillarsbrewery.com

Branding

In the early days, many microbrewers chose branding that was blokeish, jocular and often rustic. Beers had names like The Dog's Bollocks, Piston Bitter (a variation on pissed 'n' broke) and Old Fart, and the pump-clips were often not much more than photocopies of the head brewer's late-night attempts at postcard art. Often it seemed all too crass and amateurish, but it struck a chord with an ale-drinking public that was itself, in many cases, blokeish and jocular. Real ale in those days belonged in the same cultural cage as rugby club dinners and dwyle flonking; today, with beer drinking generally in decline, reading and catching a market is a much more subtle and demanding business. Today's craft brewers serves a much more self-consciously fashionable and largely American-inspired constituency and their marketing themes and designs are much more up-to-date, much bolder and much more metropolitan. This is a hard market to serve: it's more fickle, and unless you really feel a part of it, it's much easier to get wrong.

This is no place to lecture you on design, on what colours to choose, on what note to strike. Suffice it to say that unless the former life you're going into brewing to escape was in graphic design, you should hire a professional. It does make sense, though – and it's surprising how many brewers have let this obvious point fly past them – to maintain uniformity of branding across your range. In a crowded bar on a busy night, the size of the type identifying the pump-clip as yours, will defy the cursory inspection that may be all that is possible. Unless all your pump-clips have the same shape and colours, it will not be apparent that the best bitter on tap is one of yours; anybody who tried and liked your cooking bitter and would try more of your beers if given the chance will remain in ignorance. So establishing a clearly recognisable identity via a uniform pump-clip design will be a great help to drinkers who want to sample your range and to publicans who want to sell it. Some breweries take it a step further and give their whole range a common theme: Cotleigh, with its birds of prey, is perhaps the supreme example. That may be a little excessive – it seems to me a little hasty to narrow your possibilities without good reason – but for the perfect example of unobtrusive yet clearly identifiable branding across the range, check out Tunnel Brewery, (**www.tunnelbrewery.co.uk**).

As for names, jokes for blokes are as much of a turn-off as a come-on these days. Craft-brewed beer is trying to get serious and to press a whole range of contemporary buttons: it's foodie-friendly; it's got good green credentials; it's the very antithesis of all that's corporate and globalised. Perhaps because so many of these issues resonate so strongly with women, more and more are drinking beer. You are not going to appeal to them by naming your beer Maiden's Ruin, Willie Warmer or Old Horizontal (all genuine examples).

Working with CAMRA

Having created a range with names and branding calculated to appeal to the customers you have in mind, you need to find cost-effective ways of getting your name around. I have already mentioned CAMRA membership as a way of making contact with local micro-friendly licensees but CAMRA can do more for you than that (unless, of course, you're a keg- and can-toting craft brewer, in which case CAMRA will either resolutely ignore you or pronounce its dreadful anathema upon you).

The Brewery Liaison Office (BLO)

The first thing your local CAMRA branch should do for you is appoint a brewery liaison officer, or BLO. The origins of this office lie far back in the mists of the Campaign's early days, when new breweries were rare and tender shoots that CAMRA branches felt they had to nurture and fuss over. The BLO's job was to check in with the brewer from time to time, make sure that everything was all right and report back to the branch with news of new brews or looming problems. In the best of cases, the relationship between brewery and BLO would develop much further, with the BLO taking responsibility – in return for free pints and being made to feel special – for publicising and promoting the brewery. In the worst of cases, the very opposite happened, and the BLO turned out to be a curmudgeon for whom everything the brewery did was a mockery. In these, thankfully few, cases, the BLO was very soon made persona non grata at the brewery. More often, the BLO turned into a valued and indeed valuable friend who even, on occasion, ended up as a partner or employee. So provided your BLO is bearable, cultivate them. Give them things to do like writing press releases or delivering leaflets to your retail customers. They will not resent it or regard it as an imposition; they will be genuinely thrilled to help.

Every CAMRA branch also organises an annual beer festival – and some of them run a winter ales festival as well. Your local branch will undoubtedly order one or more of your range for its festival. In volume terms this is insignificant – three or four firkins at most, unless you're in one of those places like Peterborough, Cambridge or Worcester where the local beer festival is huge. So although there's not likely to be a huge amount of money involved, a presence at local festivals is great for public exposure. The local media – broadcast as well as print – will often seize on a new local brewery as the news "hook" on which to hang their festival report, especially if you have an unusual or catchy story to tell. More important still, even quite small festivals attract CAMRA members from surprisingly far afield, who are always on the look-out for new brews and will spread the news of your arrival – and their opinion of your ales – to other CAMRA members, beer festival organisers and micro-friendly licensees back home. Winning the Beer of the Festival award is better publicity still, and it's surprising how often the title goes to a new local brewery. These things are supposed to be unfixable, and in the most obvious sense they are (waving brown envelopes is likely to be counter-productive, I'm happy to affirm). But sentiment and local loyalty often play their part and who's going to complain about that?

Public Relations

Using the media is something local brewers are often very bad at. There are only 24 hours in the day, and at least two or three of them should be spent asleep; media relations tend to come far down the busy brewer's list of priorities. It shouldn't be that way, though. Building strong local awareness is one way you can help your trade accounts shift your beer, which will help you win new accounts as well.

There's no publicity like free publicity, and putting out a constant stream of news stories is one good way of getting it. Some local breweries even hire public relations agencies to do it for them, and to good effect. Wood's of Wistanstow in Shropshire has used local PR agency Seabury Salmon for years and has become one of the best-known brewers in the West Midlands as a result.

If you're doing it yourself, you need to get to know your media. Start with the CAMRA branches in your trading area, they almost all publish local newsletters – the larger branches print thousands of them – which are distributed around ale-friendly pubs for customers to browse in odd moments. Find out who the editor of your local newsletter is and keep them informed as filling these publications can be difficult and the editor will be glad of news of new brews, new members of staff, funny stories and the like. You may even get your brewery featured in a profile article.

You (or even your BLO, if he or she is canny, aware and willing) should also try to develop a relationship with a favoured reporter at each of your local newspapers and radio stations. This is, remember, a two-way street – the reporters will help you by getting you free publicity, and you will help the reporters by establishing their reputation as a keen and productive newshound.

As for what kind of stories local media are looking for – well, buy your local paper and see for yourself. New beers, especially charity brews (Wood's, that PR-canny outfit, is one of many that regularly creates special brews with part of the proceeds going to newsworthy local causes), new recruits, the brewery cat's mouse-hunting prowess – it's all grist to the local reporter's mill.

Ask yourself, also, what format your local media want to get their information in. A story is more likely to make it into the paper or onto the airwaves if it's presented in a way that needs minimum processing – as a proper press release. In the old days these would be hard copies posted by snail mail to the newsdesk; these days, a Word document attached to an email (not a cut and paste job, preferably) addressed personally to your pet reporter is probably your best bet.

Advertising

Advertising is a trickier business altogether. You're not Carlsberg, spending a fortune to establish and maintain a national brand; and you're not a scaled-down version of Carlsberg either, trying to achieve locally what it does nationally. Brand advertising doesn't work like that. It has to make your brand stand out from the others, and if it's not ubiquitous and relentless, it's a waste of money. It also only works if your brand already has excellent distribution – there's no point advertising a product no one can buy! So don't be tempted to take out big ads for your brands in the local paper, or even in specialist media such as *What's Brewing*. That's for the future, perhaps, but for now it's simply not effective.

That doesn't mean you shouldn't advertise at all; but to repay the investment, your advertising needs to be highly market-specific and well planned.

- First, make a forward planner, highlighting events such as your open day/beer festival, the launch dates of special or seasonal beers, important local dates where your beers can be highlighted and joint promotions with stockists.

- Second, set a budget. This will be based on the advertising rates of the local media you intend to use, but remember – nobody but a mug pays the ratecard price. Discounts are always available, based on repeat or regular advertising. Once you've made your budget, stick to it. You might want a small contingency fund to exploit unforseen events, but don't be tempted by slick sales patter into spending more than you have allocated.

- Third, choose your medium, basing your decision on "bangs per buck" – not the overall readership or audience of the medium, but what proportion is likely to buy your beer. Always remember: a small ad strategically placed is more effective than a big ad in a vacuum. One sure way of testing the effectiveness of each medium is to include a money-off voucher in some of your adverts (but not all of them – promotional discounts are part of your advertising budget, which is unlikely to be huge) and analyse the redemption rate.

Local CAMRA branch newsletters, distributed in hundreds to local pubs to be picked up and put down by drinkers whiling away a few idle moments, are ideal vehicles for your advertising because everybody who reads them is ipso facto in a pub and willing to buy. Local A5 newsletters of the type that are appearing in villages all over the country are also cheap and well-read; but here, as with local newspapers and local commercial radio, you need to tie your advertising to a particular event. Is the local CAMRA beer festival being covered? Is a pub where your beers are on sale being profiled? Is a special feature being published or broadcast on drinking and dining out in the district? Supporting this sort of coverage with a well-designed ad is effective both in raising your public profile and in earning brownie points with your retail partners.

Then there are specialist national media: not only beer-related titles such as *What's Brewing*, but all sorts of hobby and special interest media too. Do your beers, for instance, have a steam theme, or are you involved in a promotion with a local preserved railway? Are you donating part of the proceeds of a special ale to a good cause? Invariably there is a magazine or newsletter that will give your efforts exposure to relevant consumers, and normally at a reasonable rate too.

Even where there's no editorial involved, working with your stockists makes advertising more effective. One of your best accounts may be advertising its quiz nights, or a forthcoming beer festival, or a special menu for Valentine's Day or Father's Day. Share the cost and get your name in the ad, and you both save money and share the benefit.

One design tip: keep your ad simple. When you're paying by the column centimetre, the urge to cram in as much information as possible is almost irresistible. But do resist. Save the lingering descriptions of your hop varieties, your malt grist, your pure well-water and the rest for your website, your brochures and your back label. Your ad should be clear, uncluttered and eye-catching. You only have a split second of your customer's attention, so use it wisely! And if in doubt, use a professional graphic designer – traditionally a service provided free or at little extra cost by local newspapers.

Promotions

As with advertising, organising promotions jointly with your retail partners (and do try to think of them as partners) is often more rewarding than going solo, spreading the work and the cost and sharing the benefit. You might provide prizes – free pints, for instance, or merchandise, or brewery tours – for pub promotions such as quiz nights or charity raffles. But don't go mad with money-off or free-pint offers – they can turn out to be more popular than you anticipated and end up blowing a hole in your promotional budget.

If one of your stockists is running a beer festival, you can be of practical help by pulling pints (staff are always short on occasions like this) and providing technical support. Naturally, your beers will be on sale, and you might also be allowed to leave your dray prominently sited in the pub car park for the duration, and to put up a few posters or distribute your leaflets. If you want to run a beer festival or open day at the brewery but don't have a liquor licence of your own, a friendly publican might act as licensee for the event and also help out with cellar and dispense equipment in return for a cut of the profits and some publicity for the pub. Involving a local charity is also a good idea; it guarantees publicity, and volunteer fundraisers will both provide a workforce and drag their friends and family along.

It's all about mutuality, building relationships and creating bonds that will last. There's only a certain amount you can do alone, especially if you're a one-person band, so work with your stockists, your CAMRA branch and local voluntary groups, share both the burdens and the benefits – and make every casual customer a regular.

Online Marketing and Promotion

Marketing and promotion doesn't depend entirely on the old-fashioned print and broadcast media these days. More and more, they make use of websites, blogs and emails.

A website of your own is pretty much a must these days. It's a low-cost, low-maintenance shop window, and one that the entire world can mooch past and gaze into. Not only does it show the world what you have to offer, it can also invite them in to buy. We'll deal with e-commerce later; if you decide that it's one of your main routes to market, you'll soon find that it has problems and peculiarities of its own. But as a complement to your core business, it can be a very useful way of generating sales and awareness. It's also one way of announcing new launches and other promotions and developments.

However a website is not cost-free. Designers charge, and a webmaster will also charge to keep the site up-to-date. You can pay anything from £200 to £2,000 or even more, and in web design as in life, you get what you pay for. A cheap designer will produce a cheap-looking site that will probably break down. The best advice is to shop around and get plenty of quotes; fortunately, web designers are very easy to find. You can either Google "web designers", and literally hundreds will come up, or you can be a bit more selective and revisit a few sites you've been impressed by in the past. They'll normally have the designer's name and contact details on them somewhere (it would be odd if they didn't!) and the designers' own sites should have links to other sites they've designed.

Website Content

But before you rush in to getting quotes from designers, think of what you want your site to do. First, you want it to say who you are and what you do. A nice, chatty site with plenty of background detail is more effective than a dry, terse, and straightforwardly factual one. You want potential customers to get involved with you and your venture on a personal level – it makes the beer taste better and seem cheaper! Having engaged the public's attention, give them the facts about your beers and where people can actually buy them; keep them abreast of new and forthcoming beers, new outlets, events of your own such as brewery open days and third-party events such as beer festivals where your ales will be on sale. Using the site for e-commerce we have already touched on; but you can also use it for trade telesales, with a password-controlled page where trade customers can not only place orders but also pay for them. But do remember that if you're selling to the public, you need both a personal and a premises liquor licence. People have come badly unstuck by forgetting this tiny detail!

Other Social Media

Facebook, Twitter and other social media are apparently very effective marketing tools. But for advice on how to get the best out of them you're going to have to consult someone rather younger than this author.

Chapter Seven
Selling Packaged Beer

Local brewers have always been associated in the public mind with cask-conditioned beers or, to use the vernacular, real ale. But packaged (industry-speak for bottled and canned) beer sales are becoming more and more important both to the brewing industry as a whole and to smaller brewers in particular; and in another recent twist, thanks to the largely American-inspired craft brewing movement, canned beers are becoming increasingly respectable.

For not only have take-home sales continued to grow at the expense of pub sales (not least because beer is so much cheaper in supermarkets than in pubs), but in some sectors of the on-trade packaged beer sales have been growing at the expense of draught. Of particular importance to the craft brewer is a new generation of metropolitan cocktail and lounge bars found not only in the gentrified East End of London but in select quarters of all major cities.

Packaging some or all of your output is therefore an increasingly important string to your commercial bow, and bottles and cans do have several advantages over draught. Packaging extends a beer's life from a few days to a few months; it gives you something to stock your own shop with, if you have one; and some shops in your area – small independent grocers, especially – can usually be persuaded to stock a case or two as a showcase for (or gesture towards) local produce. Bottled and canned versions of your range make great trade samples when you're out on the road trying to drum up new business. Packaging is also relatively efficient in that you don't have to worry about your empties as you will, constantly, with casks.

But as with the pub trade, so with the packaged trade. Most of it, quite simply, will remain firmly closed to you. The Competitionand Markets Authority adamantly refuses to accept that the "multiple grocers" warrant investigation, even though the Big Five supermarkets control as large a slice of the market as the Big Six brewers did back in the late 1980s, when they were found to be a complex monopoly operating against the public interest. To pursue the analogy, the independent sector – effectively second-string supermarket chains such as Budgens – is just as restrictive as the regional brewery tied estates of the 1980s were. The take-home equivalent of the free trade – small family-run convenience stores and corner shops – is largely supplied by cash and carries that will be closed to you as firmly as Tesco or Morrisons. Nevertheless, there are opportunities out there that will almost certainly make packaging some or all of your beers – either yourself, or by a contractor – worth investigating. But before we explore these opportunities, let's take a look at the practicalities.

Short-Run Bottling

Bottling on a small scale is time-consuming and monotonous, and unless it's done carefully the beer is very prone to infection and oxidisation. On the other hand, starter-level bottling and corking machines are almost ridiculously cheap; an initial outlay of £600 will provide you with all the equipment you really need.

The most primitive four-headed hand-bottler will cost you about £400 and stands quite happily on a trestle table, leaving plenty of room for a simple crown capper (about £200) to stand next to it. The bottle filler is connected directly to a beer barrel or conditioning tank; the operative simply holds the bottles to the spouts, two at a time, and pays enough attention to make sure they don't overfill. Two operatives, one on the filler, one on the capper, can easily fill 1,500 bottles (more than an entire pallet) a day on this simplest of items; or, if you're a one-person band, you can do the whole job yourself and fill 750, which is the equivalent of nearly 10 firkins. If you do the whole thing yourself, though, remember to swap from filler to capper frequently; not only does it make the job marginally less boring, but the longer the bottles stand around without caps, the likelier they are to pick up an infection. However bored you get, remember that if you're retailing the beer yourself, either through your own shop or at farmers' markets (see below), your day of single-handed (and single-minded!) bottling equates to sales of £1,500 or more, depending on the strength of the beer.

Of course, you'll need slightly more equipment than that, but none of it is expensive. If you're filling bottles direct from the shrink-wrapped pallet on which they were delivered, they shouldn't even need sterilising. But if you're only bottling a few cases at a time, and the bottles are likely to stand around unprotected for any period before use, a simple rinser using an odourless peracetic fluid costs £30 and a plastic draining tree £25.

Consumables

Then there are the consumables, which, unfortunately, are more expensive than you might think. If you're buying in bulk – and by bulk I mean a container-load of 50-plus pallets of 1,200 bottles apiece – you can probably get your bottles for 15–16p each, with delivery thrown in. If, though, you can only afford (and store) a pallet or two at a time, you'll have to pay top dollar, with £45–£50 a pallet delivery on top, so you may be paying more than 20p for a simple brown 500ml bottle. (Always use brown glass, by the way: beer kept in clear or even green bottles is affected by ultraviolet light, producing an off-flavour known as "light-struck"). Crown corks cost a penny apiece in quantities of 1,000 or less; you could pay less than half that if you could afford and store a minimum order of 10,000. (From this I think you're beginning to see that you could get your consumables much more cheaply if you joined forces with two or three other local breweries.)

Labels

Labels are more problematic still. In bulk, they're quite cheap – but bulk, in this case, does mean quite improbable quantities. There are several firms that specialise in typesetting and printing reel upon reel of bottle labels, but the origination can be expensive. Designs stored on your personal computer (and do get a professional designer: amateur labels are rarely good enough in a market where presentation is much more important than many small brewers think) can be emailed as PDFs or taken on a USB stick to a local commercial printer and turned into self-adhesive labels at 8–9p each. The drawback is that these have to be applied by hand (the bottles carry a line to help you position the labels accurately), which you may well find repetitive and time-consuming enough to make you rethink your new career entirely. However, an entry-level automatic labelling machine can set you back £1,800, so perhaps it's something for later on. It's worth reflecting as you toil that the bottle, label and cork for a package that can retail at £2.50 should only cost about 30p.

A final point on hand-bottling – the expiry date. There is no legal formula for deciding this: most breweries opt for 12 months, or 18 months for beers of six per cent alcohol or more. But it's up to you. Set too short an expiry date and you can have trouble selling the beer to wholesale and retail accounts who are especially picky; too long and you risk beer being on the shelf when it really shouldn't, which can harm your reputation.

CASE STUDY

Redwell Brewery
Driven by love, beer and unicorn tears

Now, as one of the most popular spots to hang out in Norwich, a short few years ago it was a very different story for Redwell Brewery, which appeared to be a bit of a lost cause. However, with the support and guidance of a team of experts, the brewery is back and it's stronger than ever.

Not only is Redwell recognised for its outstanding beers, that offer quality and variety which is of paramount importance to the team, but it is also a favourite among locals and visitors alike due to its quirky setting. The brewery offers a taproom that enables its loyal customers to have a truly unique drinking experience.

Its taproom is a well-known community space which allows customers to sit and drink beer straight from source, sitting with the stainless-steel vats of beer and enjoying a friendly and relaxed atmosphere. Since launching the taproom, it has become an incredible success which is going from strength to strength and has given Redwell a reputation around Norwich as the destination to head to.

Redwell Brewery was founded in 2013 and has worked hard to ensure that it stands out in a heavily saturated market. It was one of the first UK craft breweries to make the move to create its entire range as a certified vegan and audited gluten free selection, which certainly has made a positive impact on the brand over the years.

Its beers have made the headlines numerous times, across both the country and the world, including Alltech Dublin Craft Beer Cup in 2015, The International Beer Challenge, Indie Beer Can Festival, World Beer Awards and SIBA's Independent Beer Awards in 2016, and featured again in the World Beer Awards in 2017.

The brand is driven by a love of what the brewers do and that is clear in all of their products, using their passion for brewing to create something that everyone can enjoy.

Head brewer at Redwell, Belinda Jennings, explained, "We're all about enjoying the process and spending time on creating something that others will love, as much as we love to make it... We've got capacity to expand here so we want to increase our volume but there are no real plans to move site or anything like that.

"I've always been a huge fan of Redwell – my industry experience has been in more traditional breweries, such as Adnams and Greene King, but I've always had a passion for this style of beer and in particular, this company. Our work here differs massively from those companies, positively for the most part. The team here has to put in a lot of hard work, which means we are all able to get completely involved in the entire process."

All of Redwell's beers are brewed in small batches, on site in its Norwich brewery and using locally farmed Norfolk malt. The full brewing team also includes Marcel, Steve and Will, all of whom bring something a little different to Redwell. However, one thing they all have in common is recognising the signature Redwell taste.

"I've been lucky to have received a lot of tasting training during my career," said Belinda. "Between us, we will all pick out different things, for example, some are better at picking out off-notes than others."

The brewery offers a varied selection of core beers, which include a fresh and crisp pilsner, fruity extra pale ale and a hopped west coast pale ale. They also have hybrid styles on offer, brewing steam lager with lager yeast, which is then fermented at ale temperature.

For the team, one of the best parts of being a small-batch independent brewery is utilising the flexibility to experiment with seasonal brews and collaborations, which has enabled the brand to build up great relationships with local businesses.

Belinda adds, "People are always looking for something a bit different so we have to constantly come up with something new, but that's the fun part of the job and it actually takes up a very small part of our day but is something we all love.

"We always like to talk about our new beers, so this one is our Mango Indian Pale Lager, it's a proper lager and has been fermented slowly and at a cooler temperature, so it takes a bit longer and then we have infused it with mango and lots of lovely hops. It's so traditional but with a bit of a twist.

"Unicorns Tears is another of our slightly out there ideas, from one of the founders, Amy. It's a lot of fun, individual and quirky, exactly what we like. It's such a great part of the work here that we are able to experiment a lot.

"I've worked with companies where the ideas we have to follow come from sales and marketing, whereas here they are fed from us and our whole team."

Redwell Brewery is open all year round and continues to offer a lively hub that promotes good times and good vibes. In order to keep their offering fresh and interesting, the team is constantly coming up with events, including pop-ups, free family entertainment, silent discos and more.

www.redwellbrewing.com

Bottle-Conditioned Ales (BCAs)

Which brings us neatly to bottle-conditioned ales (BCAs). In the case of the strongest BCAs, expiry dates are a complete irrelevance, since the beer is still gently working and often improves over 10 or even 20 years.

Bottle-conditioned ales are unfiltered, unpasteurised and uncarbonated, and are bottled with a certain amount of live yeast – either the original yeast with which they were fermented, or a special flocculating culture that will sink to the bottom of the bottle and form a sediment. Sometimes they are also primed with a tiny dose of sugar to help the yeast continue to work.

Some customers don't like the sediment, but if the beer is poured carefully, the yeast should stay put in the shoulder of the bottle. Actually, though, it's packed with vitamin B and is very good for you; its only deleterious effect is that it makes the beer cloudy in the glass. An old trick is to pour the beer carefully and indeed theatrically, expertly leaving all the sediment behind – then to swirl the bottle with a triumphant flourish and tip the yeast into your otherwise brilliantly clear ale.

Bottle-conditioned ales are promoted by CAMRA as "Real Ale in a Bottle" or "RAIB" (although what's wrong with the technical expression is beyond me – RAIB is a singularly graceless set of initials), and are now quite common, but until a few years ago they were in danger of dying out. When CAMRA was founded in 1972 the only BCAs (a far less clumsy expression than RAIBs, so I shall stick with it) on the market were Guinness, Gale's Prize Old Ale, Courage Russian Imperial Stout, Eldridge Pope Thomas Hardy's Ale and Worthington White Shield. Bottled Guinness is now pasteurised and carbonated, and has been for 20 years. Gale's has been bought by Fuller's, which seems disinclined to produce any more of the marvellously rich and vinous nine per cent alcohol Prize Old. The last vintage of Imperial Russian Stout was brewed in 1993, although there have been periodic rumours of another brew. Eldridge Pope of Dorchester first brewed Thomas Hardy's Ale in 1968 to commemorate the centenary of the novelist's birth but shut down long ago. The beer is now owned by Interbrau and contract brewed in London. Finally, Worthington White Shield is a classic Burton pale ale whose production has been shunted from brewery to brewery over the last decade. It was briefly contract-brewed by King & Barnes in Sussex, but when King & Barnes was closed White Shield went home to Burton, where it is now produced at the small commercial brewery which is housed in the the National Brewery Centre museum.

That was then. Thanks almost entirely to microbrewers, bottle-conditioning is now popular again, and thank goodness for that. For BCAs are usually much more complex and less gassy than pasteurised and carbonated beers, and some of the stronger ones can be laid down like a claret and will improve for years. CAMRA's *Good Bottled Beer Guide* listed over 600 examples from 143 breweries and the number continues to grow (and most CAMRA festivals these days have a bottled beer bar that stocks only BCAs, which means a few more sales and a bit more exposure for you). Some brewers won't touch BCAs because they think they're tricky to bottle and are easily spoilt, but keep everything spotless and your BCAs should be fine. Opting to bottle-condition your beers will also save you the not inconsiderable expense of installing filtration, pasteurisation and carbonation equipment.

Contract Packaging

At some stage, if things go well, you will need to move beyond the laborious and inefficient business of hand-bottling. If you have the orders, the space and the capital (or credit), you might decide to install a fully automated bottling line of your own: you can easily pick up used equipment for £3,000-£4,000, but since brand-new bottling-lines are, to an extent, custom made, in terms of finance the sky is the limit. But even if you buy second-hand it's a big step: you may well find you're paying not only for the equipment itself, but a bottling hall to accommodate it and at least one, possibly two, skilled workers to operate and maintain it. The alternative is to use a contract bottler, of which there are now quite a few.

Contract Bottlers

Contract bottlers come in all shapes and sizes: the doyen of them all, Robinson's of Stockport, advertises a minimum bottling run of 50 barrels, which is more than 16,000 500ml bottles. Staffordshire Brewing of Cheddleston, on the other hand, will cheerfully bottle a 1,000 IBC for you in 500ml, 330ml, swing-top, or almost any variation on the theme. Most contract bottlers are capable of giving you the full service from supplying labels to providing the bulk tankers to transport your beer from your brewery to their plant, and many even possess or work with studios which can do your design for you as well. Typically they'll take a week or so to process the beer – which you should supply with a few days' condition at least, but which you needn't otherwise touch – and the typical charge would be 30-35p a bottle plus 15p for the label if you aren't supplying your own. Below is a rather truncated list of contractors; there may very well be one nearer your base of operations!

Bottled in Cumbria, Cockermouth
www.bottledincumbria.co.uk

Branded Drinks, Coleford
www.brandeddrinks.co.uk

Complete Bottling, Derby
www.completebottling.co.uk

Hambleton Ales, Melmerby
www.hambletonales.co.uk

Holden's, Dudley
www.holdensbottling.co.uk

Robinsons, Stockport
www.robinsonsbrewery.com

RSM Solutions, Hartlepool
www.rsm-solutions.co.uk

South East Bottling, Broadstairs
www.southeastbottling.co.uk

Staffordshire Brewing & Bottling, Cheddleton
www.staffordshirebrewery.co.uk

Contract Canning

Canned beers, especially in the US-style 12oz can (330 or 350ml), are becoming increasingly popular for a number of reasons. They're stylish, they're lightweight and easily recyclable, and if the canning itself is competently performed, they're of good quality and will keep almost indefinitely. The difficulty is getting your beers into the can in the first place, since the packaging industry is only just waking up to the craft brewing sector's needs and requirements.

The can, whether steel or aluminium, is the mass-produced package par excellence, which makes it difficult for the packaging industry to adapt to suit the artisan producer. Some brave craft brewers, notably Fourpure and Beavertown, have actually installed their own canning lines but at eyewatering cost; once the premises are adapted and all the necessary ancillary equipment is bought and installed, think hundreds of thousands rather than tens of thousands. But contractors have been slow to emerge. Established canning plants are set up to deal in millions of units – until very recently the minimum order of blank cans has been 500,000! – while specialist newcomers have been deterred by the cost of entry. All that is about to change, though. Even as this edition goes to press the allied trades, like the US Cavalry, are galloping to the aid of the pioneers with developments that should allow even the smallest craft brewer to explore the potential of the canned beer market.

Canned Beer Market

First into the field, and already up and running, is We Can Solutions (**www.wecan.solutions**), which has launched an American-style mobile contract canning service. From its Hereford base it visits breweries all over the UK, canning minimum runs of 10 barrels at a rate of 900 cans per hour, and at a unit cost of under 50p. Close behind is Staffordshire Brewery & Bottling Supplies, which opened its own contract canning line in 2018. Staffordshire's Adrian Corke aims to offer a minimum run of 1,000 litres or 2,000 330ml cans, at about the same price as We Can Solutions. It can't be long before the packaging industry comes up with a micro-canning line; but even then many brewers might prefer to use experienced contractors since canning is a much fiddlier business than bottling.

Supermarkets

So you've bottled and/or canned your beer. Now it's time to sell it, and the most obvious first stop is the place where most people buy their packaged beer. The supermarkets, though, are not generally regarded with much fondness by microbrewers, who often claim they are either exploited or frozen out altogether. To be fair to the big multiples, though, there is only a limited amount of shelf space they can devote to premium bottled ales (PBAs), although the fact that their wine aisles are several times longer than their beer and cider aisles seems bitterly unfair. It's logical that most of the space allotted to PBAs (a fraction of the beer aisle, most of which is filled with "slab packs" of cut-price canned lager) should go to beers from the regionals, which are cheaper for the supermarkets to buy and just as attractive to an undiscerning public. While the Big Five pay lip-service to craft and microbreweries, stocking a handful of nationally distributed brands such as BrewDog and in some cases having (very short!) regional lists, the second division – notably M&S Food and the Co-op – scarcely even go that far.

Frankly, though, even if you do get on a supermarket's regional list it can be a mixed blessing. Either your stock sits on the shelf gathering dust (a listing doesn't guarantee throughput!) or there's a surge in demand that can be hard to satisfy and may mean letting down your regular customers – always something to be wary of. As with the national wholesale giants, getting paid can be a nightmare; there's a huge bureaucracy involved, in which it's all too easy for your invoice to get lost – more so if you're not a regular supplier – and mistakes once made are hard to get straightened out. Then again, it may boost your sales volumes if your beer is put on a four-for-five promotion or even declared a BOGOF, but don't think the retailer is absorbing the discount. It gets passed down to you, and even the slim margin the supermarket allows you can easily be swallowed up in this way.

Having said that, some independent brewers do very well out of the supermarket trade. But for every supermarket-friendly small brewer there are a dozen who say from experience that no spoon is long enough to sup with this particular devil. Anyway, don't build the supermarket trade into your business plan – it'll be a year or two before you're ready to start submitting samples to them, if then.

Local Stockists

Far more important to the start-up small brewer – and, indeed, the established small brewer – is to build up a strong local trade. Looking round the retail scene in your trading area, this may not at first seem too promising a strategy – you can get canned Carling anywhere, but how many off-licences stock a local beer?

That's in large part due to the fact that the big cash and carries used by many independent retailers are even less micro-friendly than the supermarkets. But in East Anglia there's a dedicated band of small brewers who have joined forces to create an alternative market for their bottled beers, under the radar of the supermarkets and cash and carries, and perhaps everybody could learn a few dodges and wrinkles from the East Anglian Brewers' Co-operative (EAB: **www.eastanglianbrewers.com**).

EAB was founded in 2002, principally as a buying consortium, and now has around 40 brewery members. It sources all kinds of equipment, services and ingredients for its members, including barley from one of the region's top growers, which is specially (and separately) processed by Crisp's, a traditional floor maltings at Great Ryburgh, Norfolk, thus guaranteeing traceability. EAB soon evolved from a buying consortium into a marketing operation helping to build collective sales of its members' bottled output, although their cask beers still compete freely in the pub trade. The philosophy is simple. While a pub may have only three or four handpumps and can only stock beers from one or two brewers at a time, beer shops and off-licences benefit from having as wide a variety of beers on the shelf as space allows. Therefore, while the EAB's members fight merrily for pub accounts, they see the wisdom of collaborating in the take-home trade. Being a "secondary co-operative", or one made up of independent members, EAB also qualifies for grants and other help from the region's Social Enterprise Board. It's been a highly successful experiment, albeit one that small brewers in other regions haven't copied.

When EAB was founded in 2002, the take-home trade in the region was as hard to penetrate as anywhere else. The group therefore set about targeting a new area of the trade: farm shops, garden centres, gift shops, post offices, delicatessens, camp-site shops and bars, traditional butcher's shops – any retailer, in fact, with a demand for genuine craft-made local produce. Many of these outlets aren't licensed: EAB therefore pays for them to get licences. The £400 it costs can quickly be recouped, and a whole new layer of retail opportunities is gradually being created.

Even if you're not a member of a co-operative like EAB, it can still be worth your while paying a shop of this kind to get a licence, and if you're paying, you can then institute an exclusive supply arrangement – a sort of tie, in fact. You might even share the cost with a local craft cidermaker or vineyard whose products will complement yours rather than compete with them. If the shopkeeper is still a little wary, there's another step you can take: consignment trading. Instead of selling them the beer in the normal way, you stock their shelves yourself and pay them commission on everything they sell. That way, the shopkeeper doesn't even have to pay upfront for stock and is taking no risk whatsoever. An inexpensive advertisement or two in the local CAMRA branch newsletter, with the cost perhaps shared by the shopkeeper, should generate enough custom to make the venture worth everybody's investment.

Farmers' Markets

Farmers' markets grew up as an evolution of farm shops, and in response to the difficulties farmers encounter in getting a decent price for their produce from the country's high street retailers. There are now around 500 regular markets throughout the UK, half of which are certified by the National Farmers' Retail & Markets Association (FARMA: **www.farma.org.uk**).

In their purest form, farmers' markets such as those certified by FARMA insist that stalls are only available to bona fide growers and producers, and there is sometimes an additional requirement that stallholders must be genuinely local. This is a source of much contention, often reaching Byzantine levels of intricacy. The purists say that shoppers who are led to believe that they're buying only local produce need to be protected from carpetbaggers who aren't really producers and aren't really local. But many small independent traders say that it only needs to be clear that all the stallholders are small and independent, and complain that they are often excluded from farmers' markets on mere technicalities.

You may well think that the ideology of farmers' markets obscures their real point – that they're not Tesco; that shoppers are guaranteed a range of interesting, unusual and top-quality products; and that producers frozen out of the mainstream can find an outlet for their products. Be that as it may, farmers' markets are proving a useful outlet for more and more small, independent brewers. The advantages are many. The overheads are low for a start. Your stall can be as simple or as elaborate as you wish, but even the most ornate is only a comparatively modest one-off cost, and your pitch fee is likely to be £50 or less – much less, in some cases. Your margin will be good; one small brewer I know charges £2.50 for a 500ml bottle of a 5% ABV beer, which is 70p more than a supermarket would charge for a similar product; and of course without the middleman, all the profit margin is his to keep.

There are drawbacks, though, says this same brewer. Markets are quite expensive in terms of time, he warns. Don't forget that you have to put up and take down your stall, which can add many hours to the proceedings. You also want to be the only brewer at that particular market. Competition from a local cidermaker or vineyard is one thing, but there's only so much people can carry away from the market, and if they're buying beer, you want to be sure it's your beer.

Then again, you are very much in the hands of the weather and the organiser. A run of rainy market-days can see takings plunge, and if the organiser is no good at promotion, you can stand there for an awfully long time without any customers. My friendly brewer's advice, though, is to stick it out for a while – if your first stall at a particular market doesn't work, give it two or three more attempts. Your first bad day may have been a one-off, so persist for long enough to see whether it's usually a busy event or not.

In licensing terms, you'll need a personal licence to run your stall. What sort of licence the promoter needs is a much more complicated question. It could be argued that the marketplace needs a premises licence, which is a virtual impossibility. It is theoretically possible to license an open space, but the owner of the marketplace (normally the district council, which also happens to be the licensing authority) is unlikely to go to the trouble. On the other hand, it might be permissible to hold a farmers' market with only a temporary event notice (TEN), and indeed many are held on precisely that basis. However, a TEN only allows for 500 people to attend at a time. Either way, there is a "due diligenc" defence for the stallholder, and provided you've done your absolute best to ensure you're operating legally, you'd be very unlucky to be prosecuted. As to whether the licensing authority would prosecute the promoter or the landowner (which is usually, as we've seen, the licensing authority) – well, Kafka must be chuckling in his grave. Meanwhile we await either a test case or, preferably, new guidance from the Department for Culture, Media and Sport (DCMS), which inexplicably is in charge of liquor licensing.

Assuming the current state of uncertainty in the licensing regime hasn't put you off, you need to find your nearest farmers' market. The FARMA website mentioned above is the best place to start, but it's an unregulated and largely unorganised (as opposed to disorganised) activity, and simply Googling "farmers' markets" will throw up many useful sites such as **www.lfm.org.uk** (farmers' markets in London) and **www.scottishfarmersmarkets.co.uk** (farmers' markets in Scotland). Other than that, it's largely a matter of local knowledge. Is there a farmers' market in your area? Has it already got a brewery stall? If the answers are (a) yes and (b) no, then pounce.

CASE STUDY

Thornbridge Brewery
Without compromise

The Thornbridge story began back in 2005 when founders Jim Harrison and Simon Webster recruited two young brewers to brew on a second-hand 10-barrel kit in the grounds of Thornbridge Hall.

The Hall brewery is based in the outbuildings of Thornbridge Hall, surrounded by beautiful gardens within the 100 acre estate. The buildings were renovated in 2004 in preparation for the brewery installation. Jim and Simon recruited two brewers, keen to kick-start their brewing careers. Their first brew was Lord Marples, a 4% classic bitter, which went on to become a core Thornbridge beer.

Next, they were tasked with brewing something a little different, an IPA which packed a punch in terms of both flavour and ABV. In mid-2005 Jaipur was born, a 5.9% IPA packed with American hops and like nothing else in the beer industry at that time. Following an array of awards and national recognition, Jaipur catapulted Thornbridge into the spotlight, demand outstripped supply and the need for investment in a new brewery became clear.

In 2009 a brand new state-of-the-art brewery was built at Riverside, Bakewell, to meet with demand and allow Thornbridge to develop its range of beers. Brewing still takes place today on the original kit at Thornbridge Hall, which allows it to experiment with new brews, create bespoke Hall brews, collaborations and assist the main brewery in Bakewell.

Thornbridge beer began to appear nationwide and export trade developed, initially to Italy but now to over 35 countries worldwide. The increase in trade both at home and abroad has led to three expansions between 2009 and today.

Thornbridge is once again looking at further expansion. A brand new Visitor Centre is being developed for 2021, which will include a retail area, extensive bar and food offering. It follows the opening of its canning line in 2019.

Thornbridge has always brewed the finest-quality beer with a passion. It recognises that not only quality but consistency and innovation are key to creating amazing and beautifully balanced beer. Consistently pushing boundaries whilst respecting the important traditions of "crafting" beer helps it to create an award-winning range of beers loved by customers all over the world. With over 350 industry-recognised awards it is proud to be part of such an exciting craft beer scene.

www.thornbridgebrewery.co.uk

Specialist Shops

Dotted around the country are 100 or so specialist beer shops, ranging from the enormous Beers of Europe (**www.beersofeurope. co.uk**) in its vast complex of former granaries at Setchey just outside King's Lynn, to the tiny Beer Essentials squeezed into a pedestrianised street in Horsham town centre.

Their number is slowly growing, but the amount of beer most of them can realistically be expected to order is measured in cases rather than pallets, and getting a few cases to an outlet on the other side of the country is prohibitively expensive. There are a handful of wholesalers that specialise in bottles, such as Beer Paradise (**www. beerparadise.co.uk**) also the parent company of the Yorkshire-based BierRitz off-licence chain (email **sales@beerparadise.co.uk**). So far, though, no one seems to have investigated the same sort of beer swaps for bottled beers that Crouch Vale and others do for cask beers – perhaps it's time someone tried. In the meantime you might consider pooling deliveries with one or more of your small brewing neighbours to target specialist shops in other parts of the country. If you can jointly rustle up an order of 60 to 70 cases (and in some cases, small shops will "share" orders with others), it's worth making up a pallet, which can be delivered anywhere in the country by a groupage distributor such as Palletways or Palletline for less than £50.

For complete details of specialist off-licences refer to the *Good Bottled Beer Guide* by Jeff Evans, published by CAMRA every two or three years and therefore reasonably up-to-date.

Hotels and Restaurants

Brewers large and small have long bemoaned the fact that however good their beers are, the foodie end of the on-trade simply won't take them seriously. Wine lovers are well catered for: no restaurant would be caught dead with Piat D'Or or Blue Nun on its list. But ask for a beer in a restaurant with a wine list that starts at £20 and you're likely to be offered a bottled international lager, take it or leave it. Chefs and sommeliers are, by and large, horribly ignorant about beer. I was consulted on what real ales Gordon Ramsay Holdings should stock in its new pub in north London, the Warrington, and Ramsay's executive chef suggested Caffrey's! I also once, many years ago, had the temerity to complain that there were no American beers on sale in the American Bar at the Savoy; I might at least have expected Budweiser or Miller, although

I suppose Sierra Nevada or Rogue would have been too much to hope for. I got a very haughty reply saying that these beers were too expensive. So does The Savoy buy its wines on price?

National newspapers are willing conspirators in this neglect of beer – all the broadsheets have wine writers; not one has a beer writer. If, grudgingly, the food and drink editor condescends once in a while to include a piece about beer, the writing is generally deputed to the wine writer.

This doesn't happen in Belgium, where top chefs as well as humble proles place craft-brewed beer among the nation's glories and regularly use it in cooking, as well as stocking it in their restaurants. In desperation, the British brewing industry declared 2004 as "The Year of Beer and Food", laying on food and beer banquets, dishing out recipe and beer-matching cards, and promoting food-friendly beers alongside the fine and not-so-fine wines in the dining rooms of their managed houses. It was a promotion that frankly sank without trace, not through lack of effort or lack of merit, but through the total indifference of the media and the catering trade.

True, a couple of high-profile restaurateurs sourced pretty skimpy beer lists almost as a token gesture. But the fact that Michel Roux Jr turned to InBev for all the beers on the highly publicised list he introduced at Le Gavroche demonstrates the scale of ignorance about beer at the top end of the catering trade.

Bottled beers ought to be the ideal way for hotels and restaurants to introduce foreign visitors and native gastronauts alike to the "wine of the country". Bottles are easy to store and dispense; they have a long shelf-life, so they won't go off; and they can be bought tentatively, a case or two at a time, so the financial risk is no more than the chef's teenage daughter's pocket money. For a restaurateur, a beer list alongside the wine list creates consumer interest and is a good point of difference.

These are strong plus points with which enterprising small brewers can tackle the more enlightened hoteliers and restaurateurs in the district. But there's more: your beer's local provenance ought to be another attraction in these days of eco-consciousness. If that isn't enough to make the sale, you could always offer the same deal you've offered the farm shop: no money upfront, but a commission on sales. If this is a market you've decided to try, you might have to work harder still to make your sales. Offer to create a beer list tailored to the individual restaurant's cuisine, with full tasting notes and a description of each beer (not too gushing, though – adjectives exist to shore up a bad product, and a good product shouldn't need them). If it doesn't work, you've wasted nothing but time; if it does, you've got your beer into a high-profile outlet that will benefit your reputation as well as your balance sheet. If the beer takes off, you might even get to install your keg font on the bar.

Mail Order and Web Sales

Mail order has always been a classic route to market for small manufacturers and traders in all sectors, including food and drink, who for one reason or another have found it difficult to break into the high street. Since the arrival of the internet mail order, or more properly e-commerce, has become an even more important alternative sales platform.

For obvious reasons, though, bottled products and couriers tend not to mix. Even those who claim to be specialists in the field can be more than a little heavy-handed. This has not deterred wine merchants, many of whom have long been enthusiastic exponents of mail order. But there's a good reason for their enthusiasm. Packaging bottles to withstand the rough handling they will undoubtedly suffer is an expensive and time-consuming business. Couriers aren't cheap either. But when you're selling high-value merchandise such as a case of 12 bottles of good-quality wine at £10 or £15 a bottle, the additional cost of packaging and delivery is a fairly, or at any rate acceptably, small addition to the price and the consumer is happy to pay it. However, the costs are exactly the same for a case of 12 bottles of beer at £2 or £3 a bottle, and suddenly the value doesn't look quite so good.

The cost of sending cases of beer around the country, and more particularly its effect on the consumer's perception of value, is one factor that deters many small brewers from getting involved in e-commerce. Dealing with couriers is an even greater one. It can take a long time to find a courier who understands that glass is fragile, according to Stuart Evans of Uncle Stuart's Brewery of Norfolk. Trying to claim insurance for the inevitable breakages is such a tangle, he says, that given the small sums involved it's not worth the effort. In fact, Uncle Stuart's eventually got out of e-commerce altogether, having tried a long list of courier companies and every variety of protective packaging under the sun.

Not all small brewers have had such an unhappy experience, though. Pitfield Brewery has had a profitable sideline in mail order sales for a quarter of century, and brewer Andy Skene says that after trying many couriers, the proportion of breakages is now well within acceptable limits. The couriers' most annoying habit, he says, is not informing the brewery of breakages. Either they're not delivered at all and are left in a corner of the depot, with brewer and customer wondering what has happened; or they're delivered, rejected and returned to the depot as above, with the brewer not knowing anything is wrong and the customer fuming for a replacement or refund.

Having said that, there are still one or two highly successful e-commerce beer sellers, probably the biggest being Beers of Europe (BoE) of Setchey in Norfolk. It did take a lot of chopping and changing before the company found a courier it could trust (it won't divulge the company's name, though); and BoE's packaging is second to none.

Not only is BoE a big company itself (by the standards of the sector, at any rate), it's also part of a much bigger one. That means there's a lot of waste cardboard on its vast site – enough to justify investing in a shredder that cost "several thousand pounds". BoE now delivers its beers in two boxes, the outer being of chemically toughened cardboard, and the whole parcel is stuffed with shredded card which not only cushions the contents against the courier's buffeting but also efficiently soaks up the spillage if a bottle does get broken. This has proved so successful that BoE now collects and shreds waste cardboard from other factories and warehouses in the area. It's not without cost, though – BoE charges its customers a standard price per delivery of whatever size. In theory the smaller orders subsidise the larger ones; actually the charges never quite cover the expenditure. On the plus side, the standard charge encourages customers to place bigger orders, so it's six of one and half-a-dozen of the other.

In conclusion, is e-commerce worth your while? Having spoken to two or three mail order/e-commerce specialists, I think Uncle Stuart's has been exceptionally unlucky; perhaps the way to find out whether your luck is equally bad is to give it a try. Certainly there are enough brewers and retailers engaged in selling beer around the country by the case to suggest it's worth their while. Thanks to the world wide web, you can now dip a toe into the mail order business without too much financial risk. In the past you had to advertise widely, persistently and expensively to get a worthwhile response, but these days your website should generate enough orders to give you sufficient experience to base a longer-term decision on.

A final word on mail order, and perhaps one that might sway you one way or the other. It's specifically mentioned as a licensable activity in the latest guidance notes from the DCMS, and that means you now need a premises licence to do it. Having said that, getting a premises licence for a mail order operation where the public don't actually come on site should (according to my local council's licensing officer) be a pretty simple procedure, and you're probably getting a premises licence anyway to enable you to hold open days and beer festivals.

Chapter Eight
A Place of Your Own

There's a widely held view in small brewing these days that anyone who opens a brewery without a pub is mad. That's because the sector has become so competitive that custom is increasingly hard to come by and wholesale beer prices have actually fallen to £50 a firkin or even less. As we saw in Chapter Two, though, owning or leasing a pub of your own isn't necessarily the key to success; in fact, the opposite can be true. For a pub is a huge investment – bigger, almost certainly, than the brewery itself; and if it turns out to be a dud, or if you're unlucky enough to appoint an unreliable manager, it can drag the whole enterprise down. The truth is that running a brewery and running a pub are quite different disciplines; despite the superficial appeal of guaranteed retail, most new brewers prefer to concentrate on what they're good at, for the simple reason that they're good at it.

Nevertheless, local brewers are either based at or very closely associated with about 200 pubs. In many of these cases, a publican has decided to turn brewer. Or, as we saw earlier, a brewer has found that a pub's outbuildings make a convenient home. Then there's the handful of local breweries including Beartown, Bath Ales, Ringwood, Butcombe and Hop Back that have made conscious decisions to go into retail wholeheartedly and have set about building up miniature tied estates of their own, although few own more than half-a-dozen or so pubs. But between them, small brewers only own a combined total of about 350 pubs, or 0.7 per cent of the national stock, so they haven't exactly been falling over themselves to invest in licensed real estate.

Still, and even if the hundreds of thousands of pounds it takes to buy a viable or potentially viable pub is a bit rich for your blood, the fact remains that building up a decent delivery route gets harder and harder, making it a good idea to take as much control as you can over the retail of your beer. A pub of your own is one way to achieve it. The whole process starts with getting a licence.

The Licensing Act 2003

The Licensing Act 2003 which came into force in November 2005 brought fundamental changes to the system. Its most highly publicised provision, and the original idea that underlay its long and tortuous journey from green paper to enactment, was the abolition of the century-old concept of "permitted hours". Pubs can now, in theory, open whenever they choose – provided, of course, the licensing authority agrees.

That was the Act's second main provision – it took the licensing function away from the magistrates and awarded it instead to district and borough councils. What this means, in practice, is that there is much wider and more detailed consultation than in the old days. The Act not only demands that licensees understand and uphold public policy on alcohol-related disorder, protection of minors and so on; it also ensures that the police and fire services as well as the local community are closely involved in granting liquor licences and imposing conditions.

In one sense this is a headache for licensees. Getting a new licence, or having an existing one varied, is far more costly and time-consuming than it used to be. On the other hand, you only have to jump through the council's hoops once; when you've done it, you're on a much more secure footing than you used to be. Provided you respect the terms of your licence, it's hard for the police or neighbours to get it reviewed or even revoked (although the Act does give the police powers to close "trouble pubs" on the spot). You've filed your flight-plan, as it were, in exhaustive detail and everyone concerned has had a chance to suggest alterations and restrictions. Everything has been openly negotiated and agreed, and as long as you stick to the operating schedule that the council has approved, nobody (in theory, at least) has a beef.

Another important provision of the 2003 Act was to split liquor licences in two, so you now have to have a personal licence as well as a premises licence. Ill-informed critics claimed this merely added another layer of bureaucracy to an already growing pile; in fact, it ended the cumbersome old system of licence transfers and made it much easier for licensees to migrate from pub to pub.

In the old days, when there was just the one licence, a "protection order" had to be granted whenever a pub fell vacant in order to allow it to trade while a new licensee was appointed. This meant a day in court for someone – normally the brewery area manager – and another when a new tenant or manager was finally appointed. If the new appointee was found to be inadequate for some reason, the procedure had to be gone through again; if a pub was proving hard to let or was going through a rough patch, there could be several licence transfers in the space of a few months. Magistrates were often critical when they had to hear serial transfers for the same premises, which they occasionally threatened to close down. Under the new system, the publican and the pub have their own licences, and the fuss of transfers has been almost entirely eliminated.

CASE STUDY

Warminster Maltings
"Warranty of Origin" points the difference

Appellation d'Origine Contrôlée (AOC or AC for short) was originally introduced by the French to restrict the use of the name Roquefort to cheese produced and matured in a defined area, by a particular method, using ewe's milk. The French then adopted the same principle for each of their wine appellations. With the clamour in the UK for "local" food, the opportunity to originate beers has never been better, and a wonderful chance for small brewers in particular to achieve another point of difference. This is why Warminster Maltings introduced its "Warranty of Origin" label.

From harvest 2006, Warminster Maltings has offered brewers the opportunity to have domain over their barley/malt supply, by creating a complimentary appellation categorised by variety of barley, geographical domain, soil type, husbandry best practice, farm assurance, and harvest quality criteria. Added to this are the malting protocols for floor-made malt.

Deliveries of malt from the scheme all carry a numbered Certificate of Compliance, and participating breweries will be licensed to use the "Warranty of Origin" logo on the bottle or even the pump clip.

Chris Garratt of Warminster Maltings modestly shares the credit for the scheme: "It was one or two of our brewer customers who first floated the idea, and it seems our first thoughts were perhaps too prescriptive.

"Since the inception of our Warranty of Origin scheme, we, together with many food producers in the UK, have experienced a huge increase in customer awareness of the provenance of their raw materials."

Reduced food miles and green credentials are important, and to be able to demonstrate this by identifying specific growers has proven to be very important.

Warminster Maltings is able to identify farms that are very pleased to be linked to a nearby brewery and to host a visit to the farm to inspect the crops. Similarly, reciprocal visits to the maltings and to the brewery help educate and inform all involved in production and marketing.

An example of this is the Cerne Abbas Brewery: its barley is grown within sight of the brewery and each year's harvest is celebrated with events within the community for the benefit of all those involved.

www.warminster-malt.co.uk

Personal Licences

A personal licence is not all that hard to get and it's worth your while holding one even if you have no immediate plans to acquire a licensed premises. Possession of a personal licence removes an otherwise almost insuperable bar to holding beer festivals or open days at the brewery; and it also allows you to retail liquor on other occasions – outdoor bars or beer-tents at the local village show, for instance. You can also hold the licence for a third party's beer festival – the local Lions Club or Rotary, or even the CAMRA branch of which you ought, by now, to be a member – where your beers will, of course, be prominently on sale. If, as many local brewers do, you run outside bars at public functions on unlicensed premises – a ceilidh at the village hall, for instance – a personal licence is now indispensable. It is also usually necessary if you sell your beer at farmers' markets – very few of them are held in venues that have premises licences.

National Certificate for Personal Licence Holders

The personal licence is issued by your local council and costs £37, and you'll also need a Disclosure and Barring Service (DBS) check at a cost of £25. Before you apply, you'll need a National Certificate for Personal Licence Holders, and to get one of those you have to attend a one-day training course which has a 40-question multiple choice exam at the end. This will cost about £300 but prices vary quite widely between the various training providers. The British Institute of Innkeeping accredits some 500 training providers who run courses at over 5,000 locations all over the country – to find one, visit **www.biiab.org**. These training providers did not appear overnight when the Act came into force; for some time previously, magistrates had been stipulating that the requirement for applicants to demonstrate that they were "fit and proper persons" included not only a clean record but also some modicum of training. Many of those who set up as trainers were extremely experienced publicans or brewery staff, so the Act's training requirement really only codified what had been existing common practice. Many times the fear has been expressed that this compulsory training would prove a turn-off to the kind of individualistic mavericks who had often made top-class licensees in the past. But a quick look at the syllabus reveals it to be an extremely practical affair and one that even the most colourful of would-be publicans should be able to complete without having the individuality entirely squeezed out of them.

The sheer number of training providers means you can shop around for the cheapest, but before enrolling do make sure that they actually teach the one-day course, rather than just the five-day National Certificate in Licensed Retailing course. Not all of them do. For general information on the subjects covered by the course click on "find a qualification" on the BIIAB home page; then click on "search" under the drop-down box at the foot of the page; and finally click "Level 2 National Certificate for Personal Licence Holders". Your local authority's liquor licensing department should give you an application form before you apply for the licence itself. The best explanation of the 2003 Licensing Act I have come across is at **www.legislation.gov.uk/ukpga/2003/17/contents**. It's long but well worth studying in detail, because even if you have been too ambitious in your plans to acquire your own pub, there are other uses for a premises licence.

Premises Licences

Your personal licence gives you leeway to indulge in a limited amount of retail on your premises – you can apply to hold up to 12 brewery open days or beer festivals a year, for instance, by submitting a temporary events notice. Increasingly, though – and especially if you've found a location that is worth visiting in its own right – some more regular form of retail is part of the local brewer's business model. It might just be selling polypins of bright beer at the door, it might be running a brewery shop, it might be establishing a visitors' centre with its own bar, it might be running a thoroughgoing brewery tap open to all and sundry. For any of these activities, you will need a premises licence for among its many revolutionary aspects, the Licensing Act 2003 swept away two previous distinctions that made a retail operation of limited scope an easy option.

Licence Definitions

The first change was to redefine the term "wholesale". Before the Act came in, this was an expression of quantity, which meant that Majestic Wines outlets didn't need to be licensed because they sold alcohol only in wholesale quantities – by the case. It also meant that breweries and cider farms could sell wholesale quantities – a 36 pint polypin or a five gallon polycask – to members of the public without a licence. Not any more. The Act redefined "wholesale" as sales by a producer or distributor to licensed retailers, not to the public – a definition which, you may feel, better reflects the real meaning of the word.

The second was to sweep away the distinctions between full on-licences (for pubs), restricted on-licences (for restaurants) and off-licences. Getting an off-licence used to be a virtual formality – an application supported by a site map would be followed by an inspection by a panel of magistrates, and then a five-minute appearance in court with the payment of a nominal fee. I myself held an off-licence for a while, and getting it was simplicity itself. But all the different categories have now been subsumed under the general heading "premises licence", and the procedure for getting one is the same whether you only intend to sell polypins at the back door or to turn part of your premises into a pub.

As mentioned earlier, the new-look licensing procedure is principally about consultation and ensuring that you understand your responsibilities. There's a fearsome-looking 16-page form to fill in, but if you download it from your local council's website and give it a thorough read you'll see that much of it isn't relevant to you.

That's one of the (admittedly slight, in this case) drawbacks to the new one-stop licensing procedure: a single form has to cover every licensable activity including showing films, putting on plays, promoting boxing matches and so on, which makes it a pretty bulky document. But most of it isn't concerned with liquor licensing at all and need not concern you, and the trickier sections, such as those to do with carrying out the council's licensing objectives, will be covered in your training course. (By the way, and although the form doesn't say so, the section covering "performance of dance" specifically excludes folk dancers such as the local morris side and their more extreme variant, molly dancers.)

The form, then, is fairly simple – you shouldn't need a solicitor to help you fill it out, and it should only take you a day or at most two. But the form is only the last part of the application process. You will also need to advertise your application in the manner prescribed by the licensing authority (which is not a new requirement); you will need to submit an accurate and intelligible plan of the premises, although hiring a proper draughtsman to do it probably won't be necessary; and you will need to submit copies to the "responsible authorities" (fire, police and so on) as stipulated by the licensing authority. Just as important as correctly observing the formalities is to consult as widely as possible in advance, both with neighbours (and the term "interested parties" includes schools and businesses as well as residents) and with the "responsible authorities" and the council's licensing officers. As with your planning application, if you do your homework thoroughly, the application you finally submit should be bomb-proof.

Council Licensing Officers

The key to dealing with council licensing officers, as with planning officers, is to be calm, rational and friendly, and not to regard them as jobsworths to be either bamboozled or placated or both.

If treated with respect, they can be – and indeed most of them want to be – extremely helpful, and can give you the advice that makes sure your application succeeds. They can suggest ways in which the four licensing policy objectives can be met, many of which you may not have thought of. They will give you many invaluable tips, such as how to present the general description of the premises (section three of the application form) and the more detailed operating schedule as flexibly as possible, so you don't have to keep varying your licence whenever you want to try something new. They will have issues of their own to raise too – you might, for instance, be in or near an area where public drinking is prohibited, and they may ask what steps you propose to deter customers from buying takeaways to drink in the street. (The best answer to this is to stress that your shop, if you have one, won't be selling cheap cans of lager or cider but extremely expensive bottles of hand-crafted ale – although once you've made this commitment you will be bound by it.) They may very well also want to know what provisions you have in mind for parking, toilets, noise abatement, control of numbers and public disorder contingency planning should you be hoping to run on-site beer festivals or open days. Going into this kind of detail may seem a bit premature, but it's as well to have considered such matters as site layout, advance publicity and limiting numbers even at this early stage.

Brewery Tours

More and more, brewers large and small are treating brewery tourism – guided tours and visitors' centres – as profitable parts of their businesses.

Brewery tours have been with us for many years, but have traditionally been seen, by established mainstream brewers and newcomers, as a sort of bolt-on – something you do as an after-hours profile-raiser for your trade customers and local CAMRA branches.

Typically, the brewer or a member of the brewing staff would be detailed to conduct the tour, which would be followed by a few sandwiches and some free samples in any space that happened to be convenient and available. Larger breweries might take on a retired employee or simply a knowledgeable enthusiast to conduct the tours, but essentially the whole thing would be pretty ad hoc. Some breweries – especially those that had grown higgledy-piggledy over the years and were an obstacle course of steps, pipes, slippery bits and so on – were unhappy about giving tours at all and only did so as an occasional necessity. But demand grew, because breweries are interesting in a way that hosiery mills and plastic extrusions factories aren't (mainly because of the nature of the product!); slowly brewers came to see that here was a way of marketing themselves not just to key accounts and special interest groups but to the general public as well.

Planning the Tour

If you're going to run tours seriously, you need to do it properly, which means devoting time, thought and investment to it. The very basics, in investment terms, are a comfortable and suitably decorated lounge where people can sit and enjoy their samples after the tour, and decent loos. You need to devote some thought to making the tour interesting too – chances are, if you're a new brewery, that your site and plant aren't going to be too picturesque or have much history, so you need to work at making the tour as entertaining as possible. A confident, well-briefed and characterful tour guide who doesn't mumble but doesn't drone on and on either can make or break the whole thing (this is a branch of showbiz, after all). Samples of hops to smell and malt to chew are essential. Posters or wall-plaques explaining each step in the process create interest. Any "breweriana" you can rustle up adds atmosphere – difficult if you're a newcomer with no history of your own, but not impossible. CAMRA beer festivals usually host breweriana stalls and auctions.

The question with tours, though, is how far to take them. Are they still an after-hours bolt-on and even a bit of a distraction, or are you going to go the whole hog and organise and promote them properly? Often, demand for tours grows by word of mouth, and you may find yourself in the position of having a decision forced on you: are you going to turn down requests for guided tours you can't manage; or are you going to give in and provide the right facilities to meet the demand? Once you've done that, you have to sustain the level of demand, or whatever investment you've made could be wasted. The time to make up your mind about the potential of your brewery itself, then, is early on.

There's also the question of whether offering free samples as part of the charge for the tour constitutes a "licensable activity" under the 2003 Act. My local licensing authority thinks it isn't, because the main purpose of the activity is not the retail of alcohol. Others might think differently, and as there has yet to be a test case to decide who's right, it's wise to check what the local line of thinking is. Even those who think it isn't licensable will warn you against abusing their good will. If you are charging enough for a five-minute tour to cover seven or eight pints as well, it will be counted as "hidden retailing" – a tried and tested concept that goes way back to the days when shops were shut on Sunday except for the sale of perishables (the test case was a furniture shop convicted of Sunday trading for selling bunches of carrots with free sofas thrown in).

Brewery Shops

The next logical step is to add a small shop. Visitors like to have something to take away with them – a branded polo-shirt, perhaps, or a brewery beer glass. Or even some of its beer. A little souvenir and merchandise counter is easy enough to organise and adds value to the tour, from both the visitor's point of view and, of course, your own. But selling bottled beer or bright beer in polypins to take away is definitely a licensable activity and one for which you will require a premises licence as well as your own personal licence.

Many breweries now run a shop selling their own beers and branded merchandise and perhaps a little local produce – honey, cheeses, jam, chutneys and the like. It can be a valuable generator of cash-flow, but there are cost implications. The most obvious one is that you have to have someone to run it, even when it's not busy. It has to be open at the stated times – nothing upsets shoppers, some of whom might have come a long way to buy your beer, like turning up when the shop says it's going to be open only to find it's shut. So someone has to be there all the time. If it's rarely busy, and you have someone at the brewery to run the office – to do the paperwork and take telephone orders – they might as well answer the shop bell too. The shop can also be the collection point for customers who have ordered polypins of bright beer for parties and other functions. The critical decision comes when the shop gets too busy to be run as an adjunct to your book-keeper's job description but not busy enough to justify a full-time employee. That's the point at which you have to decide which way to jump – whether to close down a profitable sideline, or invest in making it a separate profit-centre in its own right.

A handful of brewers have jumped in with both feet and expanded their on-site retail sideline into a thoroughgoing beer shop selling not only their own products but beers from other breweries, traditional ciders, country wines and imported speciality beers as well. It's a big investment, though. If you visit Hog's Back Brewery in Tongham, Surrey, or Tucker's Maltings in Newton Abbot, Devon (which is also home to the Teignworthy Brewery), you will find not hastily kitted-out sheds but beautifully designed and decorated boutiques with huge ranges of all sorts of wonders. They were not cheap to develop; they are not cheap to keep stocked; they are not cheap to staff, and they are not cheap to promote. Such places often acquire legendary status and generate significant custom simply by word of mouth, but you can't build that into your business plan!

Customer Car Parking

One key area for consideration when planning a shop is customer parking. There are two matters arising from this. One is that neighbours may object to your licence if they think it will mean customers having to park in the surrounding streets. Another is that customers buy more when they can load their purchases straight into their car boots. Hackney Council's decision to ban parking in Pitfield Street was a contributory factor in the demise of the Beer Shop in Hoxton. But at Beers of Europe at Setchey near King's Lynn, which has enough parking for a fleet of trucks, customers browsing among the treasure-packed aisles aren't deterred from trying one of these and a couple of those, by the knowledge that they've got to carry the whole lot 500 metres back to their car or take it all home on the bus somehow. In addition, the knowledge that there's plenty of parking brings avid beer-lovers to Setchey from astonishing distances. So if you plan to make a shop a significant part of your business, you will need adequate customer car parking.

CASE STUDY

Wild Beer Brewery
Brewing beer to get a reaction

The Wild Beer Co was born out of a love of fermentation, barrel-ageing and most importantly, flavour. The beers are brewed using modern creative techniques and ingredients while producing some of the world's oldest beer styles.

Established in 2012 in a 24 hectolitre plant on a farm in Westcombe, Somerset, the Wild nature of the beer is displayed in the alternative fermentations and unorthodox yeasts it uses alongside a barrel-ageing and blending programme. The company's house wild yeast was captured in a neighbouring cider orchard and the brewers often forage seasonal wild ingredients for their beers.

One of its more unusual one-off beers, Of The Sea, had a shellfish twist. It used 30 live lobsters, cockles, Kombu seaweed, sea salt, sea herbs, star anise and saffron to produce the 7% ABV brew.

The team like to brew beers which get an emotional reaction from people. The lobsters and other ingredients were put into the wort boil for 12 minutes. The crustaceans were removed and while staff enjoyed a team lunch of lobster rolls, the shells were grilled to intensify their flavour and then put back in at the end of the boil. They then extracted all the food debris, added saison yeast and left it to ferment for one week and to undergo a period of maturation for two weeks.

The output of the beer was limited and only 120 kegs and 8,000 bottles were put on sale. The fishy beer might not be to everyone's taste, but the reputation of the brewery has grown quickly. By the time it was only 18 months old, it had already exported to over a dozen countries with growing demand in the US, southern Europe and Scandinavia. Today the company exports to 22 countries.

In 2013, it was able to purchase extra brewing capacity and a new bottling line with the help of a grant from the REG Programme and the Rural Development Programme for England.

Wild managing director Andrew Cooper said, "The bottling process had become a real bottle-neck for the business, and with growing demand we knew we had to find some new equipment. The grant and support we have received from the REG Programme has meant that we have bought a really good piece of equipment and allowed us to grow our capacity, which will allow us to confidently plan our growth over the next few years."

The new bottling line allowed Wild Beer to increase bottle production to over 1,500 bottles an hour. Brewing director Brett Ellis said, "Far too often we had found ourselves bottling long into the night to get orders ready to go out. The new equipment means we can achieve a more consistent quality to our bottling in a fraction of the time."

Selling beer to the US has become a focus for the company. Regular consignments of bottles are sent over, but so is beer for putting into kegs. The company sends draught products out in tank containers that are kegged by the importers, B.United, at its facility in Connecticut, before being dispatched all over the United States.

Andrew said, "We're thrilled with our growing sales in America. Export is a key focus for the business; it was always at the centre of our business plan, as we felt that whilst the UK market was becoming more adventurous, some of our more esoteric beers would only ever sell in quite small volumes in the UK's very traditional beer scene.

"I have just returned from my first visit to the States so that we could get a better understanding of which of our brands would sell best and to get a better understanding of the market over there. The trip has already led to an increase in sales and helped to grow interest in some of the beers we will release in the US in the future."

The company now plans to build a new, state of the art brewery, develop its current brewery and develop its growing bar and restaurant business.

In early 2017, the brewery successfully completed an equity crowdfunding round on Crowdcube raising £1.7m. Now, it is preparing to expand and build a new 50,000 sqft, destination brewery at the Bath and West Showground, which is near Shepton Mallet, Somerset.

Andrew said, "Our aim is to stay at the forefront of the UK wild fermentation and barrel-ageing beer scene and enable us to continue growing our business, and the industry, for many years."

www.wildbeerco.com

Brewery Visitors' Centres

The need to entertain tour parties saw sample-rooms morph first into shops and then into hospitality suites with bars and loos and displays of brewery memorabilia ferreted out from dark corners – when Greene King closed its maltings, for example, enough material came to light to fill an entire museum.

Breweries had often made a modest charge for tours, to cover the guide's pay and the cost of the free samples. But they had still seen tours more as a marketing tool than as a paying part of the business. Now they saw income from extra drinks for tour parties over and above the free samples, and sales of bottled beer and branded merchandise as profitable activities in their own right. In the last 15 years many established breweries have opened visitors' centres in a bid to slot themselves into the wider tourism industry.

In time, then, your well-conducted tours and small shop counter might grow into a fully fledged visitors' centre, open throughout the day. This is a different level of operation – requiring paid staff, for one thing. Whether to take this step depends very much on your location and premises.

If you're in a new unit on an industrial estate on the edge of a northern industrial town, the chances that you'll make much of a tourist attraction are pretty slim (although even northern industrial towns have their tourism initiatives these days, so don't dismiss the possibility out of hand). If you're in a historic barn on a picturesque farm in Devon, though, or in a converted 18th-century silk mill in a quaint old Cotswold town, it's a very different proposition. Either way, before making plans, consult those who know. The local council and local tourist board will be able to provide useful information on local visitor numbers, levels of investment in local tourism and the possible availability of grants. The council and the tourist board will also be able to offer ongoing practical help in marketing and promoting your visitors' centre. You may even find that a sound and well thought-out proposal to develop your brewery as a visitor attraction is a plus-point in your planning application – especially as promoting self-sustaining rural communities is one of the 2003 Licensing Act's stated objectives.

Finally, never forget the marketing value of welcoming people into your brewery and sending them away with a story to tell their drinking buddies and, hopefully, your logo emblazoned on their glass or shirt. You've entered the tourism industry now, and it's essential to send your visitors away satisfied. That means never doing anything half-heartedly. If visitors feel they've had a substandard experience at your brewery, the feeling of dissatisfaction will embrace your products as well – and they'll be telling their friends and neighbours bad things about you when they get home.

Your Pub

All this brings us back rather neatly to where we started – whether or not to invest in a pub of your own. Running a pub, as I have said, is a very different business from running a brewery:

- You will be face to face with the public, and if you're no good at it you'll soon come unstuck.
- You will be hiring staff – maybe a manager for the pub, certainly bar staff and cleaners and possibly kitchen staff as well – and employment law is a whole new area of knowledge in itself.
- You will need to maintain investment in customer facilities – scuffed carpets and chipped urinals need to be replaced.
- There is an unimaginable tangle of compliance issues – you wouldn't believe the amount of time the average publican spends on paperwork these days. It's not something you want to slide into without thinking hard about it first.

But just by running brewery tours, a shop and maybe a visitors' centre, you will be gradually acquiring the marketing, planning, budgeting, administrative and supervisory skills you'll need to run a pub – or pubs.

One of the best ways to learn is to do, and gradually stepping up the retail side of your brewery will enable you to learn a step at a time, even leaving yourself leeway to fail without failing too disastrously. You are also, at each stage of development, increasing the sale value of your business without investing too much at a time.

Buying a pub may be your next logical step, but it's a big one. It's a very expensive and extremely complicated business and calls for detailed professional advice from one of the many specialist estate agents, correctly termed licensed trade property brokers, such as Christie & Co, Fleuret's, Guy Simmonds or Humberstone's. Like ordinary estate agents, they also offer financial advice, and in some cases run full licensed trade training courses as well.

CASE STUDY

Windsor & Eton Brewery

Never mind the castle, come and see the brewery

Windsor & Eton might be only seven years old but it has quickly made its mark, and has done much more than just restore brewing to the town of Windsor after an absence of 79 years.

The company was set up by four friends who had plenty of experience working for the big brewers as well as the food industry, who wanted to do their own thing and have some fun instead of working their socks off for a faceless machine.

One of the founders, Paddy Johnson, started in brewing back 1979 – at the original Courage brewery by Tower Bridge in London. He said, "I was straight out of university, clutching my degree in Biology. I loved it from day one and decided to get properly trained – taking an MSc in Brewing, followed by a selection of other industry exams, leading to my becoming a master brewer.

"I've worked for nine breweries across the UK as well as gaining valuable experience in breweries abroad. Windsor and Eton was my entrée into the world of small-scale craft breweries, and I haven't looked back since."

Rather than harbouring big ambitions for fast growth followed by a quick sale as others have done, the company's focus has been on building a stable, sustainable, family business that's well respected by brewers and customers.

It was on a mission to make Windsor more famous for its beer than any other attraction, whilst challenging all industry and product conventions. In the brewhouse, British tradition is married with new world pizzazz and Pacific Rim flavours. Its mash tun and fermenters are often filled with exotic flavoursome ingredients such as Imperial malts, Chinook and Simcoe hops, jaggery sugar, cardamom and coriander.

Paddy said, "Windsor and Eton has been quick to establish a reputation for traditional cask, keg and bottle beers but we also wanted to create a brand that would appeal to the exciting and emerging market for new-wave craft beers.

"My son, Kieran, joined the brewery four years ago and was really interested in all aspects of the craft beer scene, as well as cuisine. So, we let him loose to try out some edgy recipes under the Uprising brand. The name and imagery depicts young brewers as ravens

187

flying off with the brewing crown, doing things their own way and disregarding the Old Guard.

"These craft beers have been an instant success and can now be found nationally, in a range of establishments, from Wetherspoon's to Waitrose. They are designed for beer aficionados, especially our Christmas beer – ScumBag Maggot (named after a line in The Pogues' Christmas hit "Fairytale of New York") – designed to represent lead singer Shane McGowan. So, to that end it's all about imperial stout, laid down and aged in wooden Irish whiskey barrels and finished with juniper berries."

Two years ago the company canned one of its beers for the first time.

Paddy said, "On the back of critical acclaim for Uprising's Treason West Coast IPA, we were asked to enter it into a canned beer competition. A very small volume was packaged, courtesy of the can makers, especially for this competition and it did incredibly well in what's considered the competition for UK craft beer in cans – namely the Indie Beer Can Festival.

"Treason West Coast IPA won Best Ale in can; Best New Beer in can; and finally Best Overall Beer in can – effectively sweeping the board. The beer also won gold medals with SIBA and at the International Beer Challenge. These wins plus the excitement generated amongst consumers led to us being asked to supply the beer in can for every JD Wetherspoon in the country. Since then, distribution has grown, with M&S recently taking a large delivery."

According to Paddy, canning has clear benefits. "Canned beer has two main advantages: from a quality point of view, the complete lack of light interaction is especially useful in what is a very heavily hopped product, therefore susceptible to light-strike flavours. Also, a complete seal means that if we get the product packaged with low dissolved oxygen, the beer's stability is really good.

"From the marketing point of view, cans are really attractive – offering great branding coverage across the whole pack. Furthermore, cans are easy to carry and very light-weight, making them perfect for festivals and concerts – which is exactly where our consumers want to enjoy a contemporary beer."

Thus far, the company has been sending its beer out to another brewer to be canned.

"As we don't, yet, have our own can line, we tanker the beer off-site to our good friends at Fourpure Brewery in Bermondsey. Their technical knowledge has been second to none and, as with most craft brewers, we've found them to be extremely collaborative," said Paddy.

However, technically they have found that canning is not the same as putting a beer into a keg or cask. Paddy explained: "We've had to learn how to present beer to the canning line that has low enough dissolved oxygen and yeast count levels. This means extreme attention to detail, every step of the way, with nothing left to chance."

He advises other brewers to research their market before canning a beer: "Where are you going to sell the beer and at what price point? In-house canning isn't something you can achieve with very small volumes so you need to understand your market and get on the first rung for the can volumes required. Indie Beer Can Advice can help you research your choices."

The brewery continues to invest in new equipment.

"We're in the process of commissioning additional capacity (+27 per cent) here at the brewery, which follows similar increases every year since we started brewing," said Paddy

"We'll be using this additional capacity to extend our range and supply. We're also starting to trial can-conditioning, which is very exciting, especially as there's only one other brewery doing this in the UK at the moment.

"We're also planning to have a craft bar in town, with old gits like me likely to enjoy the experience as much as the hipsters."

www.webrew.co.uk
www.indiebeercanadvice.com

Freehold or Leasehold

Buying a pub outright has been made much more difficult in recent years by the fact that property prices have soared, and you're more than likely to be comfortably outbid by a developer or supermarket chain. The size of footprint and street-corner location of the typical pub makes it worth far, far more, either as a convenience store or a small residential development, than it could ever be as a going concern; and indeed a significant driver in the number of pub closures in the last decade has been their redevelopment potential.

The alternative is to lease a pub, and the obvious place to go for a leasehold pub is one of the big companies such as Punch, Enterprise or Admiral. The ingoings are, of course, many times lower than the investment required for an outright purchase. But many who have gone down this route have found that the drawbacks outweigh the advantages; and the two main drawbacks are (a) the rent and (b) the tie.

The big lease companies charge high rents because they have to. They sprang into existence in the 1990s on the back of enormous loans, and then expanded on the back of bigger loans still. Then some bright spark came up with a financial instrument called securitisation, by which the pubcos remortgaged their loans on the security of their rental streams – which was a brilliant idea when the pub trade was buoyant but has turned into something of a millstone now that times are harder. Even if they wanted to, the pubcos can't support their tenants by freezing their rents, let alone reducing them; in fact, as more and more pubs close, the more rent they have to squeeze out of the survivors. Although few if any pubcos have a formal "upwards only" clause in the rent review section of their leases, in practice it is extremely difficult to get a reduction!

Worse, you may well find that you can't even sell your own ales in your own pub. These leases are invariably tied, but you can usually negotiate an exemption by paying a higher rent for partial freedom – it's called "rentalising", and has succeeded in trebling the turnover of the iconic Whitelock's in central Leeds, which was let by the Spirit Group pubco to Mason's Brewery in 2012. But there's no guarantee such arrangements will last. One microbrewer I know did just that, leasing a pub in Epsom free of tie from a pubco and building up a very successful and popular business – until the pubco sold the pub over his head to a regional brewer, which immediately ordered him to take his beers off the bar and revert to tied status. He tried to argue his corner, but legally he didn't have a leg to stand on and found himself saddled with an expensive lease that was no good to his brewery at all.

Having said that, there are a small number of free-of-tie leasehold pubs around, often belonging to a private owner. Many stately homes also own the pub in the village outside the wrought-iron grand gates – the derelict stables might even be a base for your brewery. The National Trust actually owns a scattering of historic pubs around the country, one of which – the 15th-century King's Head in Aylesbury – is run by the Chiltern Brewery. The opportunity to acquire a free-of-tie lease like this comes but rarely, although it's worth keeping an eye out in case one does come up.

Then there's Project William. Identify a pub that will complement and enhance your business and Everard's of Leicester will actually buy it and lease it to you. You pay rent, of course, and you also stock Everard's own Tiger bitter and buy your lagers and ciders from the brewery. It's a brilliant scheme under which 10 microbrewers now lease 29 pubs between them, most of which were closed or in deep trouble when Project William came to their rescue. Everard's has invested more than £11.5m in the scheme so far. The remarkable fact about the pubs is that real ale accounts for 63 per cent of beer sales.

Micropubs

A third course of action is to set up your own micropub – that is, to acquire an unlicensed premises and turn it into a pub. This is exactly how the JD Wetherspoon empire was founded; Tim Martin, a barrister by training, started out in the 1970s by acquiring old shoe shops, garages and minimarts and turning them into characterful local pubs. His legal background stood him in good stead, because in those days it was extremely difficult to persuade magistrates to grant new licences. It's easier now, thanks in large part to him; indeed Wetherspoon's has made a speciality out of acquiring character properties such as disused banks and cinemas and turning them into splendid and often award-winning pubs – the Winter Gardens in Harrogate is a brilliant example.

Over the years, many smaller brewers have bought less grandiose historic properties, often in industrial heritage sites, and made wonderful pubs of them. Grainstore's brewery and pub next to the railway station in Oakham is an outstanding example, as is the old station at Codsall in the West Midlands, turned into a fantastic pub by local family brewer Holden's.

Scaled down, this has become the best way into the pub trade for a number of small brewers. The trick is to rent one of the many empty shops either in your high street or in the suburban parade of derelict laundrettes, fit it out as simply and cheaply as possible, and let your beer do the marketing.

The advantages are the low ingoings and the level of turnover needed to trade profitably. Much of Britain's existing pub stock is badly located, too big for the amount of trade that can reasonably be expected, and burdened by unrealistic fixed overheads in terms of pubco rent, tied trade wholesale prices and business rates. Small, in this case, is evidently extremely beautiful. The first micropub – the Butchers Arms in a former butcher's shop in Herne Village, Kent – was opened by Martyn Hillier in 2005; in 2012 he co-founded the Micropub Association (**www.micropubassociation.co.uk**); by the end of 2013 there were 50 of them; and by May 2017 there were 296.

If this rate of expansion continues, it won't be long before each of the 30 older establishments that closes each week will be replaced by a micropub more appropriate to modern trading conditions. But there is a threat on the horizon; and ironically it comes from CAMRA, which purports to be such an enthusiastic supporter. CAMRA's pub preservation wing is campaigning for pubs to be granted a use classification of their own so they can't be converted into takeaways or convenience stores without planning permission. This would allow local people to object to, and hopefully prevent, the conversion of pubs to other uses. If this succeeds, though, it will stop the micropub movement in its tracks. No commercial landlord in their right mind would rent out an empty shop as a micropub if it meant it couldn't quickly and easily be converted back to retail should the worst come to the worst. CAMRA's proposal would simplify ossify a bad situation, filling up our towns and villages with unviable, empty and derelict old pubs while preventing the opening of vibrant and profitable new ones. The Micropub Association and SIBA should be opposing it tooth and nail.

Transfer of Premises Licence

Most of the steps described above assume that you're seeking a completely new premises licence to develop the retail activities based on your brewery site. If you're taking over an existing pub or offie, of course, you won't need a new licence; you can simply transfer the existing one.

I use the word "simply" here advisedly. The sections of the 2003 Act dealing with premises licence transfer look incredibly involved, largely because the Act is seeking to cover all possible eventualities. Actually, the transfer is effected by the outgoing and incoming licensee signing a single form and one of them (you, probably) paying the council a small administration fee. That's not the end of it, though. When you move in, the existing premises licence will still be in force. That covers the opening hours, including seasonal variations as detailed in the operating schedule, and the previous licensee's choice of licensable activities – for instance, you may find you can have a disco but not a folk night, because the existing licence permits dancing but not live music.

That means that if you want to change the way your new pub is run not just substantially but even slightly, you may very well need to change the terms of the premises licence too. You can get an application form to vary the licence from the council – when you do you'll find it's almost identical to an entirely new application.

Before you fill it in, it's wise to go through a thorough consultation exercise with the interested parties and responsible authorities. You might perhaps drop a letter through all the doors within reach asking residents if they had any reservations about the way the pub was run in the past and what improvements, if any, they would like to see. Check with the local police too – there's normally an officer detailed to deal with licensing matters – to find whether the pub had a bad record and, if so, what steps they would recommend to clean it up.

Many might find this sort of consultation tedious or even an unwarranted intrusion. But remember, the best pubs are at the heart of their communities. Your neighbours are also going to be your regulars – unless, that is, you start off by picking a fight with them.

Appendix
Customs and Duty

know of two microbrewers who have been jailed for failing to pay their duty and VAT. (I also know of one who was jailed for taking part in one of those fake export scams, but that's another story.) Two out of the 1,000 or so people who have set up microbreweries in the last 40 years may not seem all that many. But neither of them set out to commit fraud – cash-flow and other problems simply overwhelmed them. The harshness of their sentences shows, nevertheless, that Her Majesty's Revenue & Customs (HMRC) is not to be trifled with. Fortunately, the world wide web makes HMRC much easier to understand and therefore satisfy. These days you no longer have to send away for copies of the various rules and regulations, or search them out in the public library and then spend hours and a small fortune photocopying them. All you have to do is visit **www.hmrc.gov.uk** and look up Notice 226 (June 2017) by clicking first on the "Excise & Other" link, then on "Information & Guides", then on "Alcohols", then on "A guide to alcohol duties & procedures", and finally on "Beer duty". This covers everything any brewer or group of breweries or packager or importer needs to know and even includes downloadable copies of all the forms you will need to fill in. It also gives access to all the relevant bits of legislation in their unintelligible full version. Unfortunately, Notice 226 runs to over 90 pages and is almost unreadable. What follows is therefore an attempt to condense and, to an extent, to translate (although not to interpret) its relevant sections. I have left out sections relating to importers, contract packagers and "connected" breweries, but I have presented my précis in the same order as the Notice (illogical though it often seems) to make it easier for you to check my version against the original.

To find out the actual rate of duty currently payable go back to "A guide to alcohol duties & procedures" and click on "Rates of duty on alcohol". This will tell you that the standard rate brought in by the 2017 Budget was £19.08 per percentage point of alcohol by volume per hectolitre, or hl%, which will have almost certainly gone up again by the time you read this, so do check! In addition, since October 2011 there has been a new rate on high-strength beers of over 7.5% ABV of 25 per cent of the general beer duty. Small brewers eligible for relief still pay the full rate of duty on these stronger beers.

The Basics

In the Alcoholic Liquor Duties Act 1979, beer is defined as including ale, porter, stout and any other description of beer, and "any liquor which is made or sold as a description of beer or as a substitute for beer" whose alcoholic strength exceeds 0.5 per cent alcohol by volume (although no duty is chargeable on beer that does not exceed 1.2 per cent). This includes mixtures such as shandy. Also classified as beer for duty purposes are certain mixtures of beer with alcoholic liquors or "other substances" of less than 5.5 per cent.

Brewers and their production premises must be registered with HMRC's National Registration Unit (address below).

Duty is charged on the quantity and alcoholic strength by volume (see hl% above) and is calculated by reference to the quantity and alcoholic strength stated on the package label or invoice. It becomes payable when the beer is released from or consumed in registered premises or excise warehouses but may also be paid on the constructive removal of beer from "duty suspense" (that is, when it is held on or moved between registered premises or to excise warehouses on registered premises).

To calculate and pay the duty, you must:

- Keep records of all beer produced
- Keep records of all beer leaving registered premises, or otherwise passing the "duty point"
- Keep a beer duty account
- Complete a beer duty return and send it to the Beer Duty Accounting Centre
- Pay by direct debit unless HMRC has agreed otherwise

If you qualify for small brewery relief, you must keep records in a beer production account as above, and records of all "small brewery beer" you handle in duty suspension.

Customs officers will make visits to ensure duty is being correctly assessed and accounted for, based on audits of your commercial, accounting and management control systems and on physical checks. Officers will also carry out physical checks on production, stock and movements of beer in duty suspension. They will normally make an appointment, and if they visit without one, the attending officer must explain why. You have to grant officers access to any area of the registered premises provided the visit is "at a reasonable time".

Your staff must be aware that officers showing the correct ID may visit without appointment.

If you fail to comply with the law or do not account for the correct amount of excise duty, HMRC's options include the issue of assessments and/or civil penalties. These are explained in Notice 208 "Excise assessment" and Notice 209 "Civil penalties: fixed, geared and daily". In many cases you will have the right to appeal. Full details of the appeals procedure are set out in Notice 990 "Excise and customs appeals".

Registration: General

The proprietor, partnership or company intending to brew beer must apply for registration at least 14 days before it starts brewing unless it is covered by one of the exemptions listed below. A separate registration is required for each premises in which beer is produced. Once any queries on the application are settled HMRC will send you a certificate of registration, which will confirm the date of registration and advise you of any conditions which are applicable. You should keep the certificate on the premises to which it refers as officers may ask to see it. Your registration will last until you stop production at the premises. You must notify HMRC in writing both if you intend to cease production and when you have actually ceased.

Except where registration is not required (if you are brewing for personal consumption or for research purposes), production of beer by an unregistered person or on unregistered premises is an offence for which there are severe penalties.

Conditions affecting registration may include:

- Limitation of the extent of registered premises
- Restriction of the classes of beer which may be received or held on registered premises
- Financial security for the duty on beer in duty suspension

If you need temporary additional storage space (for instance, due to seasonal demand), you can apply for temporary registration of any premises under your control within 5km of your registered premises.

To apply for registration, complete the form in Section 32 with a detailed plan of the proposed registered premises. If the whole site is to be registered premises, the plan need only show details of its perimeter. Send them together with a direct debit mandate to the:

National Registration Unit (Alcohol and Tobacco)
HM Revenue & Customs
Portcullis House, 21 India Street, Glasgow G2 4PZ
Tel: +44 (0) 1415 553 369; Fax: +44 (0) 1415 553 555

If you have an enquiry once your application form has been sent, contact the NRU. For enquiries before this stage, contact our National Advice Service.

To obtain a direct debit mandate form, contact the:

Beer Duty Accounting Centre
HM Revenue & Customs
Queens Dock, Liverpool, L74 4AA
Tel: +44 (0) 1517 031 375

You must make a reasonable estimate of the volume of beer that will be produced in the current calendar year in your brewery and enter details in question nine of the application form.

You must note in your business records how you have made the estimate.

If any changes affect your registration particulars, you must write to the NRU giving details. The following changes would require a new application to be completed:

- Change of legal entity, for example, formation of a limited company or
- Change in the ownership or control of your business (in the case of a sole proprietor or partnership)

Other changes that must also be notified in writing:

- Change of address of your registered and/or adjacent premises
- Change of name of the registered person, for example, change of company name
- Change of bank account details
- Change of your duty guarantor
- Cessation of production
- The production of other excisable goods on your registered premises
- Financial difficulties/impending insolvency
- You become VAT registered or de-registered
- You must apply in writing to make any changes to the classes of beer you are registered to hold

Financial Security

The financial security that may be required as a condition of registration is a guarantee by an approved guarantor who undertakes to pay HMRC in the event of an irregularity. HMRC requires financial security to safeguard the duty on all duty-suspended intra-EU movements of beer and may also require guarantees:

- For beer held in duty suspension on registered premises
- For movement of beer within the UK
- To cover beer that has passed the duty point but upon which duty has not been paid.

Further information can be obtained from the National Advice Service.

To arranging financial security, contact the Financial Securities Centre (FSC) at the NRU. Guarantees are the only form of security acceptable to HMRC, which will issue the draft wording to you when you have agreed your level of security. Only HMRC-approved companies may act as guarantors: most banks and insurance companies have this approval, but if you want to check a particular company, ask the Financial Securities Centre.

Duty Liability

Beer becomes liable to duty at the point of production, normally when the earliest of any of the following events takes place. The beer:

- Is put into any package
- Is removed from the brewery
- Is consumed
- Is lost (see Section 10)
- Reaches that state of maturity at which it is fit for consumption

However, duty only becomes payable when the beer passes the duty point: that is, when it leaves duty suspension. Duty ceases to be suspended when:

- The beer leaves registered premises, unless it is delivered to other registered premises, to an excise warehouse; for export or shipment as stores, or to entitled diplomats or members of visiting forces
- The beer is received by registered premises not entitled on their registered holder certificate to hold that class or description of beer

- The beer is constructively removed
- The beer is consumed
- The beer is lost
- The beer is irregularly diverted
- You are no longer registered
- The premises on which you are holding the beer cease to be registered
- The beer is produced and you are not registered to hold beer in duty suspense

Normally, the duty should be paid by the 25th of the month following the calendar month in which the beer passed the duty point. But if it would help your business to account for duty on duty-suspended beer in advance of delivery from registered premises, you may do so. This is known as "constructive removal". The duty should be paid by the 25th of the month following the calendar month in which the beer was constructively removed.

To work out the duty at the end of the accounting period:

- Total the quantity of beer, at each particular strength, which has passed the duty point in the accounting period
- Convert the quantity to hectolitres (hl) to two decimal places
- Multiply the result by the strength of the beer to arrive at the hectolitre percentage (hl%)
- Add together all the hl% totals for the beers of different strengths
- Multiply the total hl% by the applicable duty rate to find the duty figure

If in doubt, contact the National Advice Service.

Small Brewery Relief

Small brewery relief applies to beer, other than that brewed under licence, produced by eligible breweries whether in the UK or overseas. Beer produced under licence is always liable to the standard rate of duty.

A brewer with a single brewery not connected with other breweries must satisfy all of the following conditions for its beer to qualify as small brewery beer:

- No more than 60,000hl of beer may have been produced in the brewery in the previous calendar year

- Less than half of the beer produced in the last calendar year may have been produced under licence
- You must reasonably estimate that in the current calendar year your brewery will produce no more than 60,000hl

These conditions are the same if your brewery is "connected to" other small breweries. The definition of "connected breweries" is determined by Section 839 of the Income and Corporation Taxes Act 1988. The definition of "connection" is very wide, but examples of the circumstances in which people are connected include individuals connected by marriage, family relationships and the like, and companies under the same effective control. This is to prevent, for example, a large business being artificially split into a number of small breweries, each of which would be below the 60,000hl limit.

Estimating the Current Calendar Year's Production

An acceptable estimate must take all relevant factors into account including existing contracts to supply beer and expansion plans. It is important that you make this estimate honestly. If you make an untrue estimate by stating the brewery will produce 50,000hl in the current calendar year when you know that a reasonable estimate would be 70,000hl, HMRC can recover all the underpaid duty. You only have to inform HMRC of your estimate when you apply for registration. You don't need to notify subsequent estimates but you must note in your business records each calendar year's estimate at the time you make it, together with details of how you arrived at the estimate. This information must be kept in the form of a beer production account, which you must keep under Schedule 3(a) of the Beer Regulations 1993.

Beer Production Account

Your beer production account must show your estimate of the current year's production with details of how you arrived at it; the previous calendar year's actual production, to be recorded each month; and the total quantity (in bulk hectolitres to two decimal places) of beer that you have produced in that calendar month, split if appropriate between your own beer and beer produced under licence. The quantity should not be reduced to take account of beer you subsequently determine to be spoilt or unfit for use or for any returned spoilt beer.

At the end of each calendar year, your annual production totals shown in the beer production account will determine your continued eligibility for small brewery relief and the reduced rate for the following year. To be eligible for relief you must use the previous calendar year's production and your estimated production in the current year. Neither production total may exceed 60,000hl.

To qualify for small brewery relief, a new brewer must make a reasonable estimate of the amount of beer that will be produced in the current year which, where appropriate, must be grossed up to arrive at a full calendar year's figure using the formula $E \div (365 - N) \times 365$ where E = the amount of your estimate and N = the number of days in the calendar year before the brewery started production. For example, if you intend to start brewing on 1 August and you estimate, based on the size of the plant, business plans and workforce, that in the five months to 31 December the brewery will produce 6,400hl, the grossed-up estimate is 15,268hl.

Provided that you reasonably estimated that production would not exceed 60,000hl in the current year, then the first 60,000hl will be small brewery beer and subject to a reduced rate of duty. Any beer over that amount will not be small brewery beer and will be subject to the standard rate of duty.

If you share a brewery, the production figure for the purposes of small brewery relief will be the total production within the brewery in that year.

Calculating Duty Relief

If your actual or honestly estimated annual production figure is less than 5,000hl, the reduced rate is quite simply 50 per cent of the standard rate, rounded up to the nearest penny. (Remember, though, that any beer you brew from a third party is charged at the full rate; if beer produced under licence exceeds half of your output, you lose your eligibility for relief altogether.)

If your production figure or estimate (P) is between 5,000hl and 30,000hl, you can calculate the duty per hectolitre as follows: $(P - 2,500)$ over P times the standard rate. If your production figure is, say, 7,500hl then the calculation is: $7,500 - 2,500 = 5,000$; divided by $7,500 = 0.6$ recurring; multiplied by £16.15 = £10.96 per hectolitre times the % ABV.

The calculation for production of 30,000-60,000hl is more complicated still. You will find it expressed as a proper equation on the HMRC website; translated into step-by-step sums, it goes like this.

First, subtract 30,000 from your production figure or estimate P. Let's say P = 45,000hl. Divide the result (15,000) by 100 and multiply by 8.33 to get 1,249.5. Subtract 1,249.5 from 2,500 to get 1,250.5. Subtract 1,250.5 from P (45,000hl, remember?) and get 43,749.5. Divide 43,749.5 by P and you get 0.97221; which multiplied by the standard rate of £16.47 gives you a duty payable figure of £16 per hectolitre, a saving of 47p per hectolitre or, assuming the average strength of your output is about 4% ABV, nearly £85,000 for the year. Even if you're useless at sums, £85,000 is well worth a few minutes' struggle with a calculator.

Irregularities, Losses and Deficiencies

As a registered brewer, you are responsible for the control of beer in your premises. You must have the necessary systems to control and safeguard your stocks and examine critically all losses and deficiencies.

Your records of production and processing should indicate how much beer you lose during routine operations, for example, the losses you normally incur during packaging. For accidental losses, Regulation 14(3) of the Beer Regulations 1993 requires you to record the date and time the loss occurred; a description (product name) and the volume of beer lost, and the alcoholic strength if the loss occurred after production has been completed; and the reason why the accidental loss occurred. If beer cannot be accounted for after the start of production and there is no acceptable explanation, you are liable for duty on the missing beer. You cannot normally offset stock losses against production surpluses.

Normally there is no duty relief of beer that is lost after it has passed the duty point. But if duty-suspended beer is spoilt, you do not have to pay the duty providing HMRC is satisfied that it was unintentionally spoilt, contaminated or otherwise rendered unfit for consumption in the registered premises and has not been consumed.

Measurement of Quantity

HMRC can require duty to be paid on the actual quantity of beer in each container as it passes the duty point. However most brewers do not measure the quantity in each container, but use the "average system" common throughout Europe.

Under this arrangement, the average contents of packages must not be less than the declared contents marked on the can, bottle or label or, in the case of draught beer, on the invoice or delivery note. Within limits the actual contents of each container may be more or less than the declared contents. Packagers using the system must conform to weights and measures codes of practice issued by the British Beer & Pub Association and agreed with Trading Standards. SIBA has a similar code of practice on the contents of kegs and casks. Packagers are obliged to monitor and record the actual quantity of beer in a proportion of packages to ensure they fulfil the code's requirement.

Small Packages

Under the average system of quantity control, duty will normally be charged on the quantity declared on the container for beer delivered in small packages such as cans and bottles. Evidence of compliance with weights and measures legislation will be sufficient to accept the labelled contents as the duty base, unless there are grounds for believing that deliberate duty avoidance is involved. Packagers should exercise "due diligence" to ensure that the can or bottle contains on average at least the amount of beer stated on its label, and that volume in excess of the declared contents is minimised.

To demonstrate that "due diligence" has been observed, you must monitor the filling process to ensure that the quantity put into the package does not regularly or excessively exceed the amount declared on the container. You should record these checks and provide an adequate audit trail to satisfy HMRC that due diligence is being exercised. Where there is evidence of consistent excessive overfilling, additional duty will be due.

Large Pack

To ascertain the quantity in large pack – containers from 10,400 litre capacity such as kegs and casks – packagers customarily fill the containers in accordance with the average contents rules. The quantity of beer in a container will be treated as the average of the samples taken for the purpose of complying with these rules, which permit some latitude in the sampling regime adopted. However, in determining volume for duty purposes, packagers will be expected to maintain a minimum sampling rate of one container per filling head per operating day or 0.1 per cent of a production run of 4,000 containers or more; the samples to be representative of the mix of containers filled. A copy of the sampling protocol you intend to use to assure compliance with average contents rules and for duty purposes should be sent to HMRC.

Some smaller packagers do not take samples but use their containers as capacity measures. To meet HMRC's tolerance requirements, they should ensure that the average capacity of their containers is such that they are operating within the set limits.

Sediment in Cask-Conditioned Beer

Duty need not be charged on undrinkable sediment in cask-conditioned beer provided the customer (for example, the publican) is made fully aware in writing, at or before the time of receipt, of the quantity of beer on which duty has been charged. If, for example, a barrel (163.7 litres) is likely to contain 2.3 litres of sediment, the customer must be made aware by a statement on the label, delivery note or price list etc. that duty has been charged on 161.4 litres (a copy of the notification to customers must be retained). Any sediment on which duty has not been charged cannot be included in any subsequent claims for relief on spoilt beer.

There is no prescribed method for calculating the proportion of undrinkable sediment, but you must be able to satisfy HMRC that the method you use gives equitable results. Sediment levels for each quality of beer and container size must be regularly monitored by brewers and reviewed/amended (as necessary) at least annually and agreed with HMRC. Any changes to recipes/ingredients etc. during the year, that would significantly affect sediment levels must be notified to HMRC and the allowance adjusted accordingly. There is no undrinkable sediment allowance for polypins and mini-pins sold by brewers to the public or on bottle-conditioned beer.

Alcoholic Strength

For duty purposes alcoholic strength is the percentage of alcohol by volume (ABV) in the beer expressed to one decimal place, for example, 4.19% ABV becomes 4.1% ABV. Ignore figures after the first decimal place.

You may use any method you wish to measure the strength of beer as long as it produces results that agree with those that would be achieved using one of HMRC's preferred reference methods (described below). Additionally, if using these or any other methods not based on laboratory analysis, an independent analyst must test the ABV of each of your products at least annually to ensure consistency with calculated results. The results of the independent analyses must be held in your business records.

You must continuously monitor and record your ABV results, which should normally fall randomly on either side of the target strength. The average of your results should equate closely with the declared strength.

It is recognised that ABV may occasionally vary, but provided appropriate action is taken quickly to return the strength of the beer to within its normal specification, due diligence will have been demonstrated. You must keep records of action taken to maintain product strength within control limits.

You must establish the strength of each batch for each of your products. Where beer from one batch is packaged into different container types, such as cans and bottles, you may combine the results. If you can demonstrate to HMRC that based on available information and experience, due care was taken when deciding target ABVs for new and/or infrequently brewed products (and that all decisions, actions etc. were properly recorded), HMRC will accept the label/invoice/ delivery note strength for duty purposes. Customs officers will examine your results and your record of actions taken. Where the results have consistently fallen above your target, they will wish to confirm that action was taken as soon as the problem was identified to bring the process back into control or to change the declared ABV. If you have failed to take such action, an assessment will be raised for the additional duty due. If there is a dispute over the strength, officers may take samples of beer to be analysed to establish the actual dutiable strength of the beer.

Cask- and bottle-conditioned beers will continue to ferment after removal from registered premises, resulting in an increase in strength. You must account for duty on the strength at which you expect the beer to be when it is consumed. This is also the strength that must be shown on the label/invoice/delivery note. And in addition to procedures to establish the ABV at packaging, you must regularly monitor and record the actual strength of each quality of cask and bottled conditioned beer at the expected time of consumption, to establish its alcoholic strength. The precise method and frequency of checking is a matter for you, but you must be able to satisfy HMRC of the accuracy of your results.

Beer Duty Account

A beer duty account is a summary of the beer duty due in each accounting period and must contain the following information:

- The amount of duty due on all beer which leaves duty suspension
- The amount of duty reclaimed on spoilt beer which has been reprocessed or destroyed
- The amount of duty reclaimed on drawback
- The amount of underdeclarations and overdeclarations from previous periods
- The net amount of duty due for the period and the date and method of payment

You should keep the beer duty account in a specific book or ledger opening or on computer, providing you can print a satisfactory legible copy of the account when required.

Records

As a revenue trader you need to keep and preserve certain records and accounts as evidence of your business activities (Revenue Traders Accounts and Records) Regulations 1992. You also have to allow HMRC access to all your business records.

You have to keep a record of:

- Production
- Stock
- Handling
- Buying

- Selling
- Importation
- Exportation of beer

You must normally keep your records for six years. If, however, this causes problems, ask HMRC's National Advice Service if you can keep some records for a shorter period. You must get HMRC's agreement before destroying any business records that are less than six years old. You can keep your records on any form of storage technology, provided that copies can be easily produced and there are adequate facilities for allowing a Customs officer to view them when required. Obtain agreement from the National Advice Service before transferring records. You may be required to operate the old and new systems side by side for a limited period, and HMRC may refuse or withdraw approval if its requirements are not met.

You can keep your records on a computer provided they can be readily converted into a satisfactory form and made available to HMRC when required. If you do keep your records on a computer, HMRC requires access to it.

Beer Duty Returns

The beer duty return (EX46) is the form on which you declare your liability for beer duty in each accounting period. You must make a return of your beer duty liability each accounting period, which will normally be a calendar month. If your duty liability for the month is nil, you must still send a return. If you fail to submit a return on time, you will be liable to penalties. HMRC may estimate the duty which would have been due and to pursue the debt through the civil courts.

If you foresee any problems, you should immediately contact the Beer Duty Accounting Centre.

EX46s are routinely sent out to all registered brewers and packers. If you do not receive a return, you should contact the Beer Duty Accounting Centre.

Each copy of the form has full instructions on how to complete it. You must complete all boxes, writing "none" where necessary. Returns must be completed in ink and any changes must be initialled and dated by the person who signs the declaration – the proprietor, partner, company secretary, director of the company or any other authorised person.

You must ensure that beer duty returns are completed accurately. Failure to exercise due care in completing returns may result in civil penalties. If you deliberately make a false beer duty return you may face prosecution for the offence and incur heavy penalties. You must submit your return so that it arrives not later than the 15th of the month following the accounting period. When the 15th falls at a weekend or on a public holiday the return must be received by the previous working day.

Mixing Beers from Different Brews and of Different Strengths

- Beer that is not in duty suspension may not be mixed with duty-suspended beer
- Beers of different strengths that have passed the duty point may not be mixed until they are sold to the consumer
- You may mix duty-suspended beers only on registered premises or in an excise warehouse
- There are no restrictions on the mixing of beers of the same strength that have passed the duty point
- You may mix small brewery beer with beer of a different rate of duty in duty suspension
- The mixture will not be small brewery beer and therefore will be liable to the standard rate of duty

Additions to Beer

Beer can be primed with sugar to boost its alcohol content on registered premises. A registered brewer planning to prime beer on unregistered premises must seek HMRC approval and keep a record of any such premises at which priming takes place. If you are not a registered brewer or registered holder, you may not prime beer unless HMRC has approved the arrangements. For approval write to the National Advice Service stating the address of the premises at which you wish to undertake priming; the addresses of registered premises from which the beer will be received; estimated annual quantities of the beer to be primed; and the destination of the primed beer. Your records must include the date and time of the priming; the type of beer (product name) that is primed; the quantity and strength of beer that is primed; the type and quantity of primings added; and the quantity and expected strength of the resulting product. These records should be kept on the premises where priming is carried out and made available to Customs officers when requested.

Beer in duty suspension on registered premises can be diluted with water. If you wish to add water to beer elsewhere, before it is sold or supplied to the consumer, you must obtain approval by writing to the National Advice Service. However, if you add water to small brewery beer after it has left the registered premises where it was produced, it will no longer be small brewery beer.

You can add finings (provided they do not contain alcohol) to beer on any premises.

If you wish to mix beer with any substance, including non-alcoholic beverages, after the duty point, you must seek prior approval from the National Advice Service. However, if you only intend to produce drinks whose alcoholic strength is not more than 1.2% ABV, you do not need approval. Shandy of more than 1.2% and its variants are classified as beer. These include shandy made with lemonade, lemon cordial, lemon flavourings, lemon juice or lemon squash; lager and lime made with lime cordial, lime flavouring, lime juice, lime squash or limeade; ginger beer shandy, shandygaff or a mixture of beer and ginger, ginger cordial, ginger flavouring, ginger squash or unfermented ginger beer; beer and fruit cordial, fruit flavourings, fruit-flavoured carbonated water, fruit juice or fruit squash; or beer and any alcoholic liquor or substance other than spirits.

Mixtures containing alcohol other than spirits – for instance, alcopops based on beer – where the end strength is 5.5 per cent or more are liable at the appropriate made-wine rate of duty. Beer mixed with spirits is liable to the spirits rate of duty. This applies even if the majority of the product is beer rather than spirit. There are only two instances where an element of spirit may be used without incurring the spirits rate. These are where there are no spirits in the final product – for example, the spirits are used as a carrier for a flavouring added at an early stage of production – or where the spirits are added in such a small quantity they do not increase the alcoholic strength of the beer.

If you are unsure of the duty category that will apply to any blend or mixture you intend to produce, you should consult the National Advice Service beforehand. It will also advise you of any additional approvals you may need (for example, a made-wine producer's licence).

You can claim duty relief on any beer that has been charged with duty and has subsequently been spoilt or is otherwise unfit for use, provided it is presented for duty reclaim in the same container in which it left duty suspension (unless delivered in bulk). However, where this is not possible for health and safety or other practical reasons, and subject to prior approval from HMRC, the beer may be transferred to other containers.

If a registered brewer buys duty-paid beer that becomes spoilt and they wish to destroy it and claim spoilt beer relief, they must apply to HMRC for approval to do so. In the case of beer imported on payment of duty, only the person who accounted for the duty on importation will normally be entitled to claim relief, but the National Advice Service will be able to provide further information in these circumstances. NB: Spoilt beer does not have to be destroyed if duty relief is to be claimed. It can also be reprocessed – mixed with other beer on registered premises or filtered and/or repasteurised.

You can only claim for the actual quantity of beer destroyed or reprocessed on which duty has been charged. This will depend on whether you use a spoilt beer vessel; destroy directly from cask, keg or other package; or a combination of both. If you wish to decant beer to determine the volume for relief, you must use a gauged and tabulated spoilt beer vessel or establish the volume by using a properly calibrated meter. If you use a spoilt beer vessel to claim relief, you must take a sample for laboratory testing to establish its alcoholic strength. This must be recorded in support of your claim. If you destroy or decant for reprocessing directly from cask, keg or other containers, you can only claim for the actual quantity of beer returned on which duty has been charged. In the case of unbroached containers, you should use the declared contents. Broached containers and depot leakers, which may be unbroached, should have their actual contents measured for duty reclaim purposes. Remember to exclude any undrinkable sediment allowance from the quantity claimed.

To make a claim, total the entries in the spoilt beer record (including those for destructions and reprocessings of spoilt beer) and at the end of the accounting period transfer the total to your beer duty account. To claim relief, enter this total (that is, the spoilt beer relief claimed) in box 12 of your beer duty return.

The following are ineligible for relief:

- Unconsumable beer (for example, sediment in cask-conditioned beer) on which duty was not charged
- Diluted beer (unless HMRC approved the addition of water)
- Adulterated beer (beer containing additions which HMRC did not approve)
- Where no satisfactory audit trail is available

Destroying Spoilt Beer

You must destroy the beer in a way acceptable to HMRC and which makes it unsaleable as a beverage. A Customs officer will advise you if you need to give notice; otherwise you can destroy spoilt beer whenever you wish provided that the following conditions are met:

- A full audit trail is maintained
- The requirements of other regulatory authorities (including the Environment Agency) are observed
- Proper control practices are maintained, including appropriate action at management and supervisory levels

If you are destroying the beer away from your registered premises, the operation must be supervised by a representative of the brewery.

Repayment of the duty will normally require evidence of a full credit of the duty paid value, or replacement of the goods to your customer (or owner of the goods at the time they became spoilt). In cases where an abatement is made to the amount of credit given, you must be able to demonstrate that the abatement is not due to accidental loss, adulteration, dilution after the duty point or similar circumstances.

The minimum amount of relief that you can claim in any accounting period is £50. If you destroy beer on which the amount of relief is less than £50 during an accounting period, wait until the total amount of relief reaches at least £50 before making a claim. This means that one claim may cover beer destroyed during several accounting periods. If the accounting periods cover a change in duty rates, separate entries must be made in the spoilt beer record for beer charged with duty at the old and new rates.

HMRC does not object to bulking of beer at two rates in one

destruction, so long as a system to apportion the total has been agreed in advance.

When beer is either returned to the brewery for destruction or destroyed remotely, Regulation 33(1) of the Beer Regulations 1993 requires you to enter the following details in the destruction section of your spoilt beer record:

- The total volume of spoilt beer destroyed
- The strength of the spoilt beer destroyed
- The date and time of the destruction
- The volume and strength of the beer in each container from which the spoilt beer was directly destroyed
- Evidence of duty charged or paid
- The amount of remission or repayment claimed
- The description of the beer returned by each purchaser for which a claim is made
- The name and address of each purchaser
- The numbers and sizes of each container in which the beer was returned by each purchaser returning the beer

When beer is returned for reprocessing, enter the following particulars in a reprocessing section of your spoilt beer record:

- The date and time the beer was returned for reprocessing
- The volume and strength of the beer, in each container, in which it was returned for processing
- The total volume and strength of the beer reprocessed
- Evidence of the duty charged or paid
- The amount of remission or repayment claimed
- The description of the beer returned by each purchaser for which a claim is made
- The name and address of each purchaser
- The numbers and sizes of each container in which the beer was returned by each purchaser returning the beer

Unless HMRC allows a longer period, the spoilt beer record must be completed within one hour of reprocessing taking place.

Returning Duty-Paid Beer to Duty Suspension

Duty-paid beer cannot be returned to duty suspension unless it is spoilt and comes back for reprocessing. If duty-paid beer is returned to registered premises because of a failed delivery, for example, because a customer is unwilling or unable to accept a delivery or an erroneous delivery has been made, the beer must be separately identified from duty-suspended stock in your records, for example in a failed delivery account.

Beer on which duty has been paid can, subject to certain conditions, be stored with duty suspended beer in your registered premises. No physical segregation of duty suspended and duty-paid beer is necessary. The change of status of any beer from duty suspended to duty-paid must be recorded and the product(s) clearly identified in your records.

Exports

All exports from the UK must be made using the Excise Movement & Control System (EMCS) and be covered by a movement guarantee. The usual practice is to export alcohol under bond from a registered bonded warehouse, which means that exports are conducted without duty having been paid.

Exports of excise goods from the UK to the EU will be treated the same as exports to the rest of the world. This includes moving excise goods to a place of export in the UK.

EMCS is a UK- and EU-wide computer system that is used to record duty suspended movements of excise goods taking place within the UK and the EU. It captures and processes information about the movements online, validates the data entered and allows real-time notification of the dispatch and receipt of duty suspended excise goods.

Exporters must register and enrol for EMCS even if they choose to use a commercial software package or in-house-designed software to record any consignments of duty suspended excise goods they will be sending or receiving.

To export beers, businesses will either need to appoint an export/import agent, or buy software which will allow them to make export declerations themselves. This software interacts directly with HMRC's systems to make export declarations which clear the goods, pay the excise and deal with duty suspension. An agent with access to this software can also do this on your behalf.

All exporters will need an EORI number to continue trading. EORI stands for Economic Operator Registration and Identification. It will allow you to interact with HMRC's systems for export, customs, excise and VAT.

From 1 January 2021 all exporters have needed to submit an electronic export declaration. Brewers should be e able to recover the excise duty on the exported goods by claiming excise duty drawback.

Italy, France, Sweden, Germany, Norway and Spain are the top destinations for exporters of UK craft beer. It is important to ensure the labelling requirements for each country are covered. This will add to the cost especially at the beginning when orders are small. Get it wrong and it can prove to be costly

Determining the Strength of Beer

Method One

(a) A representative sample is to be taken and, after first being cleared of sediment and gas by filtration in an approved manner, a definite quantity thereof by measure at the temperature of 20° C shall be distilled.

(b) The distillate shall be made up at the temperature of 20° C with distilled water to the original measure of the quantity before distillation.

(c) The strength of the distillate made up in accordance with paragraph (b) shall be ascertained by determining its density in air at the temperature of 20° C by means of an approved pycnometer used in an approved manner; and

(d) The strength of beer shall be taken to be the percentage of alcohol by volume in the table entitled "Laboratory Alcohol Table" which corresponds to the density determined in accordance with paragraph (c), except that where the density so determined is between two consecutive numbers in the table aforesaid the strength shall be determined by linear interpolation.

NB: Where the result ascertained by the method specified above is rendered inaccurate by the presence of substances other than alcohol, that method shall be adjusted in such manner as may be approved for the purpose of producing an accurate result.

Method Two

You may calculate the alcoholic strength of your beer by multiplying the number of degrees by which the beer has attenuated by a factor. In order to ensure accurate calculations, the original gravity must be established as soon as possible after collection and before fermentation commences – normally be within one hour of filling the fermenting vessel.

NB: If you add priming sugar to promote secondary fermentation, you will need to calculate the alcoholic strength of the finished product as outlined below.

Step action:

1. Measure the original gravity (OG) within one hour of collection
2. Wait until fermentation is completed – for cask- conditioned beer this will be after secondary fermentation in the casks; then:
3. Measure the present gravity (PG – also known as the specific or final gravity)
4. When you have taken your readings, calculate the alcoholic strength using the formula: $(OG – PG) \times f = a\%$ ABV where:

- OG is the original gravity of the beer
- PG is the present gravity of the beer
- a is the beer's alcoholic strength; and
- f is the factor connecting the change in gravity to alcoholic strength

The value of f is not constant because the yield of alcohol is not constant for all fermentations. In lower-strength beers, more of the sugars available for fermentation are consumed in yeast reproduction than in producing alcohol.

Complaints and Suggestions

If you have a complaint that you cannot resolve on the spot with the Customs officer, or have a suggestion about how HMRC can improve its service, contact one of its Regional Complaints Units.

The Adjudicator, whose services are free, is a fair and unbiased referee whose recommendations are independent of HMRC. You can contact the Adjudicator at:

The Adjudicator's Office
Haymarket House, 28 Haymarket, London, SW1Y 4SP
Tel: + 44 (0) 2079 302 292; Fax: + 44 (0) 2079 302 298
E-mail: adjudicators@gtnet.gov.uk
www.adjudicatorsoffices.gov.uk

Further Information

The British Beer & Pub Association (BBPA) has a series of guidelines offering advice to brewers and packagers. Copies from:

BBPA
Ground Floor, 61 Queen Street, London, EC4R 1EB
Tel: + 44 (0) 2076 279 191; Fax: + 44 (0) 2076 279 123
Email: contact@beerandpub.com
www.beerandpub.com

Further Help and Advice

If you need general advice or more copies of HM Revenue & Customs notices, ring the National Advice Service on **+44 (0) 8450 109 000**, 8am-8pm Mon-Fri.

Directory of Services and Supplies

Please note: The following list is as complete as our research team could make it at the time of going to press. However, it is not exhaustive, and we apologise to any suppliers and services that have been omitted. Many of the firms listed operate in more than one category; however, we have listed them once in the category we believe best represents their sector. It is therefore always worth a thorough check of their websites to see just how wide and varied their activities are. If you would like to be listed in the next edition please email **info@paragraph.co.uk**.

ASSOCIATIONS, CLUBS & SOCIETIES

Brewing, Food & Beverages Suppliers Association (BFBi)
11 Sidestrand, Pendeford Business Park, Wolverhampton, West Midlands, WV9 5HD
www.bfbi.org.uk
+44 (0) 1902 422 303

British Beer & Pub Association
Ground Floor, 61 Queen Street London, EC4R 1EB
www.beerandpub.com
+44 (0) 2076 279 191

Campaign for Real Ale
230 Hatfield Road, St Albans, Hertfordshire, AL1 4LW
www.camra.org.uk
+44 (0) 1727 867 201

Cask Marque
B10 Seedbed Centre, Severalls Park, Colchester, Essex, CO4 9HI
www.cask-marque.co.uk
+44 (0) 1206 752 212

Institute of Brewing & Distilling
44A Curlew Street, London, SE1 2ND
www.ibd.org.uk
+44 (0) 20 7499 8144

SIBA
PO Box 136, Ripon, North Yorkshire, HG4 5WW
www.siba.co.uk
+44 (0) 1765 640 441

BOTTLING MACHINES & SUNDRIES

Advanced Bottling UK Limited (ABUK)
Unit 21, Lincoln Enterprise Park, Newark Road, Lincoln, Lincolnshire, LN5 9FP
www.abuk.co.uk
+44 (0) 1427 890 099

Carlson Filtration
Butts Mill, Barnoldswick, Lancashire, BB18 5HP
www.carlson.co.uk
+44 (0) 1282 811 000

Enterprise Tondelli
Unit 7 College Farm Buildings,
Barton Road, Pulloxhill,
Bedfordshire, MK45 5HP
www.enterprisetondelli.co.uk
+44 (0) 1525 718 288

Krones UK Ltd
Westregen House, Great Bank
Road, Wingates Industrial Park,
Bolton, Lancashire BL5 3XB
www.krones.com
+44 (0) 1942 845 000

Oakbank Products Ltd
6 Fairbairn Road,
Livingston, EH54 6TS
www.oakbankproducts.com
+44 (0) 1506 412 937

BREWING CONSULTANCY & INSTALLATION

Brewing Services Ltd
6 Church Street, Copmanthorpe,
Yorkshire, YO23 3SE
www.brewingservices.co.uk
+44 (0) 1904 706 778

Brewlab Ltd
Unit 1, West Quay Court,
Enterprise Park, Sunderland,
Tyne & Wear, SR5 2TE
www.brewlab.co.uk
+44 (0) 1915 499 450

FlavorActiV Ltd
Parkwood Stud, Aston Park,
Aston Rowant, Oxfordshire, OX49 5SP
www.flavoractiv.com
+44 (0) 1844 396 113

PBC Brewery Solutions Ltd
Unit 1 & 2, Foundry Business Park,
Ordsall Lane, Salford M5 3LW
www.pbcbreweryinstallations.com
+44 (0) 7740 094 677

BREWING PLANT & EQUIPMENT

Abbott & Co (Newark) Ltd
Newark Boiler Works, Newark,
Nottinghamshire, NG24 2EJ
www.air-receivers.co.uk
+44 (0) 1636 704 208

Alan Ruddock Engineering
Unit 6 Shepherds Grove Ind.
Estate, Stanton, Bury St Edmunds,
Suffolk, IP31 2AR
www.brewing-equipment.co.uk
+44 (0) 1359 250 989

Alfa Laval Ltd
7 Doman Road, Camberley,
Surrey, GU15 3DN
www.alfalaval.co.uk
+44 (0) 1276 633 833

Axflow
820 Yeovil Road, Slough Trading Estate,
Slough, SL1 4JA
www.axflow.com
+44 (0) 1753 255 600

Bellingham + Stanley Ltd
Longfield Road, North Farm
Industrial Estate, Tunbridge Wells,
Kent, TN2 3EY
www.bellinghamandstanley.com
+44 (0) 1892 500 400

Brupaks
Unit C2, Rail Mill Way, Parkgate,
Rotherham S62 6JQ
www.brupaks.com
+44 (0) 1709 780 888

Buhler Ltd
20 Atlantis Avenue, London,
Greater London, E16 2BF
www.buhlergroup.com
+44 (0) 2070 556 650

BW Container Systems
Plumtree Farm Industrial Estate,
Bircotes, Doncaster,
South Yorkshire, DN11 8EW
www.bwcontainersystems.com
+44 (0) 1302 711 056

Cockayne Systems Limited
Glenearn Works, Glenearn Road,
Perth, Perthshire, PH2 0NJ
www.cockayne.co.uk
+44 (0) 3330 058 491

Dixon Group Europe Ltd
350 Leach Place, Walton Summit Centre,
Bamber Bridge, Preston,
Lancashire PR5 8AS
www.dixoneurope.co.uk
+44 (0) 1772 323 529

Don Valley Engineering
Sandall Stones Road, Doncaster,
South Yorkshire, DN3 1QR
www.donvalleyeng.com
+44 (0) 1302 881 188

Eastfield Process Equipment
Eastfield Farm, Tickhill, Doncaster,
South Yorkshire, DN11 9JD
www.eastfieldprocessequipment.co.uk
+44 (0) 1302 751 444

Fulton UK
5 Fernhurst Road, Fishponds,
Bristol, BS5 7FG
www.fulton.co.uk
+44 (0) 1179 723 322

Hi-Line Services
56 Britannia Way, Lichfield,
Staffordshire, WS14 9UY
www.hilineservices.co.uk
+44 (0) 1543 258 741

J & E Hall International
Questor House, 191 Hawley
Road, Dartford, Kent, DA1 1PU
www.jehall.com
+44 (0) 1322 394 420

Johnson Controls Inc
72 Buckingham Avenue, Slough,
Berkshire, SL1 4PN
www.johnsoncontrols.com
+44 (0) 1753 693 919

MDM Pumps Ltd
Spring Lane, Malvern,
Worcestershire, WR14 1BP
www.mdmpumps.co.uk
+44 (0) 1684 892 678

Mettler-Toledo Ltd
64 Boston Road, Beaumont Leys,
Leicester, Leicestershire, LE4 1AW
www.mt.com
+44 (0) 116 2 357 070

Moeschle U.K.
Unit 1b, Parkway Rise,
Sheffield, S9 4WQ
www.moeschle.com
+44 (0) 1142 434 463

Samson Controls Ltd
Perrywood Business Park,
Honeycrock Lane, Surrey, RH1 5JQ
www.samsoncontrols.co.uk
+44 (0) 1737 766 391

Seepex UK Ltd
3 Armtech Row, Houndstone
Business Park, Yeovil, Somerset,
BA22 8RW
www.seepex.com
+44 (0) 1935 472 376

**Tanks And Vessels
Industries Limited**
Bankwood Lane Trading Estate,
Bankwood Lane, Doncaster
South Yorkshire, DN11 0PS
www.tanksandvessels.com
+44 (0) 1302 867 328

Verder (UK) Ltd
3 California Drive, Castleford,
West Yorkshire, WF10 5QH
www.verderliquids.com
+44 (0) 1924 221 001

Vigo Limited
Dunkeswell, Honiton,
Devon, EX14 4LF
www.vigoltd.com
+44 (0) 1404 892 100

CANS, CERAMICS, GLASS
BOTTLES & GLASSWARE

Allied Glass Containers
South Accommodation Road,
Leeds, LS10 1NQ
www.allied-glass.com
+44 (0) 1132 451 568

Ardagh Group
Headlands Lane, Knottingley,
West Yorkshire, WF11 0HP
www.ardaghgroup.com
+44 (0) 1977 674 111

Bottle Company (South) Ltd
Unit 1, Pixash Business Centre,
Pixash lane, Keynsham,
Bristol, BS31 1TP
www.bottlecompanysouth.co.uk
+44 (0) 1179 869 667

Burns Crystal Glass
(See Glencairn Crystal)

Dartington Crystal
Torrington, Devon, EX38 7AN
www.dartington.co.uk
+44 (0) 1805 626 262

Forever Crystal
12 Lancaster Rise, Belper,
Derbyshire, DE56 1HF
www.forevercrystal.co.uk
+44 (0) 1773 820 287

Glencairn Crystal
11 Langlands Avenue, Kelvin
South Business Park, East Kilbride,
South Lanarkshire, G75 0YG
www.glencairn.co.uk
+44 (0) 1355 279 717

Pont Packaying Ltd
2 Steuber Drive,
Irlam, Manchester,
M44 5AL
www.ponteurope.com
+44 (0) 1618 741 930

Owens-Illinois Inc
P.O. Box 6068, Edinburgh Way,
Harlow, Essex, CM20 2UG
www.o-i.com
+44 (0) 1279 422 222

Schott Glass
Science Centre Pd106, Glaisher Drive,
Wolverhampton, Staffordshire, WV10 9RU
www.schott.com/uk
+44 (0) 3300 021 340

Urban Bar Ltd
The Glasshouse, Highfields
Business Park, Kneesworth,
Royston, Hertfordshire, SG8 5JT
www.urbanbar.com
+44 (0) 1763 244 473

Riedel Crystal
RSN UK Ltd, Lakeside House -
Trentham Office Village, Trentham
Lakes South, Stoke-on-Trent,
Staffordshire, ST4 8GH
www.riedel.com
+44 (0) 1782 646 105

Wade Ceramics
Bessemer Drive, Stoke-on-Trent,
Staffordshire,
www.wade.co.uk
+44 (0) 8454 810 206

William Croxson & Son Limited
c/o SPACES, 6 Sutton Plaza,
Sutton, Surrey, SM1 4FS
www.croxsons.com
+44 (0) 20 83372 945

CASKS & KEGS

Keg Logistics
Gladden Place, West Gillibrands
Industrial Estate, Skelmersdale,
Lancashire, WN8 9SY
www.keglogistics.com/united-kingdom
+44 (0) 7728 720 478

Rotech (Swindon) Ltd
10 Blackworth Industrial Park,
Highworth, Swindon, SN6 7NA
www.rotechkeg.co.uk
+44 (0) 1793 764 700

**Speyside Cooperage
Visitor Centre**
Dufftown Road, Craigellachie,
Aberlour, Banffshire, AB38 9RS
www.speysidecooperage.co.uk
+44 (0) 1340 871 108

CLOSURES
Bruni Erben
Lady Lane, Hadleigh, Ipswich,
Suffolk, IP7 6AS
www.erben.co.uk
+44 (0) 1473 823 011

Global Closure Systems UK Ltd
Staines One, Station Approach,
Staines, Middlesex, TW18 4LY
+44 (0) 1784 415 200

Herti UK Ltd
Astra House, The Common
Cranleigh, Surrey, GU6 8RZ
www.herti.co.uk
+44 (0) 1483 266 617

Rankin Brothers & Sons
3c Drakes Farm, Drakes Drive,
Long Crendon, Buckinghamshire, HP18 9BA
www.rankincork.co.uk
+44 (0) 1844 203 100

United Closures & Plastics Ltd
1 Stewart Road, Bridge of Allan,
Stirling, Stirlingshire, FK9 4JG
www.ucplimited.com
+44 (0) 1786 796 393

Viscose Closures Ltd
Ferryboat Close, Enterprise Park,
Swansea, SA6 8QN
www.viscose.co.uk
+44 (0) 1792 796 393

COMPUTER SERVICES

Merlin Business Software Ltd
Chatsworth House, Millennium
Way, Chesterfield, S41 8ND
www.merlinbusinesssoftware.com
+44 (0) 1246 457 150

Premier Systems Limited
Whiteside Farm, Fritham,
Lyndhurst, Hampshire, SO43 7HH
www.premiersystems.ltd.uk
+44 (0) 2380 811 100

Vintner Systems
16 Station Road, Chesham,
Buckinghamshire, HP5 1DH
www.vintner.co.uk
+44 (0) 1494 792 539

DISPENSE SYSTEMS

Hallamshire Brewery Services
Liverpool Street, Sheffield, South
Yorkshire, S9 2PU
www.hallamshire.co.uk
+44 (0) 1142 431 721

John Guest
Horton Road, West Drayton,
Middlesex, UB7 8JL
www.johnguest.com
+44 (0) 1895 449 233

ENGINEERING SERVICES

ABM Ltd
Pitt Street, Widnes, Cheshire, WA8 0TG
www.abm.ltd.uk
+44 (0) 1514 202 829

NIRAS
St. Giles Court, 24 Castle Street,
Cambridge, CB3 0AJ
www.niras.com/offices/united-kingdom/
+44 (0) 1223 803 750

Bevisol
Orchard Business Park, Bromyard Road,
Ledbury, Herefordshire, HR8 1LG
www.bevisol.com
+44 (0) 1531 637 820

Briggs
Briggs House, Derby Street,
Burton-upon-Trent, Staffordshire, DE14 2LH
www.briggsplc.co.uk
+44 (0) 1283 566 661

CypherCo Ltd
Unit 19 Rural Enterprise Centre,
Vincent Carey Road, Rotherwas
Industrial Estate, Hereford,
Herefordshire, HR2 6FE
www.cypherco.com
+44 (0) 1432 343 340

Endress+Hauser Ltd
Floats Road, Manchester, Greater
Manchester, M23 9NF
www.uk.endress.com
+44 (0) 1612 865 000

GEA Process Engineering Ltd
Leacroft House, Leacroft Road,
Birchwood, Warrington, Cheshire, WA3 6JF
www.gea.com/united-kingdom
+44 (0) 1925 812 650

Gilbert Gilkes & Gordon Ltd
Canal Head North, Kendal,
Cumbria, LA9 7BZ
www.gilkes.com
+44 (0) 1539 720 028

Hanovia
780 Buckingham Avenue, Slough,
Berkshire, SL1 4LA
www.hanovia.com
+44 (0) 1753 515 300

LH Stainless Ltd
Towiemore, Drummuir, Keith,
Banffshire, AB55 5JA
www.l-h-s.co.uk
+44 (0) 1466 792 222

Logistex
2700 Kettering Parkway, Kettering,
Northamptonshire, NN15 6XR
www.logistex.com
+44 (0) 1536 480 600

Lorien Engineering
Solutions Ltd
Millennium Court, First Avenue,
Centrum 100, Burton-upon-Trent,
Staffordshire, DE14 2WH
www.lorienengineering.com
+44 (0) 1283 485 100

Malone Group
Skyline Court, Third Avenue,
Centrum 100, Burton-upon-Trent,
Staffordshire, DE14 2BZ
malonegroup.com
+44 (0) 1283 688 083

Moody Direct Ltd.
West Carr Road, Retford,
Nottinghamshire, DN22 7SN
www.moodydirect.com
+44 (0) 1777 701 141

Orapi Applied Ltd
Spring Road, Smethwick,
West Midlands, B66 1PT
www.orapiapplied.com
+44 (0) 1215 254 000

Pall Food and Beverage
Europa House, Havant Street,
Portsmouth, Hampshire, PO1 3PD
www.pall.com
+44 (0) 2392 303 303

Parker Hannifin Ltd
Tachbrook Park Drive, Tachbrook,
Park, Warwick, CV34 6TU
www.parker.com
+44 (0) 1926 317 878

Scott Process Technology Ltd
Ovenstone Works, Ovenstone,
Ansthruther, Scotland, KY10 2RR
www.scottprotec.com
+44 (0) 1333 311 394

Standfast Precision Engineering
Victoria Street, Craigellachie,
Banffshire, AB38 9SR
www.spe.switchedonsystems.com
+44 (0) 1340 881 371

Sterling Fluid Systems (UK) Ltd
Europe House, Second Avenue,
Trafford Park, Manchester, M17 1EE
www.sterlingsihi.com
+44 (0) 1619 286 371

Tomlinson Hall & Co Ltd
Lagonda Road, Billingham, North
Yorkshire, TS23 4JA
www.tomlinson-hall.co.uk
+44 (0) 1642 379 500

Veolia Water Solutions & Technologies
Aqua House, 2620 Kings Court,
Birmingham Business Park,
Birmingham, B37 7YE
www.veoliawatertechnologies.co.uk
+44 (0)1642 379 500

HOP MERCHANTS

Botanix Ltd, Barth-Haas Group
Hop Pocket Lane, Paddock
Wood, Kent, TN12 6DQ
www.barthhaasgroup.com
+44 (0) 1892 833 415

Brewers Select
Fengate Place,
Peterborough, PE1 5PE
www.brewersselect.co.uk
+44 (0) 1733 889 100

Charles Faram & Co. Ltd
The Hopstore, Monksfield Lane, Newland,
Malvern, Worcestershire, WR13 5BB
www.charlesfaram.co.uk
+44 (0) 1905 830 734

Lupofresh Ltd
Benover Road, Yalding,
Maidstone, Kent, ME18 6ET
+44 (0) 1622 815 720

Steiner Hops Ltd
185-189 High Street, Epping,
Essex, CM16 4BL
www.hopsteiner.com
+44 (0) 1992 572 331

LABELLING & PRINTING

Advanced Labelling Systems
Unit B Bandet Way, Thame,
Oxfordshire, OX9 3SJ
www.als.eu.com
+44 (0) 1844 213 177

Antalis McNaughton
Interlink Way West, Coalville,
Leicestershire, LE67 1LE
www.antalis.co.uk
+44 (0) 3706 079 014

APi Laminates Ltd
Second Avenue, Poynton
Industrial Estate, Stockport,
Cheshire, SK12 1ND
www.apilaminates.com
+44 (0) 1625 650 500

CCL Decorative Sleeves
Rollesby Road, Hardwick
Industrial Estate, Kings Lynn,
PE30 4LS
www.ccl-label.com
+44 (0) 1553 769 319

Clarifoil
1, Holme Lane, Spondon, Derby,
Derbyshire, DE21 7BS
www.clarifoil.com
+44 (0) 1332 681 329

CS Labels
Unit D Bay 2, Willenhall, Trading Estate,
Midacre, Willenhall, Willenhall,
West Midlands, WV13 2JW
www.cslabels.co.uk
+44 (0) 1902 365 840

Darley Ltd
Wellington Road, Burton-upon-Trent,
Staffordshire DE14 2AD
www.darleylimited.co.uk
+44 (0) 1283 564 936

Denny Bros Group
Kempson Way, Bury St Edmunds,
Suffolk, IP32 7AR
www.dennybros.com
+44 (0) 1284 701 381

Domino Printing Sciences Plc
Trafalgar Way, Bar Hill,
Cambridge, CB23 8TU
www.dennybros.com
+44 (0) 1954 781 888

Duncan Print
Broadwater House, Mundells,
Welwyn Garden City, Herts, AL7 1EU
www.duncanprint.co.uk
+44 (0) 1707 336 271

Esko UK (Solihull)
The Rhodium, Blythe Valley Park,
Solihull, West Midlands, B90 8AS
www.esko.com
+44 (0) 1216 674 200

G. & A. Kirsten Ltd
Suite 8 Pelmark House, 11 Amwell
End, Ware, Hertfordshire, SG12 9HP
+44 (0) 1920 487 300

Gavin Watson & Reid Printers
79-109 Glasgow Road, Glasgow,
Glasgow G72 0LY
www.gavinwatson.co.uk
+44 (0) 1698 826 000

Hewlett-Packard
Amen Corner, Cain Road,
Bracknell, Berkshire, RG12 1HN
www.hp.com
+44 (0) 3452 704 567

Herma Labelling Systems
The Hollands Centre, Hollands
Road, Haverhill, Suffolk, CB9 8PR
www.herma.co.uk
+44 (0) 1440 763 366

Label Apeel Ltd
Bo House, 17 Pinfold Road, Thurmaston,
Leicester, Leicestershire, LE4 8AS
www.labelapeel.co.uk
+44 (0) 1162 314 555

Labels Plus
Unit 22 Botany Business Park,
Macclesfield Road, Whaley
Bridge, Derbyshire, SK23 7DQ
www.labelsplus.co.uk
+44 (0) 1663 736 250

Linx Printing Technologies
8 Stocks Bridge Way, Compass
Point Business Park, St Ives,
Cambridgeshire, PE27 5JL
www.linxglobal.com
+44 (0) 1480 302 100

Logopak International Ltd
Enterprise House, George Cayley Drive,
Clifton Moor Industrial Estate,
York, YO30 4XE
www.logopak.co.uk
+44 (0) 1904 692 333

Markem-Imaje Limited
4th Floor, Centenary House
1 Centenary Way, Manchester, M50 1RF
www.markem-imaje.co.uk
+44 (0) 1618 648 111

Mercian Labels
Unit 2 Plant Lane Business Park,
Burnswood, Staffordshire, WS7 3GN
www.mercianlabels.com
+44 (0) 1543 431 070

Multi-Color Labels Daventry
Newnham Drive, Daventry,
Northamptonshire, NN11 8YG
www.mcclabel.com
+44 (0) 1327 301 181

NSD International
Dalkeith, Midlothian, EH22 4AF
www.nsdinternational.com/en
+44 (0) 1316 542 800

OKI Systems (UK) Ltd
Blays House, Wuck Road, Egham,
Surrey, TW20 0HJ
www.oki.co.uk
+44 (0) 1784 274 300

OPM (Labels & Packaging) Group
The Colour Box, 55 Gelderd
Road, Leeds, LS12 6LS
www.opm.co.uk
+44 (0) 1132 311 000

Reflex Label Plus
Moat Way, Barwell,
Leicestershire, LE9 8EY
www.reflexlabelplus.co.uk
+44 (0) 1455 852 400

Royston Labels
Unit 17 - 20 Greenfield,
Royston, SG8 5HN
www.roystonlabels.co.uk
+44 (0)1763 212 020

The Label Makers
Labmak House, Prince Street,
Bradford, BD4 6HQ
www.labmak.co.uk
+44 (0) 1274 681 151

Tullis Russell
Church Street, Bollington,
Macclesfield, Cheshire, SK10 5QF
www.tullisrussell.com
+44 (0) 1625 573 051

Weber Marking System UK
Macmerry Industrial Estate,
East Lothian, EH33 1HD
www.webermarking.com
+44 (0) 1875 611 111

LABORATORY ANALYSIS & TECHNICAL SUPPORT

Anton Paar
Unit F, The Courtyard, St Albans, AL4 0LA
www.anton-paar.com
+44 (0) 1992 514 730

Cara Technology
Mole Business Park, Bluebird House
Station Road, Leatherhead,
Surrey, KT22 7BA
www.cara-online.com
+44 (0) 1372 439 990

Teledyne Gas Measurement Instruments Ltd.
Inchinnan Business Park, Renfrew,
Renfrewshire, PA4 9RG
www.teledynegasandflamedetection.com/en
+44 (0) 1418 123 211

Hach Ultra Analytics
Laser House, Ground Floor,
Suite B, Waterfront Quay, Salford
Quays, Manchester, M50 3XW
www.uk.hach.com
+44 (0) 1618 721 487

Integrated Scientific Ltd
Unit 3, Aspen Court, Aspen
Way, Centurion Business Park,
Templeborough, Rotherham,
South Yorkshire, S60 1FB
www.integsci.com
+44 (0) 1709 830 493

Lovibond
Lovibond House, Sun Rise Way,
Amesbury, Wiltshire, SP4 7GR
www.lovibond.com/en
+44 (0) 1980 664 800

Murphy & Son Ltd
Alpine Street, Old Basford,
Nottingham NG6 0HQ
www.murphyandson.co.uk
+44 (0) 1159 785 494

Skalar (UK) Ltd
8 Warren Yard, Warren Park,
Wolverton Mill, Milton Keynes, MK12 5NW
www.skalar.com
+44 (0) 1908 410 168

Stevenson Reeves Ltd
40 Oxgangs Bank, Edinburgh, EH13 9LH
www.stevenson-reeves.co.uk
+44 (0) 1314 457 151

Strathkelvin Instruments Ltd
Rowantree Avenue, Motherwell,
North Lanarkshire, ML1 5RX
www.strathkelvin.com
+44 (0) 1698 730 400

LOGISTICS

Anchor Freight
109 Barrie Road, Glasgow,
Lanarkshire, G52 4PX
www.anchor-freight.co.uk
+44 (0) 1418 922 080

Culina Ambient
Hellaby Lane,
Rotherham, S66 8HN
www.culina.co.uk
+44 (0) 1630 695 407

Dachser
Northampton Logistics Centre,
Thomas Dachser Way, Brackmills,
Northamptonshire, NN4 7HT
www.dachser.co.uk
+44 (0) 1604 433 400

Hellmann Worldwide Logistics
26/27 Market Square,
Dover, Kent, CT16 1NG
www.hellmann.com/en/united-kingdom
+44 (0) 1304 248 390

Hillebrand
Dissegna House, Weston Avenue,
West Thurrock, Grays, Essex, RM20 3ZP
www.hillebrand.com
+44 (0) 1708 689 000

Kammac plc
Gladden Place, West Gillibrands
Industrial Estate, Skelmersdale,
Lancashire, WN8 9SY
www.kammac.com
+44 (0) 1695 727 272

Kuehne + Nagel
1 Union Business Park, Uxbridge,
Middlesex, UB8 2LS
www.kuehne-nagel.com
+44 (0) 1895 552 000

Macintyre Scott Xtra
Testwood House, Testwood Park, Salisbury
Road, Totton, Hampshire, SO40 2RW
www.macintyrescott.com
+44 (0) 23 8066 0074

MALTS, SUGARS & ADJUNCTS

Bairds Malt Ltd
Station Malting, Station Road,
Witham, Essex, CM8 2DU
www.bairds-malt.co.uk
+44 (0) 1376 513 566

Crisp Malting Group Ltd
Great Ryburgh, Fakenham,
Norfolk, NR21 7AS
www.crispmalt.co
+44 (0) 1328 829 391

DDW The Colour House
Trafford Park, Manchester,
Greater Manchester, M17 1PA
www.ddwcolour.com
+44 (0) 1618 863 345

French & Jupps
The Maltings, Stanstead Abbotts,
Ware, Hertfordshire, SG12 8HG
www.frenchandjupps.com
+44 (0) 1920 870 015

Micronized Food Products
Standard Way, Northallerton,
North Yorkshire, DL6 2XA
www.micronizedfoodproducts.co.uk
+44 (0) 1609 751 000

Muntons plc
Cedars Maltings, Stowmarket,
Suffolk, IP14 2AG
www.muntons.com
+44 (0) 1449 618 300

Pauls Malt Ltd
24-25 Eastern Way,
Bury St Edmunds, Suffolk, IP32 7AD
www.paulsmalt.co.uk
+44 (0) 7935 524 305

Simpsons Malt Ltd
Tweed Valley Maltings, Berwick-upon-
Tweed, Northumberland TD15 2UZ
www.simpsonsmalt.co.uk
+44 (0) 1289 330 033

Thomas Fawcett & Sons Ltd
Eastfield Lane, Castleford, West
Yorkshire WF10 4LE
www.fawcett-maltsters.co.uk
+44 (0) 1977 552 490

Tuckers
Commercial Road, Crediton,
Devon EX17 1ER
www.tuckersmaltings.co.uk
+44 (0) 1363 772 202

Warminster Maltings Ltd
39 Pound Street, Warminster,
Wiltshire BA12 8NN
www.warminster-malt.co.uk
+44 (0) 1985 212 014

PACKAGING

HSM UK Ltd
Burntwood Business Park,
Burntwood, Staffordshire, WS7 9GJ
www.hsm.eu/uk
+44 (0) 1543 272 480

LINPAC Packaging
Wakefield Road, Featherstone,
West Yorkshire, WF7 5DE
www.linpacpackaging.com
+44 (0) 1977 692 111

PROMOTIONAL ITEMS

Festival Glass Ltd
Unit 6 Calderdale Business Park, Club Lane,
Ovenden, Halifax, HX2 8DB
www.festivalglass.co.uk
+44 (0) 1422 382 696

Mail Boxes Etc.
6 Wilmslow Road, Rusholme,
Manchester, M14 5TP
www.mbe.co.uk/manchesterrusholme/
print/beer-mats
+44 (0) 1612 243 355

Mosaic Board Printers Ltd
1-2, Pytchley Lodge Road, Pytchley Lodge
Road, Industrial Estate, Kettering,
Northamptonshire NN15 6JQ
www.mosaic-boardprint.com
+44 (0) 1536 312 800

Screen Works Ltd
Homefield Road, Haverhill,
Suffolk, CB9 8QP
www.screenworks.co.uk
+44 (0) 1440 702 022

Willis Publicity
Unit 2, Allied Business Centre,
Coldharbour Lane, Harpenden,
Hertfordshire, AL5 4UT
www.willispublicity.co.uk
+44 (0) 1582 764 040

RESEARCH

Campden BRI (Brewing
Research International)
Station Road, Chipping Camden,
Gloucestershire, GL55 6LD
www.campdenbri.co.uk
+44 (0) 1386 842 000

International Centre for
Brewing & Distilling
Heriot-Watt University, Riccarton,
Edinburgh, EH14 4AS
www.icbd.hw.ac.uk
+44 (0) 1314 495 111

National Brewing Library
Journals Office, Oxford Brookes
University Library, Gipsy Lane
Campus, Oxfordshire, OX3 0BP
www.brookes.ac.uk/library/
special-collections
+44 (0) 1865 741 111

The IWSR
5 Fleet Place, London, EC4M 7RD
www.iwsr.co.uk
+44 (0) 2038 555 477

Index

Page numbers in bold refer to case histories